First Edition

International Association of Electrical Inspectors
Richardson, Texas

First Edition
Copyright © 2005 by
International Association of Electrical Inspectors
901 Waterfall Way, Suite 602
Richardson, TX 75080-7702

All rights reserved. First Edition published 2005
Printed in the United States of America
09 08 07 06 05   5 4 3 2 1

ISBN: 1-890659-39-8

Notice to the Reader

This book has not been processed in accordance with NFPA Regulations Governing Committee Projects. Therefore, the text and commentary in it shall not be considered the official position of the NFPA or any of its committees and shall not be considered to be, nor relied upon as a formal interpretation of the meaning or intent of any specific provision or provisions of the 2005 edition of NFPA 70, *National Electrical Code.*[1]

Publishers do not warrant or guarantee any of the products described herein or perform any independent analysis in connection with any of the product information contained herein. Publisher does not assume, and expressly disclaims, any obligation to obtain and include information referenced in this work.

The reader is expressly warned to consider carefully and adopt all safety precautions that might be indicated by the activities described herein and to avoid all potential hazards. By following the instructions contained herein, the reader willingly assumes all risks in connection with such instructions.

THE PUBLISHERS MAKE NO REPRESENTATIONS OR WARRANTIES OF ANY KIND, INCLUDING, BUT NOT LIMITED TO, THE IMPLIED WARRANTIES OF FITNESS FOR PARTICULAR PURPOSE, MERCHANTABILITY OR NON-INFRINGEMENT, NOR ARE ANY SUCH REPRESENTATIONS IMPLIED WITH RESPECT TO SUCH MATERIAL. THE PUBLISHERS SHALL NOT BE LIABLE FOR ANY SPECIAL, INCIDENTAL, CONSEQUENTIAL OR EXEMPLARY DAMAGES RESULTING, IN WHOLE OR IN PART, FROM THE READER'S USES OF OR RELIANCE UPON THIS MATERIAL.

[1]*National Electrical Code* and *NEC* are registered trademarks of the
National Fire Protection Association, Inc., Quincy, MA 02269

HAZARDOUS LOCATIONS · **TABLE OF CONTENTS**

Large photo courtesy of Thomas and Betts

Introduction and History

The intent of this book is to provide training material and resources for students in the classroom or seminar setting and to assist those involved with designing, installing, inspecting and maintaining electrical systems in hazardous (classified) locations. It includes information on area classification, methods of protection, interaction of protection techniques with specific types of electrical equipment, wiring requirements, and information on specific occupancies and industries.

The study of any subject related to the *National Electrical Code* should include a basic review of the information from Article 90. The purpose of the *NEC* as stated in 90.1 is "the practical safeguarding of persons and property from hazards arising from the use of electricity." Therefore, everything in chapter 5 of that document should relate to that purpose.

Scope of the *Code*

The scope of the *NEC*, in 90.2, is to provide the reader guidance on what is covered by the *Code*. Not all of the electrical hazards associated with hazardous (classified) locations are within its scope. This book, although primarily concerned with proper application of the *Code*, will also include information related to electrical safety that is outside the scope of the *NEC*. A basic understanding of such information located in other standards and recommended practices is critical to properly applying the requirements and concepts covered by the *NEC*. Since many *NEC* users do not have ready access to those documents, one of the goals of this book will be to provide applicable information and proper references to specific requirements in other documents and resources to assist in proper applications.

Arrangement of the *Code*

The arrangement of the requirements in the *NEC* is critical to proper application of those requirements and is covered in 90.3, which reads: "This *Code* is divided into

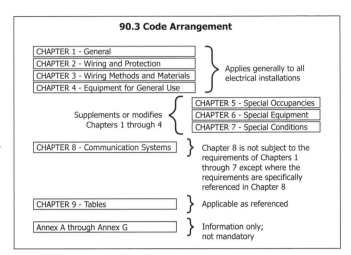

Figure 1. *Code* **Arrangement** (Reproduction of *NEC* Figure 90.3)

the introduction and nine chapters, as shown in Figure 90.3. Chapters 1, 2, 3, and 4 apply generally; Chapters 5, 6, and 7 apply to special occupancies, special equipment, or other special conditions. These latter chapters supplement or modify the general rules. Chapters 1 through 4 apply except as amended by Chapters 5, 6, and 7 for the particular conditions (see figure 1).

"Chapter 8 covers communications systems and is not subject to the requirements of Chapters 1 through 7 except where the requirements are specifically referenced in Chapter 8.

"Chapter 9 consists of tables."

When 90.3 is applied to an installation related to a hazardous (classified) location, it is obvious that all of the general requirements of chapters 1 through 4 of the *NEC* apply, unless they are modified by the special occupancy requirements in chapter 5. Section 800.3(B) refers to applicable requirements in chapter 5 for communications circuits and equipment installed in hazardous (classified) locations.

Enforcement of *Code*

Enforcement is addressed in 90.4: "This *Code* is intended to be suitable for mandatory application by governmental bodies that exercise legal jurisdiction over electrical installations, including signaling and communications systems, and for use by insurance inspectors. The authority having jurisdiction for enforcement of the *Code* has the responsibility for making interpretations of the rules, for deciding on the approval of equipment and materials, and for granting the special permission contemplated in a number of the rules."

Readers should be aware that *approval of* and *design of* electrical installations in hazardous locations are two different tasks and responsibilities. Readers should also realize that the area classification part of design would likely include a design team rather than a single electrical design person. This design team could easily include electrical, process, mechanical, fire protection and structural design contributors. Area classification and design of the electrical system installed within that area is the responsibility of the owner's representative(s), the design team. That design should include proper documentation. Approval of the classification and design is the responsibility of the AHJ. Proper application of the *NEC* requirements will necessitate everyone involved in the project working together for the installation to be effectively completed.

Common Language of Communication
An additional goal of this book will be to collect and use defined terms to minimize confusion. A study of any *NEC* topic requires all participants to use common, defined terms to insure proper exchange of information. Some terms related to hazardous (classified) locations are found in the text of the *NEC*, while others are found in various other standards or documents. The term *hazardous (classified) location* for example, as used in Articles 500–517, is "a location where fire or explosion hazards may exist due to flammable gases or vapors, flammable liquids, combustible dust, or ignitible fibers or flyings." A review of other codes and standards reveals that *hazardous locations* include health hazards, flammability hazards, and instability hazards (see NFPA 704).

Another primary goal of this training material is to offer a systematic outline for the exchange of information related to electrical installations in hazardous (classified) locations. Such a systematic approach will allow everyone involved in the process to realize that all applicable variables related to the project have been considered in order to minimize the chance of fires and explosions being caused by the electrical system.

Approvals
The *Code* indicates (requires) that conductors and electrical equipment are acceptable only where approved by the authority having jurisdiction. This authority could be a federal, state, local or regional department, or an individual such as a fire chief, fire marshal, building official, electrical inspector, or others having statutory authority. Often, the AHJ bases approvals on the use of listed equipment. For electrical installations in hazardous (classified) locations, however, the approval process can involve utilizing other acceptable alternatives. The terms *approved*, *identified*, and *listed* are all used throughout the *Code* rules that apply to hazardous locations and the specific meaning of each should be understood for proper application.

Definitions
Approved means being acceptable to the authority having jurisdiction.

Identified, as applied to equipment, is being recognizable as suitable for the specific purpose, function, use, environment, application, and so forth, where described in a particular *Code* requirement.

"FPN: Some examples of ways to determine suitability of equipment for a specific purpose, environment, or application include investigations by a qualified testing laboratory (listing and labeling), an inspection agency, or other organizations concerned with product evaluation."

Listed is when equipment, materials, or services are included in a list published by an organization that is acceptable to the authority having jurisdiction and concerned with evaluation of products or services, that maintains periodic inspection of production of listed equipment or materials or periodic evaluation of services, and whose listing states that the equipment, material, or services either meets appropriate designated standards or has been tested and found suitable for a specified purpose.

"FPN: The means for identifying listed equipment may vary for each organization concerned with product evaluation, some of which do not recognize equipment as listed unless it is also labeled. Use of the system employed by the listing organization allows the authority having jurisdiction to identify a listed product" (Article 100).

History and Timeline

The following brief history and timeline of events from the 1920s to the current edition of *NEC* indicate when events happened and how *Code* requirements for hazardous (classified) locations evolved over time. This information, furnished by Underwriters Laboratories Inc., provides a basic idea of the evolution of key codes and standards related to hazardous (classified) locations.

1920s–1930s

In the early years, hazardous (classified) locations were referred to in the *NEC* as "Extra Hazardous Locations." Everything else regarding the use of electricity at that time was considered to be hazardous, but for reasons of shock and fire, not explosions. *NEC* rules addressed rooms or compartments in which highly flammable gases, liquids, mixtures or other substances were manufactured, used or stored. At that time, Underwriters Laboratories had been evaluating and certifying equipment for use in such areas for about two years. One of the first hazardous (classified) location requirements in the *NEC* was associated with inhalation of flammable gases for anesthetizing locations in health care facilities.

1931

Classifications of Class I materials, including gases and vapors, and Class II for dusts were defined and covered by the *NEC*. Also, Class III and Class IV locations were defined for fibers.

1935

Groups were first defined for Class I locations, based on explosive pressure and flame transmission. At this time the gases were designated into groups as follows:

- Group A—Acetylene
- Group B—Hydrogen or gases and vapors of equivalent hazard
- Group C—Ethyl ether or gases and vapors of equivalent hazard
- Group D—Gasoline, petroleum, naphtha, alcohol, acetone, lacquers, solvent vapors

1937

Groups for Class II locations were first defined and designated as follows:

- Group E—metal dusts
- Group F—coal and other carbonaceous dusts
- Group G—grain, wood, plastic, etc.

1947

The concept of the Division system was introduced to the *Code*. Classified locations were divided into separate divisions based on the degree of hazard involved. For Class I and Class II locations, Divisions 1 and 2 locations were designated. At this time Class III and IV were combined into Class III locations.

1960

Underwriters Laboratories developed Westerberg Explosion Test Vessel (WETV). The WETV was designed to determine two quantities for any gas or vapor, and flame transmission properties by measuring the maximum experimental safe gap (MESG) under explosion pressure.

The WETV was and still is used to determine certain explosion characteristics of gases and vapors. The chamber is equipped with two blocks of metal that can be adjusted to obtain air gaps between them; by igniting the gas in the first chamber it may ignite the gas in the second chamber after passing through the metal-to-metal gapped joint (see photos 1 and 2). The largest clearance that will not allow passage of

Photo 1. Westerberg Explosion Test Vessel (WETV) Courtesy of Underwriters Laboratories Inc.

Photo 2. Westerberg Explosion Test Vessel (inside view)
Courtesy of Underwriters Laboratories Inc.

flame is called the MESG. The WETV data enables classification of gases and vapors into defined groups by comparing the MESG and explosion pressure to those of materials already defining the group.

1969

UL published *Bulletin of Research* No. 58. This bulletin summarized a UL investigation of fifteen flammable gases or vapors based on WETV test data. The materials (groups) were added to *NEC*–1971. The International Electrotechnical Commission published IEC 79-1A that defines a different type of apparatus to classify gases and vapors, based on MESG only. Autoignition temperature limits for group classification of gases and vapors were removed from the *NEC*. Equipment-operating temperatures, or "T codes," were established. External temperatures of equipment in these locations cannot exceed autoignition temperature of material.

1970s

UL published *Research Bulletins* 58A and 58B. These bulletins summarize investigations of approximately 30 additional gases and vapors based on Westerberg Explosion Test Vessel data. These 30 additional gases and vapors were then added to *NEC*–1978.

1983

The National Fire Protection Association published NFPA Standard 497M, *Classification of Gases, Vapors and Dusts for Electrical Equipment in Hazardous (Classified) Locations.*

NFPA Standard 497M classified hazardous materials based on test data from the Westerberg Explosion Test Vessel, and it was used to establish similarity to a tested material or chemical family.

1993

The maximum allowable temperature for Class II groups, which relied on comparing "T codes" and ignition temperatures of dusts was removed from the *NEC.*

1996

The International Zone Classification system was added to the *NEC* by including a new Article 505. This new article covered Class I only and included three gas groups—IIC, IIB, and IIA. It also included three Zones— 0, 1, and 2, which were comparable to the Division system with some small differences. Underwriters Laboratories began certifying equip-ment for use in areas classified under the IEC Zone classification system.

1997

NFPA combined their standards NFPA 497A, B, and M into two separate standards: NFPA 497 (for gases) and NFPA 499 (for dusts).

1999

Some new definitions of Class I groups were added in *NEC*–1999, based on the following information:
- Historical perspectives
- MESG data from WETV & IEC 79
- Minimum igniting current (MIC) ratio

Article 505 was also revised to introduce the IEC protection techniques and marking scheme.

2002

Article 505 was completely rewritten and re-structured, making it independent of other articles.

2005

NEC–2005 was revised to provide clarification about area classification in the earth below a motor fuel dispensing facility and a commercial repair garage. These areas are unclassified due to the lack of air in those locations.

Articles 500 through 505 were restructured to provide a common numbering sequence between the articles; and a new Article 506 has been added to provide an alternative method of addressing concerns for electrical installations where fire and explosion hazards may exist due to combustible dusts, fibers and flyings. Article 506 does not provide any IEC protection techniques. The addition of Article 506 is a continuation of the efforts toward harmonization between the *NEC* and the IEC requirements for electrical installations in hazardous (classified) locations.

IAEI intends to revise this work to complement each new edition of the *National Electrical Code,* so this will be an on-going project. Any suggestions for additional pertinent material or comments about how this work could be improved, would be most welcome.

Chapter 1

Classification of Areas and Locations

One of the most important actions associated with safe electrical installations in hazardous (classified) locations is to determine the area classification and the extent of such areas. Before electrical wiring and equipment is installed in a hazardous location, the hazardous area classification must be known. Some of these classified locations are clearly defined in the *National Electrical Code* (NFPA 70), while others require research and reference to other applicable codes and standards.

A rea classification is often the result of a risk analysis of a particular location or area to determine the likelihood that an explosion hazard exists. Areas are generally hazardous (classified) locations if ignitible concentrations of flammable gases or vapors, flammable liquids, combustible liquids, or combustible dust, fibers or flyings, either in suspension in the air or in other accumulations that present explosion or fire hazards, exist, or could exist.

Degree of the Hazard

The degree of the hazard is usually determined by the particular gas, vapor, or other substance and associated process that will produce, or is likely to produce, atmospheres or accumulations of these materials that can be ignited. Electricity presents an ignition source to these areas, and installations of electrical equipment and materials in these locations are much more restrictive and specific. This chapter provides some general insight into the various classified areas that are determined either under the Division system or the Zone system of classifying hazardous locations. The various levels of area classification and details of each will be provided later in this chapter. Figure 1-01 shows a Class I, Division 1 area with a boundary against a Class I, Division 2 area that extends out to an unclassified area. Areas without any classification are defined as *unclassified locations* as provided in Section 500.2 (see figure 1-01 and photo 1-01).

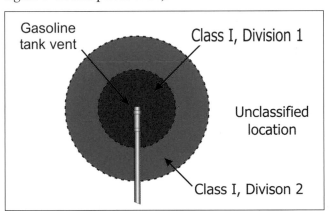

Figure 1-01. Typical Class I, Division 1 and Division 2 areas with a boundary against an unclassified area

At this point, it is necessary to familiarize one-self with the common terms used in determining area classification. These are the terms used by the applicable standards. When discussions or planning related to area classification are taking place, it is vital to use a common language of communication, the language used in the applicable *Code* or standard.

15

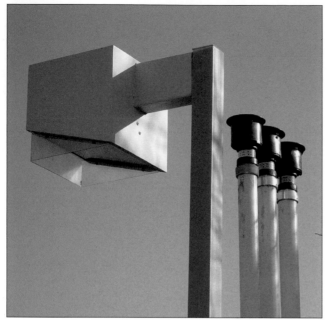

Photo 1-01. Class I, Divisions 1 and 2 areas within determined distances from underground gasoline tank vents.

Definitions

Flammable gases are those that will burn in air[1] and as gases that are flammable at atmospheric temperature and pressure in a mixture of 13 percent or less (by volume) with air, or that has a flammable range with air wider than 12 percent, regardless of the lower limit.[2]

Flammable vapors are those "given off from a flammable liquid at and above its flash point."[3]

Flammable liquids are defined as Class I liquids having a flash point below 37.8°C (100°F) and having a vapor pressure not exceeding 40 psia at 37.8°C (100°F).[4]

Combustible liquids have a flash point at or above 37.8°C (100°F).[5] These liquids will form an ignitible mixture only when heated above their flash point.

Combustible dust is finely divided solid material 420 microns or less in diameter (i.e., material passing through a U.S. No. 40 standard sieve) that presents a fire or explosion hazard when dispersed.[6]

Easily ignitible fibers and flyings are not defined in any NFPA document or in any other industry document.

Unclassified locations are "determined to be neither Class I, Division 1; Class I, Division 2; Class I, Zone 0; Class I, Zone 1; Class I, Zone 2; Class II, Division 1; Class II, Division 2; Class III, Division 1; Class III, Division 2; or any combination thereof. "[7]

Predetermined Classification Areas

The *NEC* identifies several predetermined hazardous (classified) locations associated with various special occupancies and conditions. Where the area classification is already predetermined and provided in a *Code* rule or standard, one can proceed with a design or installation with an understanding of the extent (boundaries) of the hazardous (classified) location. For example, in Article 514, there is a predetermined classified area at a motor fuel dispenser identified in Table 514.3(B)(1). This table indicates that the area extending up to 450 mm (18 in.) above grade level within 6.0 m (20 ft) horizontally of an edge of the dispenser enclosure is a Class I, Division 2 location (see figure 1-02 and photo 1-02). With that information, the installer or design team can plan an electrical design or installation for the dispensing equipment. Electrical wiring and equipment installed in this classified location must be done with the appropriate wiring methods and equipment. Chapter five of this book provides more detailed information about the wiring methods installed in hazardous (classified) locations. The above example is just one of many classified (hazardous) locations predetermined and delineated in *NEC* rules. Several other special occupancies with hazardous locations have well defined boundaries identified in the *NEC*, such as aircraft hangars, commercial repair garages, and spray paint booths. Chapter six takes a more detailed look at these special occupancies and their associated requirements for the hazardous (classified) locations in each.

Risk Assessment and Analysis

Many other locations and conditions in industry require a more analytical and careful approach to determining area classifications. For these areas not defined by a particular code or standard, the process of determining a classified area is more complicated. The first step of which is usually an assessment or risk analysis associated with the area in question. In addition to determining the likelihood that an ignitible concentration exists, the area classification provides an accurate and defined description of the material (gas, vapor, dust, etc.) so that appropriate electrical

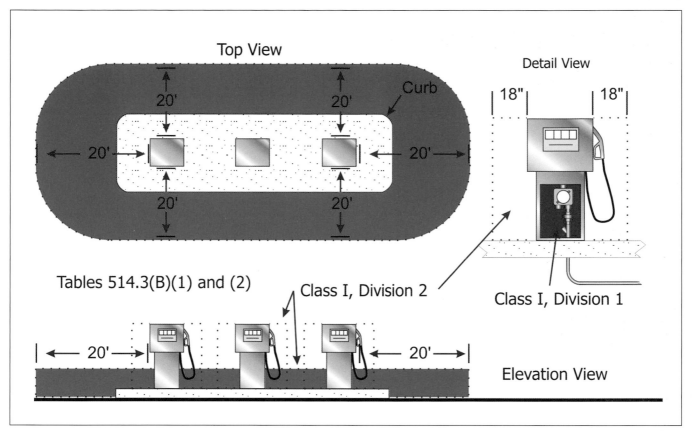

Top View

20'

20'

20'

20'

Curb

Detail View

18"   18"

20'

20'

20'

Tables 514.3(B)(1) and (2)

Class I, Division 2

Class I, Division 1

20'   20'

Elevation View

Figure 1-02. Motor fuel dispensing equipment showing the classification of the area and the extent (boundary) of the hazardous classified) location as identified in Table 514.3(B)(1) in Article 514.

systems and equipment can be selected for the design and installation. Determining who is responsible for the risk analysis is a common question. More than one individual is often responsible for determining the area classification.

When it has been established that any flammable or combustible materials are present, then an assessment must determine if the material is likely (1) to be released, and (2) to form an ignitible concentration with air (oxygen), and whether (3) an ignition source by the electrical system is a threat to

Photo 1-02. Typical motor fuel dispensing facilities fall under the requirements of Article 514 of the *NEC*; NFPA 30A is the associated standard.

persons and property. In some cases this assessment process is simple in nature; and in others, it can be quite complex. It is important to carefully consider all possible situations that present ignition risks that might result in explosions and fire.

Documentation of Hazardous (Classified) Locations

The *NEC* requires, in 500.4(A), proper documentation of areas designated as hazardous (classified) locations. This documentation can be in several acceptable formats, but it must be acceptable to the approving authority (see the definition of *authority having jurisdiction* in Article 100). Usually, it is in the form of written documents, accompanied by blueprints or drawings that graphically show the area classification (see figure 1-03). This documentation must be available to those authorized to design, install, inspect, maintain, or operate electrical equipment at that location [500.4(A)]. This requirement and the general information provided in this chapter will assist readers and reinforce the understanding that risk analysis and determination of hazardous locations is not a process that should be performed in the field during installation.

The Design Team

Educated design and ingenuity are critical to making these determinations and, generally, include work by various professionals involved in this type of work. As all of the information and facts are gathered that relate to determining the extent of a hazardous location, it becomes obvious that the process will likely involve more than just the electrical component of the facility design and installation. In many installations it will require involvement from one or more of the following engineering or design professionals: chemical, process, mechanical, fire protection, civil, environmental, structural, architectural and electrical.

The owner has a responsibility to assist the design team by disclosing all pertinent information about the materials to be used and how they will assist in implementing an adequate design. Any change of design in any of these disciplines can impact the area classification. Communication and full disclosure is imperative in accurate determination of hazardous (classified) locations and the extent of those areas. It is also important that owners and operators of facilities that include hazardous locations be familiar with the hazards and the determined locations.

Important Design Reference Information

The process of determining a hazardous (classified) location involves identifying combustible or flammable materials. These two important references are essential to the process of area classification:

NFPA 497-2004, *Recommended Practice for the Classification of Flammable Liquids, Gases, or Vapors and of Hazardous (Classified) Locations for Electrical Installations in Chemical Process Areas*

NFPA 499-2004, *Recommended Practice for the Classification of Combustible Dusts and of Hazardous (Classified) Locations for Electrical Installations in Chemical Process Areas*

Much of the information contained in these recommended practices has been extracted and inserted into other applicable and mandatory codes

and standards. NFPA 497 and NFPA 499 serve as the primary basis of hazardous area classification. Many of the requirements in the *NEC* have been extracted from either NFPA 497 or 499 and inserted as rules. Where the *NEC* provides extracted information from other standards, brackets containing the standard and the section number of the standard from which it was derived will follow the rule. Most who are involved in the electrical industry are usually familiar with *NEC* (NFPA 70) but are far less familiar with other standards applicable to hazardous locations. When dealing with hazardous locations, especially when it comes to determining area classification, one needs to be familiar with recorded industrial experience as well as with the other applicable standards of the National Fire Protection Association (NFPA), the American Petroleum Institute (API), and the Instrumentation, Systems, and Automation Society (ISA) that may be of use in the classification of various locations. Information about determining adequate ventilation, and the various forms of protection against static electricity and lightning hazards as well as other important protection methods and techniques are also described in these standards [*NEC*, 500.4(B) FPN].

These two common primary references are useful in assisting in the determination of hazardous locations. Table 4.4.2 of NFPA 497 provides a fairly complete list of combustible and flammable liquids. Appendix C to NFPA 497 gives several additional references that could also assist in judging materials for purposes of area classification because of flammable or combustible liquids. Table 4.5.2 of NFPA 499 presents an extensive list of common materials defined as combustible dusts. Appendix B to NFPA 499 offers several additional references to assist in judging materials for purposes of area classification because of combustible dust [see Annex, table A-01 that reproduces NFPA 497, Table 4.4.2 and table A-02 that reproduces NFPA 499, Table 4.5.2].

The Fire Triangle

To develop an understanding of the hazards associated with the use of electricity in hazardous locations, a review of the components (oxygen, heat or ignition, and fuel) of the fire triangle is in order.

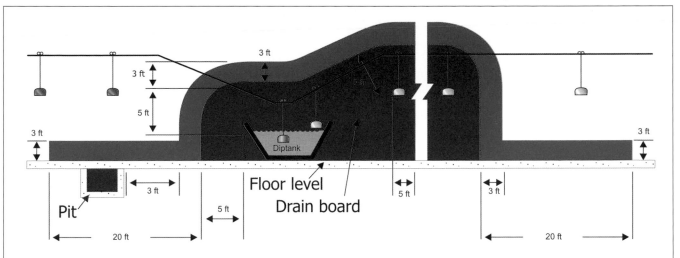

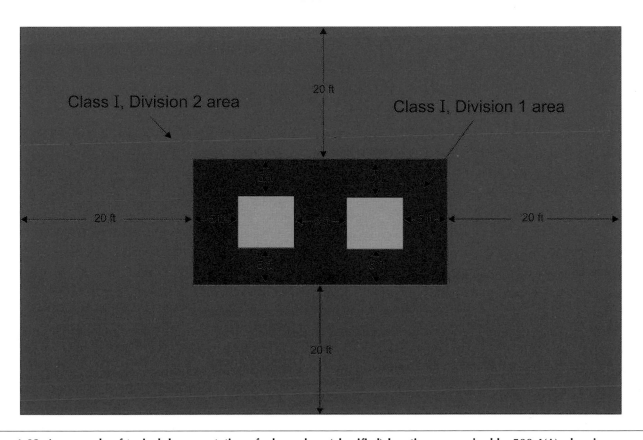

Figure 1-03. An example of typical documentation of a hazardous (classified) location as required by 500.4(A), showing a small schematic and a legend that provides information about the area classification. Documentation should provide material involved, autoignition temperature, gas group, and vapor density.

All three elements of the triangle must be present in specific ratios for ignition and explosion to occur (see figure 1-04). Vapor density will impact the likelihood that an ignitible concentration will develop; this will be covered in detail later in this chapter. Approximately 21 percent of earth's atmosphere is oxygen. For the focus of this text, the heat or ignition source is the electrical system; although it could be open flame or other heat sources that exceed the ignition levels of the materials involved. The fuel leg of the triangle could be one or a combination of the various volatile materials listed in the tables provided in NFPA 497 and 499.

Requirements in standards related to hazardous (classified) locations are based on *normal* atmospheric quantities of oxygen. It should be noted that these normal requirements have not considered situations involving oxygen-enriched or oxygen-deprived atmospheres. Identifying those conditions is part of the risk assessment and analysis process when determining area classification.

Other General Safety Concerns

Although the electrical system is the source of ignition considered by this text, those performing electrical work in hazardous (classified) locations must be aware that many non-electrical items that occur in an electrical installation (vehicle use, smoking, cutting and burning, mechanical sparks, welding, etc.) are also regulated in the codes, standards, and recommended practices developed by many industries that include hazardous (classified) locations. A thorough review of those requirements for working safely in hazardous (classified) locations must be made. An additional general statement applies to all locations where flammable and combustible materials are present: Catastrophic failures or discharges of the materials from containment have not been considered in the area classification of a facility. If catastrophic events—hurricanes, tornados, earthquakes, military or terrorist attacks, etc.—occur, providing special electrical equipment would probably have little impact on the ignition of the material.

Unclassified Areas

As briefly discussed earlier in this chapter, *unclassified locations* are defined in *NEC* 500.2 and

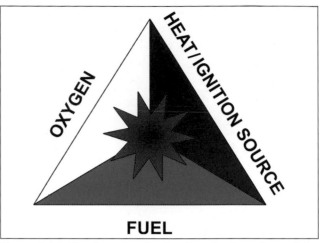

Figure 1-04. The fire triangle showing the three legs of the triangle: fuel, heat/ignition, and oxygen.

505.2 as "locations determined to be neither Class I, Division 1; Class I, Division 2; Class I, Zone 0; Class I, Zone 1; Class I, Zone 2; Class II, Division 1; Class II, Division 2; Class III, Division 1; Class III, Division 2; or any combination thereof." These locations are not necessarily void of combustible materials. If those materials are present but not expected to exist in a quantity and concentration, under normal or abnormal conditions, that would allow electrical systems to become an undesirable ignition source, the area could be unclassified. Almost all facilities have some presence of combustible dust, ignitible fibers and flyings, and even combustible liquids and vapors, but all are not hazardous (classified) locations.

Desirable ignitible mixtures occur in all types of occupancies, with many types of equipment, on a regular basis in normal operating conditions. For example, many types of heating equipment, both large and small, use flammable materials (see photo 1-03). Those include water heaters, boilers, air heaters, dryers, kilns, incinerators, furnaces, etc. Where the purpose of the equipment involves the need for a flame, area classification resulting in special electrical equipment in the immediate area of that equipment would not be appropriate. This concept assumes that all of the applicable requirements in the governing document [NFPA 497, 3-3.3] have been met, including storage of the fuel, piping of the fuel supply, control of the fuel supply; valves, regulators, safety devices, etc.; installation of equipment and evaluation of the equipment. Even though classification of spaces

Photo 1-03. A natural gas boiler with a sealed gas piping system

around this type installation is usually not done, locating electrical circuits and systems away from potential leaks is a wise choice.

Limited quantities of combustible materials are also stored in approved containers in many buildings without requiring area classification and/or special electrical equipment. The volume of the container and material from which it is made will vary, depending on the combustible material stored in it. Use of storage lockers will also impact the storage of combustible materials. Chapter four of NFPA 30, *Flammable and Combustible Liquids Code*, provides specific requirements and conditions that will affect an area where combustible materials are stored.

Sealed Systems

Because the release of ignitible mixtures from some operations and apparatus is so infrequent, these areas are considered unclassified. Some examples of unclassified locations where combustible materials are processed, stored, or handled include piping systems that do not include valves, fittings, flanges or similar fittings that are prone to leak (sealed systems). If the piping system did not include potential release points, it could be located in a well-ventilated or non-ventilated area and the space would remain unclassified. Where piping systems include fittings subject to minor releases of combustible material that occur in an outdoor area which provides adequate ventilation, the space may be considered unclassified. Even spaces not completely outdoors that include adequate ventilation may be considered unclassified. Keep in mind that adequate ventilation is a condition where the concentration of combustible material does not exceed 25 percent of the lower flammable limit of the material being considered.

Also considered unclassified, are the locations where Class IIB liquids are processed, stored, or handled. These materials seldom evolve enough vapors to form ignitible mixtures even when heated, and they are seldom ignited by properly installed and maintained general-purpose electrical equipment.

Some halogenated liquid hydrocarbons have a flammable range but do not have a flash point. For practical purposes, including selection of electrical equipment, these are considered unclassified areas and do not require special electrical equipment for hazardous (classified) locations.

Like unclassified facilities that include combustible or flammable liquids, gases or vapors, there are unclassified facilities where combustible dusts are processed, stored, or handled. Some of those include areas where materials are stored in sealed containers (e.g., bags, drums, or fiber packs on pallets or racks, closed tanks, and well maintained closed piping systems). These containers minimize the release of the product into the atmosphere.

Ventilation and Area Classification
Ventilation in Areas Hazardous with Gases or Vapors
Effective use of ventilation to keep an area or location purged of the fuel component of the fire triangle will reduce or eliminate a hazardous location. This

Photo 1-04. Typical dust control system at an industrial facility

method of reducing hazardous area classification is generally part of engineering designs that include moving a minimum amount of air [measured in cubic feet per minute (cfm)] in the area of concern. Two key considerations for such designs are the method of interlocks and hours of operation, among others. An example of this method of reclassification of hazardous locations can be found in *NEC* 511.3(A). In a commercial repair facility, the area is unclassified if there are fewer than four air changes per hour provided in that area. Thus, if there are more than four air changes per hour, the area is classified. The AHJ, as a general practice, often requires documentation from a mechanical engineer that demonstrates that amount of air movement [see Section 511.3(A)].

Ventilation in Hazardous Areas with Combustible Dusts
Controlling the amount of dust particles in suspension in the air and preventing excessive accumulations (blanketing) can reduce the risks in Class II locations. By providing dust removal systems, visual dust clouds and layer accumulations that make surface colors indiscernible can be minimized to a point where the space is considered unclassified. These dust removal systems should have adequate safeguards and warnings against failure (see photo 1-04). Excellent housekeeping that prevents visual dust clouds and layer accumulations that make surface colors indiscernible may also result in a space being considered unclassified. Housekeeping, in every situation, should be provided as a supplement to dust source elimination and ventilation. It should never be the primary method of dust control.

Contributing Factors for Area Classification
Combustible Dust Explosions
Combustible dust explosions can be violent and destructive. They can cause serious injury or death and result in fires that can destroy property. Once ignition of dust has occurred either in a cloud suspension or in a layer, an explosion is likely. Often the initial explosion is followed by another much more violent explosion fueled from dust accumulations on structural beams and equipment surfaces being

thrown into suspension by the initial blast. For this reason, good housekeeping in all areas handling dust is vitally important and is assumed throughout recommended practices. Dust control systems help in controlling the amount of dust, but should not be considered a substitute for frequent housekeeping.

Classification of Class II locations depends both on the presence of dust clouds (suspension in the air) and on the presence of hazardous accumulations of dust in layer form. Presence of a combustible dust cloud under normal conditions of operation, or due to frequent repair or maintenance, requires the area to be a Division 1 classification. Abnormal conditions or operation of machinery and equipment that could simultaneously produce a dust cloud or suspension and a source of ignition also predicates Division 1 area classification. In other words, if a dust cloud is present at any time, it is assumed to be ignitible; and, generally, all that is necessary for electrical ignition and a resulting explosion is failure of the electrical system. If dust clouds or hazardous dust accumulations are present only as a result of infrequent malfunctioning of handling or processing equipment, and ignition can result only from abnormal operation or failure of electrical equipment, these locations can be classified as Class II, Division 2 [NFPA 499, 2-3.3].

Some utilization equipment, such as boilers and heaters, is fueled by solid combustible fuels (dust). Just as it is with a gas water heater, area classification resulting in special electrical equipment in the immediate area of that equipment would not be appropriate.

Locations are unclassified where pyrophoric materials (those that ignite spontaneously in contact with air) are the only materials used or handled [NEC, 500.5(A)]. When these materials are released, ignition will occur regardless of the type of electrical equipment installed. In some cases, owner/operators will use hazardous location equipment in these areas. It is possible that because of the heavy construction characteristics of explosionproof or dust-ignitionproof enclosures (able to contain explosions that occur inside), the owner or operators assume that less damage might occur to the electrical equipment from an outside explosion. There is no known test data to substantiate that thought and no other "special electrical equipment" evaluated for use in those applications.

Vapor Density

An issue related to the specific gas or vapor involves the behavior of the material when it is released. Some materials are lighter than air, while others are heavier than air. Table 4.4.2 of NFPA 497 also identifies the vapor density for many common materials. Lighter-than-air gases, those with a vapor density less than 1.0, tend to dissipate rapidly and rarely accumulate to form an ignitible atmosphere near electrical equipment, unless they are released in an enclosed area and are not permitted to escape. Because of their rate of dissipation, classified areas for these materials tend to be smaller. Often these materials have less effect on the electrical installation because it will be located closer to the ground; and this material, when released naturally, leaves the location of the electrical equipment. It should be recognized that lighter-than-air gas that has been cooled sufficiently might behave as a heavier-than-air gas until it absorbs heat from the surrounding atmosphere.

Heavier-than-air gases, those with a vapor density greater than 1.0, tend to fall to grade level when released, and may remain for a significant period unless dispersed by natural or forced ventilation (see figure 1-05). This collection of gas near the ground is more likely to occur in the location of electrical equipment. If heavier-than-air gas has been heated sufficiently to decrease its density, it may behave as a lighter-than-air gas until cooled by the surrounding atmosphere. As gases of all densities diffuse into the surrounding air, the density of the mixture approaches that of air.

In many industries, the user or operator affects vapor density by controlling the temperature and pressure of the material. For example, compressed liquefied gases are those that are stored above their normal boiling point but are kept in the liquid state by pressure. When released, liquid immediately expands and vaporizes, creating large volumes of cold gas. Cold gas behaves like a heavier-than-air gas. Cryogenic liquids are generally handled below

-101°C (-150°F). They behave like flammable liquids when spilled. Small spills vaporize immediately, but larger spills may remain in the liquid state for extended periods. As liquid absorbs heat, it vaporizes and may form an ignitible mixture.

It is easy to understand how vapor density would affect the likelihood that an ignitible concentration of a material could be formed. Vapor density will have a major influence on the rate of dispersion if the material is released. If the material is heavier-than-air and the location includes areas where the material could collect that are close to the ground, the likelihood that an ignitible concentration can form increases. If the material is lighter-than-air and the location is outdoors without a roof or other place for a release to collect, the likelihood of an ignitible concentration forming decreases.

Flash Point

Another unique characteristic of materials that affects area classification is a *flash point*, the lowest temperature at which sufficient vapor of a liquid is generated to form an ignitible concentration. Table 4.4.2 of NFPA 497 identifies the flash point of many common materials. When flammable liquids [those having a flash point below 37.8°C (100°F) and having a vapor pressure not exceeding 40 psia at 37.8°C (100°F)] are released in appreciable quantity, they begin to evaporate at a rate that depends on its volatility.

More volatile materials evaporate faster and therefore have a lower flash point. Vapors of flammable liquids form ignitible mixtures with air at ambient temperatures more or less readily. Even when evolved rapidly, vapors tend to disperse rapidly, becoming diluted to a concentration below the lower flammable limit. Until this dispersion takes place, however, these vapors will behave like heavier-than-air gases. Flammable liquids normally will produce ignitible mixtures that will travel some finite distance from the point of origin; thus, they will normally require area classification for proper electrical system design.

Combustible Liquids

Combustible liquids [those having a flash point at or above 37.8°C (100°F)] will form an ignitible mixture

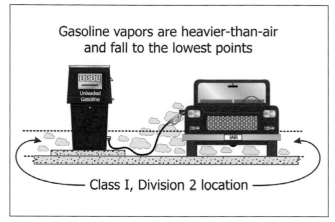

Figure 1-05. Gasoline vapors are heavier than air, which results in classification of hazardous areas for motor fuel (gasoline) dispensers at grade level.

only when heated above their flash point. It is possible that some of these materials under the right set of conditions warrant area classification, while others would never require special electrical equipment. Again, it is obvious that one flammable or combustible material released in a specific set of conditions might vaporize and form an ignitible atmosphere, while a different material might not vaporize nor form an ignitible atmosphere.

Flammable Liquids

Liquids designated as Class I have a flash point *below* 37.8°C (100°F) and a vapor pressure not exceeding 40 psia at 37.8°C (100°F). Class I liquids are subdivided as follows:

- Class IA liquids are those having flash points *below* 22.8°C (73°F) and boiling points *below* 37.8°C (100°F).

- Class IB liquids are those having flash points *below* 22.8°C (73°F) and boiling points *at or above* 37.8°C (100°F).

- Class IC liquids are those having flash points *at or above* 22.8°C (73°F) and *below* 37.8°C (100°F).

Ignitible Mixture is a combustible material that is within its flammable range.

Maximum Experimental Safe Gap (MESG). The maximum clearance between two parallel metal surfaces that has been found, under specified test conditions, to prevent an explosion in a test chamber from being propagated to a secondary chamber containing the same gas or vapor at the same concentration.

Minimum Igniting Current (MIC) Ratio. The ratio of the minimum current required from an inductive spark discharge to ignite the most easily ignitible mixture of a gas or vapor, divided by the minimum current required from an inductive spark discharge to ignite methane under the same test conditions [see IEC, 79-3].

Minimum Ignition Energy (MIE). The minimum energy required from a capacitive spark discharge to ignite the most easily ignitible mixture of a gas or vapor.

Classified Locations

When it has been determined that flammable or combustible liquids; gases or vapors; or combustible dust are present at the location of an electrical installation, an additional sorting of those materials must be considered prior to selecting equipment and wiring components. Although electrical designers, installers, and authorities having jurisdiction normally will not be involved in classifying the material group, it is critical that this information be provided to them so that proper electrical equipment can be selected and installed. There are three area classifications, Class I, Class II, and Class III. These classifications are further divided into divisions or zones, depending on the classification system being used in the design and installation.

The *NEC* currently permits several options for area classification in a Class I location. A location could be classified using the *Division System* or the *Zone System.* Both systems could be used in the same facility as long as they do not overlap. The traditional North American, Division system divides materials into four groups: A, B, C, and D. The traditional International Electrotechnical Commission (IEC), Zone system divides those same materials into three groups: IIC, IIB, and IIA. These group designations overlap as follows: Once it is established that combustible or flammable liquids, gases or vapors are present and the area will not qualify as unclassified, the next step involves gathering pertinent information to determine the proper classification. The extent of a Division 1 or Division 2 or Zone 0, Zone 1, or Zone 2 area requires careful consideration of the following factors: combustible material, vapor

Division System		Zone System
Groups A and B	=	IIC
Group C	=	IIB
Group D	=	IIA

Table 1-01. Systems and Groups Comparison

density, temperature, process or storage pressure, size of release, and ventilation.

Division System of Area Classification
Class I Locations
Locations in which flammable gases or vapors are, or may be, present in the air in quantities sufficient to produce explosive or ignitible mixtures are Class I locations. Class I locations are subdivided into either Division 1 or 2 locations [*NEC,* 500.5(B)(1) and (B)(2)].

Class I, Division 1. Combustible material is present normally or frequently. A Class I, Division 1 location is one where ignitible concentrations of flammable gases or vapors can exist under normal operating conditions, or where ignitible concentrations of gases or vapors exist frequently because of repair or maintenance operations or because of leakage. Locations or areas in which breakdown or faulty operation of equipment or processes could release ignitible concentrations of flammable gases or vapors and might also cause simultaneous failure of electrical equipment in such a way as to directly cause the electrical equipment to become a source of ignition are also considered as Class I, Division 1 locations [*NEC,* 500.5(B)(1)].

Some examples of Class I, Division 1 locations are listed in the fine print note (FPN) to 500.5(B)(1) and include areas where volatile flammable liquids or gases are transferred from one container to another, interiors of spray paint booths, or drying rooms or compartments for the evaporation of flammable solvents, to name a few.

Class I, Division 2. Combustible material is present as a result of infrequent failure of equipment or containers. A Class I, Division 2 location is where volatile flammable liquids or flammable gases are handled, processed, or used, but will normally be confined within closed containers or closed systems

Photo 1-05. Grain and feed handling facility for loading rail cars

from which they can escape only through accidental rupture or breakdown of such containers or systems, or because of abnormal operation of equipment. A Class I, Division 2 location can also be one in which ignitible concentrations of gases or vapors are normally prevented by positive mechanical ventilation, but which might become hazardous through failure or abnormal operation of the ventilating equipment; or one adjacent to a Class I, Division 1 location from which ignitible concentrations of gases or vapors might occasionally be communicated, unless such communication is prevented by adequate positive-pressure ventilation from a source of clean air and effective safeguards against ventilation failure are provided [*NEC*, 500.5(B)(2)].

Class II Locations

Class II locations are those that are hazardous because of the presence of combustible dust. Class II locations shall include those specified in *NEC* 500.5(C)(1) and (C)(2).

CONDITIONS:

(1) Class I, Division 1 hazard exists during normal operation conditions.

• Open air mixing tank
• Products stored in work area

(2) Area is classified based on properties of vapors present.

(3) Electrical equipment must use approved Division 1 *NEC* protection techniques and wiring methods.

Figure 1-06. Example of area classification under the Division System (Class I, Division 1) Concept by Appleton

A Class II, Division 1 location is where combustible dust is in the air under normal operating conditions in quantities sufficient to produce explosive or ignitible mixtures. A Class II, Division 1 location can also exist where mechanical failure or abnormal operation of machinery or equipment might cause such explosive or ignitible mixtures to be produced, and might also provide a source of ignition through simultaneous failure of electric equipment, through operation of

Hazardous Locations

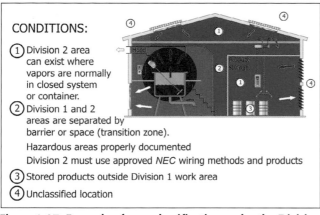

CONDITIONS:

① Division 2 area can exist where vapors are normally in closed system or container.

② Division 1 and 2 areas are separated by barrier or space (transition zone).

Hazardous areas properly documented

Division 2 must use approved *NEC* wiring methods and products

③ Stored products outside Division 1 work area

④ Unclassified location

Figure 1-07. Example of area classification under the Division System (Class I, Divisions 1 and 2) Concept by Appleton

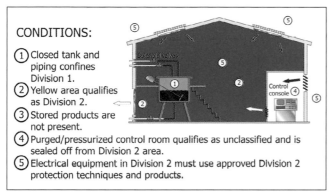

CONDITIONS:

① Closed tank and piping confines Division 1.

② Yellow area qualifies as Division 2.

③ Stored products are not present.

④ Purged/pressurized control room qualifies as unclassified and is sealed off from Division 2 area.

⑤ Electrical equipment in Division 2 must use approved Division 2 protection techniques and products.

Figure 1-08. Example of area classification under the Division System (Class I, Divisions 1 and 2) Concept by Appleton

protection devices, or from other causes. Class II, Division 1 locations can also be those in which combustible dusts of an electrically conductive nature may be present in hazardous quantities [see *NEC*, 500.5(C)(1) and photo 1-05].

A Class II, Division 2 location is where combustible dust is not normally in the air in quantities sufficient to produce explosive or ignitible mixtures, and dust accumulations are normally insufficient to interfere with the normal operation of electrical equipment or other apparatus; but combustible dust may be in suspension in the air as a result of infrequent malfunctioning of handling or processing equipment.

Locations where combustible dust accumulations on, in, or in the vicinity of the electrical equipment may be sufficient to interfere with the safe dissipation of heat from electrical equipment or may be ignitible by abnormal operation or failure of electrical equipment are also Class II, Division 2 locations [*NEC*, 500.5(C)(2)].

The quantity of combustible dust that may be present and the adequacy of dust removal systems are

factors that merit consideration in determining the classification and may result in an unclassified area.

Class III Locations

Class III locations are those that are hazardous because of the presence of easily ignitible fibers or flyings, but in which such fibers or flyings are not likely to be in suspension in the air in quantities sufficient to produce ignitible mixtures. Class III locations shall include those specified in 500.5(D)(1) and (D)(2).

A Class III, Division 1 location is one in which easily ignitible fibers or materials producing combustible flyings are handled, manufactured, or used. Class III, Division 1 locations usually include some parts of rayon, cotton, and other textile mills; combustible fiber manufacturing and processing plants; cotton gins and cotton-seed mills; flax-processing plants; clothing manufacturing plants; woodworking plants; and establishments and industries involving similar hazardous processes or conditions [*NEC*, 500.5(D)(1) FPN].

A Class III, Division 2 location is one in which easily ignitible fibers are stored or handled other than in the process of manufacture (see figures A-01, A-02, A-03 in the annex that are diagrams of area classifications and groups under the Division system).

Groups in the Division System

Materials are grouped to permit classification of locations depending on the properties of the flammable vapors, liquids, or gases, and to permit testing and approval of the equipment for such locations (see table 1-02). There are four material groups provided for Class I locations, and three material groups for Class II locations as follows:

Class I, Groups A, B, C, and D include the following gases [*NEC*, 500.6(A)(1) through (4)].

Group A. Acetylene [NFPA 497, 1-3]

Group B. Flammable gas, flammable liquid–produced vapor, or combustible liquid–produced vapor mixed with air that may burn or explode, having either a maximum experimental safe gap (MESG) value less than or equal to 0.45 mm or a minimum igniting current ratio (MIC ratio) less than or equal to 0.40 [NFPA 497, 1-3]. A typical Class I, Group B material is hydrogen.

Group C. Flammable gas, flammable liquid–produced vapor, or combustible liquid–produced vapor mixed with air that may burn or explode, having either a maximum experimental safe gap (MESG) value greater than 0.45 mm and less than or equal to 0.75 mm, or a minimum igniting current ratio (MIC ratio) greater than 0.40 and less than or equal to 0.80 [NFPA 497, 1-3]. A typical Class I, Group C material is ethylene.

Group D. Flammable gas, flammable liquid–produced vapor, or combustible liquid–produced vapor mixed with air that may burn or explode, having either a maximum experimental safe gap (MESG) value greater than 0.75 mm or a minimum igniting current ratio (MIC ratio) greater than 0.80 [NFPA 497, 1-3].

Class II, Groups E, F, and G

There are three material groups provided for Class II locations as follows:

Group E. Atmospheres containing combustible metal dusts, including aluminum, magnesium, and their commercial alloys, or other combustible dusts whose particle size, abrasiveness, and conductivity present similar hazards in the use of electrical equipment.

Group F. Atmospheres containing combustible carbonaceous dusts that have more than 8 percent total entrapped volatiles [see ASTM D3175-02 for coal and coke dusts] or those sensitized by other materials so that they present an explosion hazard.

Substance 500.1 Scope	Gas	Dust	Fibers and Flyings
Class	I 500.5(B)	II 500.5(C)	III 500.5(D)
Division 1 (Normally Harzardous)	Flammable or combustible concentrations exist under normal operating conditions	Group E Groups F & G Normally in air in ignitible concentrations	Where they are manufactured
Division 2 (Normally Harzardous)	Confined within closed systems and closed containers	Groups F & G Not normally in air in ignitible quantities	Where they are stored
Groups	A, B, C, and D NEC 500.6(A)	E, F, and G NEC 500.6(B)	No Groups
NEC Article	501	502	503

Table 1-02. Class I and II, and III locations and divisions and the relationships to the various groups associated with each.

Coal, carbon black, charcoal, and coke dusts are examples of carbonaceous dusts.

Group G. Atmospheres containing other combustible dusts, including flour, grain, wood flour, plastic, and chemicals.

Class III Groups

There are no groups for Class III locations.

Zone System of Area Classification

The Zone system of classifying a hazardous location is fairly new to the NEC and is part of a larger effort to harmonize the rules contained in the NEC with other international (IEC) standards. It is incorporated in the Code to provide another method of hazardous area classification other than the division system. The two systems (Zone and Division) are similar with some small differences. The Zone classification system is seldom used in North America, but is often used beyond its boundaries. Some offshore oil rigs and refineries have incorporated this method of classifying hazardous locations, but it is not used much in the United States. The NEC is the most widely adopted code in the world and is being used in many other countries and often applied to hazardous locations using the Zone system of classification. The following is an overview of Class I, Zone 0, 1, and 2 locations as provided in the NEC (see figure 1-06).

An important factor for utilizing the Zone system of classification of hazardous locations is that it is required to be done under the supervision of a registered professional engineer, as required by 505.7. All electrical equipment and wiring methods must also be selected under the supervision of a registered professional engineer. This is not a requirement for locations or areas classified under the Division system.

Dual Classification and Reclassification

When areas within the same facility are classified separately, Class I, Zone 2 locations shall be permitted to abut, but not overlap Class I, Division 2 locations. Class I, Zone 0 or Zone 1 locations shall not abut against classified locations [NEC, 505.7(B)].

A Class I, Division 1 or Division 2 location can also be reclassified as a Class I, Zone 0, Zone 1, or Zone 2 location provided all of the space classified because of a single flammable gas or vapor source is reclassified under the requirements of *NEC* Article 505.

Class I, Zone 0. Combustible material is present continuously or for long periods. Class I, Zone 0 locations must meet the following conditions: (1) ignitible concentrations of flammable gases or vapors are present continuously; or (2) ignitible concentrations of flammable gases or vapors are present for long periods of time [*NEC*, 505.5(B)(1)].

Class I, Zone 1. Combustible material is likely to be present normally or frequently because of repair or maintenance operations or because of leakage. Class I, Zone 1 locations are those meeting the following conditions:

• Ignitible concentrations of flammable gases or vapors are not likely to occur in normal operation, and if they do occur, they will exist only for a short period.

• Volatile flammable liquids, flammable gases, or flammable vapors are handled, processed, or used, but the liquids, gases, or vapors normally are confined within closed containers or closed systems from which they can escape only as a result of accidental rupture or breakdown of the containers or system, or as the result of the abnormal operation of the equipment with which the liquids or gases are handled, processed, or used.

• Ignitible concentrations of flammable gases or vapors normally are prevented by positive mechanical ventilation, but may become hazardous as the result of failure or abnormal operation of the ventilation equipment.

• Being adjacent to a Class I, Zone 0 location from which ignitible concentrations of flammable gases or vapors could be communicated, unless such communication is prevented by adequate positive-pressure ventilation from a source of clean air, and effective safeguards against ventilation failure are provided [*NEC*, 505.5(B)(2)].

Class I, Zone 2. Combustible material is not likely to occur in normal operation, and if it does occur, it will exist only for a short period. A Class I, Zone 2 location is one in which:

• ignitible concentrations of flammable gases or vapors are not likely to occur in normal operation and,

if they do occur, will exist only for a short period; or

• volatile flammable liquids, flammable gases, or flammable vapors are handled, processed, or used but the liquids, gases, or vapors normally are confined within closed containers of closed systems from which they can escape, only as a result of accidental rupture or breakdown of the containers or system, or as a result of the abnormal operation of the equipment with which the liquids or gases are handled, processed, or used; or

• ignitible concentrations of flammable gases or vapors normally are prevented by positive mechanical ventilation but may become hazardous as a result of failure or abnormal operation of the ventilation equipment; or

• ignitible concentrations of flammable gases or vapors from an adjacent Class I, Zone 1 location could be communicated, unless such communication is prevented by adequate positive-pressure ventilation from a source of clean air and effective safeguards against ventilation failure are provided [*NEC*, 505.5(B)(3)].

Zone 2 classified areas usually include locations where volatile flammable liquids or flammable gases or vapors are used, but would become hazardous only in case of an accident or of some unusual operating condition.

Groups in the Zone System

There are three Class I, Zone groups of combustible materials listed in Table 4.4.2 from NFPA 497:

Group IIC. Atmospheres containing acetylene, hydrogen, or flammable gas, flammable liquid-produced vapor, or combustible liquid-produced vapor mixed with air that may burn or explode, having either a maximum experimental safe gap (MESG) value less than or equal to 0.50 mm or minimum igniting current ratio (MIC ratio) less than or equal to 0.45.

Group IIB. Atmospheres containing ace-taldehyde, ethylene, or flammable gas, flammable liquid-produced vapor, or combustible liquid-produced vapor mixed with air that may burn or explode, having either maximum experimental safe gap (MESG) values greater than 0.50 mm and less than or equal to 0.90 mm or minimum igniting current ratio (MIC ratio) greater than 0.45 and less than or equal to 0.80.

Group IIC	Group IIB	Group IIA
Acetylene Hydrogen Carbon Disulfide	Ethylene Diethyl Ether 1, 3 Butadiene Ethylene Oxide Cyclopropane Methyl Acetate	Propane Benzene Styrene Hexane Ethanol Methane Kerosene Ethyl Acrylate

Table 1-03. Class 1, Zone Groups

Article 500 Groups	Typical Material	Article 505 Groups
A	Acetylene	IIC
B	Hydrogen	IIC
C	Ethylene	IIB
D	Gasoline-Propane-Methane	IIA

Table 1-04. Basic Articles 500 and 505 Group Comparsion

Group IIA. Atmospheres containing acetone, ammonia, ethyl alcohol, gasoline, methane, propane, or flammable gas, flammable liquid-produced vapor, or combustible liquid-produced vapor mixed with air that may burn or explode, having either a maximum experimental safe gap (MESG) value greater than 0.90 mm or minimum igniting current ratio (MIC ratio) greater than 0.80.

Article 506, Zones 20, 21, and 22

This article is new to the *NEC* for the 2005 cycle and provides another method for classification of hazardous areas with combustible dusts, fibers and flyings. This article does not replace the current provisions in Articles 500, 502, and 503 for such classified locations, but is in addition to them (see table 1-05 for the basic arrangement of Article 506). Note that this new article is incomplete in some areas; for example, there are no protection techniques offered.

General Procedure for Classifying Areas

The following guideline of general procedures should be used for each room, section, or area being classified as a hazardous location. It is important that this process of determining the extent of a hazardous (classified) location be performed by a team of experts qualified in this area. Each hazardous location will require its own study, analysis, and solutions depending on the conditions of that particular facility or location. It should be noted that this basic guideline might not be adequate for all situations or conditions. Many design teams have their own well-established methods of determining hazardous (classified) locations.

Usually, the first challenge is to verify if the location is a hazardous (classified) location in accordance with any applicable code or standard, or to determine the need for classification as a hazardous location based on the material in question. An example of a predetermined hazardous location is a motor fuel dispensing facility. In this case, refer to *NEC* Articles 510 and 514 for the defined classified locations and requirements for electrical installations.

The area should be classified if flammable liquids, gases or vapors or combustible material such as dusts are processed, handled, or stored there. Reference NFPA 497 or NFPA 499 as necessary, depending on the type of material and how it is being used.

Second, gather the information based on sound research and information about the characteristics of the material.

Facility Information

For a proposed facility that exists on drawings only, a preliminary area classification can be done so that

Article 506 Zone 20, 21, and 22 Locations for Combustible Dusts, Fibers, and Flyings		
Zone 20 Hazardous (Classified) Location	**Zone 21 Hazardous (Classified) Location**	**Zone 22 Hazardous (Classified) Location**
An area where combustable dust or ingnitible fibers and flyings are present continuously or for long periods of time in quantities sufficient to be hazardous as classified by 506.5(B)(1)	An area where combustible dust or ignitible fibers and flyings are likely to exist occasionally under normal operation in quantities sufficient to be hazardous as classified by 506.5(B)(2)	An area where combustible dust or ignitible fibers and flyings are likely to occur under normal operation in quantities sufficient to be hazardous as classified by 506.5(B)(3)

Alternate methods to the requirements in Articles 500, 502, and 503 for these specific environments

Table 1-05. Zones 20, 21, and 22 in Article 506

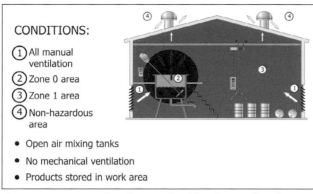

CONDITIONS:
1. All manual ventilation
2. Zone 0 area
3. Zone 1 area
4. Non-hazardous area

- Open air mixing tanks
- No mechanical ventilation
- Products stored in work area

Figure 1-09. Example of area classification under the Zone system (Class I, Zones 0 and 1) Concept by Appleton

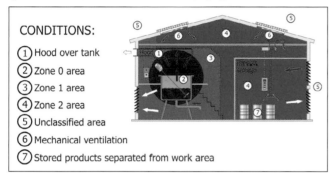

CONDITIONS:
1. Hood over tank
2. Zone 0 area
3. Zone 1 area
4. Zone 2 area
5. Unclassified area
6. Mechanical ventilation
7. Stored products separated from work area

Figure 1-10. Example of area classification under the Zone system (Class I, Zones 0, 1, and 2) Concept by Appleton

suitable electrical equipment and instrumentation can be purchased. Plants are rarely built exactly as the drawings portray, and the area classification should be later modified based upon the actual facility. Owners and operators can provide critical information at this stage of the process.

Existing Plant or Facility History

For an existing facility, the individual plant experience is extremely important in classifying areas within the plant or facility. Both operation and maintenance personnel in the actual plant should be asked the following questions:

Class I and II Locations

Is a flammable liquid, gas or vapor or combustible material (gas, vapor, or dust) likely to be in suspension in air continuously, periodically, or intermittently under normal conditions in quantities sufficient to produce ignitible concentrations or mixtures?

Class II Locations (Dust)

Are there dust layers or accumulations on surfaces deeper than 3 mm (1/8 in.)?

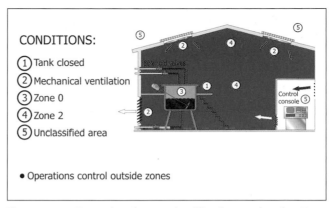

CONDITIONS:
1. Tank closed
2. Mechanical ventilation
3. Zone 0
4. Zone 2
5. Unclassified area

- Operations control outside zones

Figure 1-11. Example of area classification under the Zone system (Class I, Zones 0 and 2) Concept by Appleton

Are there dust layers or accumulations on surfaces that make the colors of floor or equipment surfaces indiscernible?

What is the 24-hr dust accumulation?

Is the equipment in good condition? questionable condition? or in need of repair? Are equipment enclosures in good repair and preventing the entrance of dust?

Do maintenance practices result in the formation of ignitible mixtures?

What equipment is used for dust collection?

Material Density

Determine the vapor density (of the particular gas or vapor).

Determine if the specific particle density of the dust is at least 40 lb/ft^3.

Plot Plan

A plot plan (or similar drawing) is needed showing all vessels, tanks, building structures, partitions, and similar items that would affect dispersion or promote accumulation of the dust.

Fire Hazard Properties of Flammable Gases or Vapors or Combustible Material (Dusts)

First determine the *NEC* group and the ignition temperature, vapor density, and other applicable data or information as shown in NFPA 497 Table 4.4.2 for many Class I materials (see table A-01 in the annex).

The *NEC* group and the layer or cloud ignition temperature are shown in NFPA 499 Table 4.5.2 for many Class II materials.

Second contact the material supplier to determine if the material has been group classified.

Have the material tested to determine if the ignition sensitivity is less than 0.2 and the explosion severity is less than 0.5. Area classification is not considered necessary for dusts that meet both criteria.

Third, select the appropriate area classification. Then determine whether the process equipment is open or enclosed.

Determine whether the gas or vapor is Group A, B, C, or D.

Determine whether the dust is Group E, F, or G.

Determine whether the area is for storage.

Fourth, determine the extent of the classified area. The extent of the classified area should be determined using sound engineering judgment and research about the flammable liquid, gas, or vapor, or combustible dust.

Locate the potential sources of leaks on the plan drawing or at the actual location. These sources could include rotating or reciprocating shafts, doors and covers on process equipment, and so forth.

For each leakage source, find an equivalent example on the selected classification diagram to determine the minimum extent of classification around the leakage source.

The extent can be modified by considering the following:

• Whether an ignitible mixture is likely to occur frequently due to repair, maintenance, or leakage

• Where conditions of maintenance and supervision are such that leaks are likely to occur in process equipment, storage vessels, and piping systems containing combustible material

• Ventilation or prevailing wind in the specific area and the dispersion rates of the combustible materials

Once the classification is made and the minimum extent of the classified area is determined, for practical reasons utilize distinct landmarks (e.g., curbs, dikes, walls, structural supports, edges of roads, etc.) for the actual boundaries of the area classification. These landmarks permit easy identification of the boundaries of the hazardous areas for electricians, instrument technicians, operators, and other personnel in the future.

Summary

Electrical installations in hazardous (classified) locations if not installed to meet the minimum requirements of the applicable codes and standards can be hazardous to persons and property. Electricity is a source of ignition for atmospheres that can explode. Various hazardous (classified) locations are delineated in the *NEC*. This chapter has provided a review of the basics of determining area classification as well as the characteristics of the various classified locations under the Zone system and under the Division system Often area classification is not covered by the *NEC* and requires reference to other applicable standards to determine the classification of a hazardous area and the extent of that area or location. This process should include a team of professionals (experts in their fields) in the risk analysis and assessment. NFPA 497 and 499 are among the other standards that have to be used. Classification of hazardous areas or locations is not the responsibility of the authority having jurisdiction or the installing contractor. There is a process that calls for careful exercises in ingenuity, sound engineering, designs for the best results, and electrical safety. Before electrical equipment and wiring is installed in a hazardous (classified) location, the classification or the area must be known. Various specific methods of protection are required for electrical installations in hazardous locations and those are covered in chapter two.

---

1 NFPA 45-2002, Section 14.22

2 NFPA 50-2001, Section 13.6; NFPA 50; and NFPA 55 -1998, Section 1-4

3 NFPA 497-1997, Section 1-3

4 NFPA 497-1997, Section 1-3

5 NFPA 497-1997, Section 1-3

6 NFPA 499-1997, Section 1-3

7 NFPA 70, 2005 *National Electrical Code*, 500.2 and 505.2

Courtesy of Thomas & Betts

Classification of Areas and Locations

Review Questions

1. Flammable or combustible liquids must be heated above their _____ to become an explosion risk.

    a.   boiling point
    b.   melting point
    c.   flash point
    d.   freezing point

2. In order for an explosion to occur, the concentration of flammable vapor and oxygen must be between _____ for the material involved.

    a.   10 and 15 percent vapor
    b.   greater than 50 percent vapor
    c.   the upper and lower flammable limit
    d.   the freezing and boiling point

3. Where flammable vapors with a vapor density greater than one are released inside a building, the risk of reaching an ignitible concentration will be greater_____.

    a.   near the floor
    b.   near the ceiling
    c.   in heated spaces
    d.   in ventilated spaces

4. The _____has no affect on area classification where flammable liquid is handled.

    a.   ventilation of the space
    b.   storage pressure
    c.   electrical equipment installed
    d.   size of a potential release point

5. The minimum temperature required to initiate combustion is referred to as the _____ of the material.

    a.   boiling point
    b.   flash point
    c.   combustion point
    d.   autoignition temperature

6. A Class I location that included ignitible concentrations of Group D materials under abnormal conditions would be a _____ location.

    a.   Zone 0
    b.   Division 2
    c.   Zone 2
    d.   Division 1

7. A Class I location that included ignitible concentration of Group IIC materials under abnormal conditions would be a _____ location.

    a.   Zone 2
    b.   Division 1
    c.   Division 2
    d.   Zone 0

8. Group __ includes the greatest number of flammable liquids, gases and vapors.

    a.   D
    b.   C
    c.   B
    d.   A

9. Where combustible dust layers on electrical equipment are greater than _____ under normal conditions, the space would be a Class II, Division 1, location.

    a.   ½ inch
    b.   1/3 inch
    c.   ¼ inch
    d.   1/8 inch

10. Combustible dusts are finely divided solid materials _____ in diameter that present a fire or explosion hazard when dispersed.

    a.   600 microns or greater
    b.   420 microns or less
    c.   1/8 inch or less
    d.   1/32 inch or less

11. Locations that include sufficient quantities of aluminum dust under abnormal conditions to become hazardous would be a _____ ___ location.

    a.   Class II, Division 1
    b.   Class II, Division 2
    c.   Class I, Division 2
    d.   Class III, Division 2

12. Where users choose to apply Article 506 and ignitible concentrations if ignitible fibers are present for long periods of time, the space would be classed a_____ location.

    a.   Zone 0
    b.   Zone 22
    c.   Zone 21
    d.   Zone 20

13. Atmospheres that include combustible metal dust will be Group __ locations.

    a.   D
    b.   E
    c.   F
    d.   G

14. When ignitible fibers are present _____ _____ the space will be a Class III, Division 1, location.

    a.   under normal operating conditions
    b.   under abnormal operating conditions
    c.   in a manufacturing application
    d.   in a storage application

15. Locations that include sufficient quantities of grain dust under abnormal conditions to become hazardous would be a_____.

    a.   Class III, Division 1
    b.   Class III, Division 2
    c.   Class II, Division 1
    d.   Class II, Division 2

16. Combustible dust are divided into __ material groups when the when the Division System is used.

    a.   1
    b.   2
    c.   3
    d.   4

17. Combustible dust and ignitible fibers are classified exactly the same using the_____ _____.

    a.   Zone System covered by *NEC*, Article 506
    b.   Division System covered by *NEC*, Article 500
    c.   Division System covered by *NEC*, Article 502
    d.   Division System covered by *NEC*, Article 503

18. Where flammable liquids, gases, or vapors; combustible dust; or ignitible fibers or flyings are present, but the presence of the material does not present a fire or explosion hazard, the location is considered_____.

    a.   non-hazardous
    b.   non-classified
    c.   normal
    d.   unclassified

19. The Zone classification scheme used in Article 505 divides flammable liquids, gases and vapors into __ zones based on how likely and how often an ignitible concentration will exist.

    a.   4
    b.   3
    c.   2
    d.   1

20. The Zone classification scheme used in Article 506 divides combustible dust and ignitible fibers and flyings into __ zone(s) based on how likely and how often an ignitible quantity will exist.

    a.   4
    b.   3
    c.   2
    d.   1

Chapter 2

Methods of Protection

When the fire triangle, discussed in chapter one, is reviewed, it becomes obvious that in order to minimize the chance of a fire or explosion, one or more of the components of the triangle must be removed. At the same time, it is obvious that all three elements of the fire triangle must be present in specific quantities, simultaneously, for fire or explosion to occur. In hazardous (classified) locations, the electrical system will often be the ignition component of the triangle. Acceptable protection of facilities involves control of these three elements to a point that one or more is not present at any given time. An unwritten rule of thumb, used to provide reasonable assurance that ignition will not take place, states that a minimum of two faults or system failures should occur prior to ignition.

Special electrical equipment is available for many tasks that must be accomplished within most hazardous (classified) locations; however, in some situations it is not easy to use the normal protection techniques. For example, some electrical equipment is not available using those protection techniques, such as motors. In Group D locations, motors are listed and available for Class I, Division 1 locations. If the application was Division 1 based on infrequent but normal releases, the designer might accept the Division 1 classification, specify an explosionproof motor and move forward with the design. If the facility included Group A or B materials, and had motors located where infrequent but normal releases occur, an option other than an explosionproof motor would have to be selected. UL 674, *Electric Motors and Generators for Use in Hazardous Locations, Class I, Groups B, C and D, Class II, Groups E, F, and G* does not include requirements for Group A locations. *NEC* 501.125(A)(2), (A)(3), and (A)(4) provide additional options to protect motors in Class I, Division 1 locations. It would also be possible to provide adequate ventilation or possibly adequate ventilation and gas detection and change the classification to Division 2. *NEC* 501.125(B) permits squirrel-cage induction motors without brushes, switching mechanisms, or other arc producing devices to be installed in Division 2 locations without explosionproof enclosures.

In some cases, a combination of more than one method of protection may be used to prevent the electrical equipment from becoming an ignition source in classified areas.

It is not always necessary to provide special electrical equipment to provide protection. In areas classed Division 2, Zone 2, or Zone 22, an abnormal condition (1st fault) would have to occur in the containment system for the flammable or combustible material before an ignitible concentration could occur. Some electrical equipment does not include arcing and sparking parts or provide elevated temperatures in its normal operation (junction boxes) and, therefore, an abnormal condition (2nd fault) such as an insulation failure in a splice or conductor would have to occur simultaneously with the failure in the

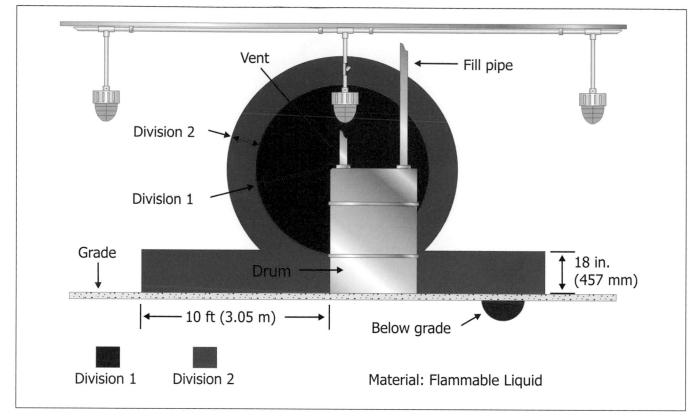

Figure 2-01. Luminaires (light fixtures) installed in Class I, Division 1 locations must be suitable for that location.

containment system to produce ignition. Hence, ordinary location electrical equipment is permitted under those conditions.

This chapter will look at several methods of protection that can be utilized to prevent electrical systems from becoming ignition sources at facilities that include hazardous (classified) locations.

Location of Electrical Equipment

One means of removing a component of the fire triangle that is not included as a protection technique is covered in *NEC* 500.5(A) FPN and 505.5(A) FPN No. 2. It involves designing the electrical system so that much or all of it is located outside the classified areas. This would involve accurate area classification of the space and careful placement of the electrical equipment. Depending on the type of process and facility involved, this option could eliminate some, or all, special electrical equipment. This option should be used whenever possible, because it should be cost effective and, in all cases, result in safer installations. However, this means of protection cannot be used in all cases since electrical components in some cases

must be installed within the process, e.g., pumps, compressors, instrumentation, etc. In other cases, the electrical equipment can be located to an area less likely to include ignitible concentrations. In many cases, relocating equipment a relatively short distance could result in decreased costs and have a major impact on safety and equipment requirements (figures 2-01, 2-02, and 2-03).

For example, figure 2-01 shows a luminaire installation that must be suitable for Class I, Division 1 locations. This installation is costly and also provides an ignition source at the most likely place for an ignitible concentration to develop. This ignition source must be protected by one of the few protection techniques that are permitted in Class I, Division 1 locations, and the only practical option for lighting is explosionproof.

However, figure 2-02 shows the same installation with the luminaire located in the Class I, Division 2 location. This relocation of 5 feet or less will decrease the cost of the installation and also increase the safety of the installation by placing the possible ignition source in a location that will only include

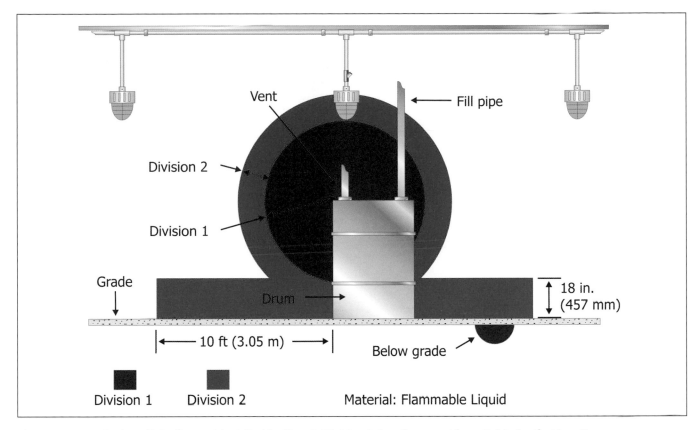

Figure 2.02. Luminaires (light fixtures) installed in Class I, Division 2 locations must be suitable for that location.

ignitible concentrations under abnormal conditions. Many protection techniques are permitted in Class I, Division 2 locations, providing options for owners and installers.

But figure 2-03 shows the best option for locating the luminaire (light fixture). This lighting installation will perform the electrical function that was required (lighting the area) and can be installed with ordinary location equipment. The relocation of just more than 5 feet allows a decrease in cost and completely removes the ignition source from the classified space.

The principles are exactly the same for space classified using *NEC* 505, the Zone system. An accurate area classification and careful placement of electrical devices will always reduce both cost and risk of ignition in Class I locations. As the equipment location moves from a Zone 0 area to a location classified as Zone 2, the number of permitted protection techniques increases. This provides more flexibility for the installation, a decrease in cost, and a safer installation. Just like the Division system, a relatively minor relocation of many electrical devices could result in the use of ordinary

location equipment. It should also be noted that Article 505 allows only electrical equipment that is protected by the *intrinsic safety* technique in Zone 0 spaces. That prohibits many electrical functions from taking place in that space.

With accurate area classification, much of the electrical equipment—lighting, alarm devices, security devices and communication devices—can be relocated to less classified or unclassified locations in many facilities. One common application where design can easily be used for protection involves the location of the exhaust fan motor when ventilation is provided in hazardous (classified) locations. A review of *NEC* 500.5(B)(1) FPN No. 2, item (5) and 505.5(B)(1) FPN No. 2 identifies the "interior of an exhaust duct that is used to vent ignitible concentrations of gases or vapors" as a Division 1 or Zone 0 location. Figure 2-04 shows the exhaust fan motor located inside the duct, which is permitted in a Division system if the fan is explosionproof. In almost all applications, the motor could be located outside the duct in a Division 2 or unclassified location, as shown in figure 2-05, and achieve the same purpose using an ordinary

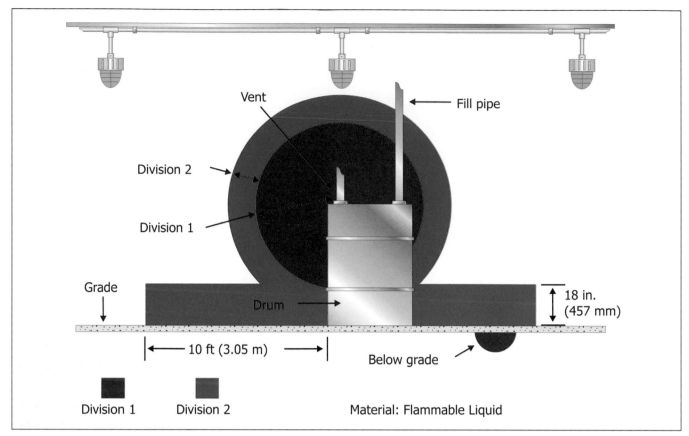

Figure 2.03. Luminaires (light fixtures) installed outside a Class I, Division 1 or 2 location can be suitable for general use.

location motor. If the Zone system were used, only intrinsic safety protection technique would be permitted in Zone 0. This requirement would force the motor to be located outside the duct.

Containment of Combustible Materials

In the United States over the past several decades,

containment of combustible materials as a result of environmental protection laws has certainly lessened the likelihood that ignitible concentrations of those materials are present during normal operations. Although reducing area classification is not the primary purpose for those laws, a byproduct is that many industries have been able to reduce their area

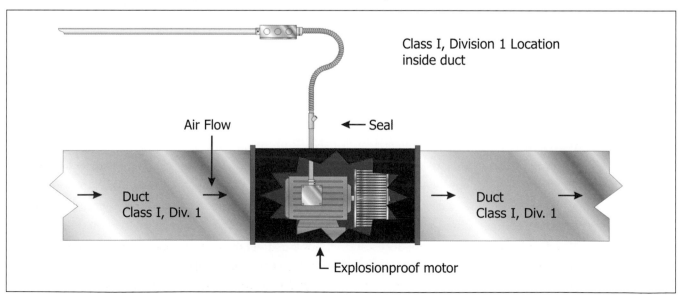

Figure 2-04. Exhaust duct with the electric fan motor installed inside the duct (hazardous location)

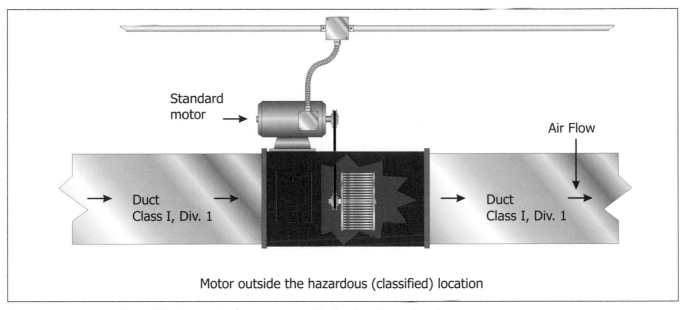

Figure 2-05. Exhaust duct with the electric fan motor outside the duct (hazardous location)

classification because they release fewer particles into the atmosphere. While the Environmental Protection Agency regulations address release of particles into the atmosphere in a different way than area classification, any control of release will have an impact on the area classification. Many people in the petrochemical industries today indicate that large "normal" releases of combustible materials would never be allowed under current EPA guidelines. This is not to say Division 1, Zone 0 or Zone 1 areas do not exist, but large-scale areas are not as common as they were in the past. It is no longer environmentally acceptable to vent waste products from a process, which could include flammable and combustible vapors in some industries, into the atmosphere. These EPA requirements have led to greater control of *fugitive emissions*, defined in American Petroleum Institute (API) Recommended Practice (RP) 500, Section 3.2.24 as "continuous flammable gas and vapor releases that are relatively small compared to releases due to equipment failures. These releases occur during normal operations of closed systems from components such as pump seals, valve packing and flange gaskets."

NFPA 30, *Flammable and Combustible Liquids Code,* defines fugitive emissions in somewhat broader terms as it covers both continuous and intermittent releases and includes additional components that may be the source of release. As the environmental requirements evolved, manufacturers of various

types of process equipment improved their products. The cumulative effect is that less flammable vapor is released into the atmosphere.

For many years, flammable and combustible liquids were delivered to sites and transferred to storage tanks for use upon demand. As liquid was added to the partially empty storage tanks, vapors above the liquid level were forced out the tank vents into the atmosphere. Today vapor recovery is provided with many fill operations involving flammable or combustible liquids. Consequently, a much smaller volume of flammable or combustible vapor is released into the atmosphere.

A common example of vapor recovery is used with gasoline delivery at gasoline stations all over the country. All new gas tanks and most existing gas tanks that are still in use are provided with tight fill connections. As the gasoline tanks are filled, the vapors located above the liquid level in the tank are recovered into the tanker trucks, rather than being forced out the tank vents. These recovered vapors are then taken back to the bulk storage facilities. Photos 2-01 and 2-02 show a typical tight fill delivery application.

When the tanker delivery truck returns, vapor recovery is provided at the bulk storage facility also. Photo 2-03 shows the vapor recovery operation at the bulk storage facility.

It should be noted that adoption and enforcement of EPA regulations could have a different impact on

Photo 2-01. Tight fill combustible liquid transfer

area classification from state to state or region to region. The affect of environmental regulations could also vary from industry to industry since the goal of those regulations is environmental not prevention of ignitible concentrations as it relates to electrical installations. It should also be noted that the *National Electrical Code* is used both inside and outside the United States, and that other countries will likely have different regulations, and that some

may have no environmental regulations at all.

For Class II and Class III locations, dust collection systems and housekeeping both have a major affect on area classification through the containment of combustible or ignitible material. These concepts also provide greater mechanical life for moving equipment, health benefits to employees, and minimize overheating of electrical equipment that would otherwise be covered with layers of dust or fibers.

In order to realize the benefit of dust collection and housekeeping and also use this as a method of protection by controlling the fuel side of the fire triangle, the installation must comply with the standards and recommended practices for the specific industry involved (see sidebar 2-01).

For electrical designers, installers, and inspection authorities, dust collection and housekeeping may be difficult to accept as protection techniques since they take place after the electrical installation is completed. Proper documentation of housekeeping policies and procedures could be requested from operators prior to relying on this method of protection. Section 3-3.2 of NFPA 499 indicates that areas designated as unclassified based on dust collection should be required to include adequate safeguards and warnings against failure. This might include some method to turn dust-producing equipment off when dust collection equipment is inoperable.

Photo 2-04 shows a dust collection system that limits the dust cloud in this operation and, in turn, minimizes the dust layering. That in combination with housekeeping can greatly limit the amount of special electrical equipment needed for this operation.

In many facilities that include classified locations, the classified areas can be limited by providing closed storage vessels and transporting flammable and combustible materials in well maintained closed piping systems. NFPA 497 and 499 both recognize these situations as unclassified areas. Special electrical equipment in the closed systems

Photo 2-02. Tight fill combustible liquid transfer

Photo 2-03. Vapor recovery operation at the bulk storage facility

Photo 2-04. Typical dust collection system (equipment shown inside of structure)

might be limited to instrumentation devices.

Separating hazardous locations with walls, enclosed vaults, or other solid partitions is another means to contain combustible materials and limit area classification. This method of containing the flammable or combustible materials is possible

Dust Collection and Housekeeping

- Construction requirements for hoods, capture devices, and enclosures
- Duct construction requirements
- Inspection and cleaning for exhaust vents
- Sludge removal requirements
- Prohibition of electrostatic duct collectors in certain industries
- Moisture control in certain industries
- Cleaning requirements for the dust collection system
- Inspection, testing and maintenance program requirements
- Employee training requirements
- Housekeeping
- Specific schedules for cleaning, i.e., concurrently with operations, at regular intervals
- Specific tools permitted for cleanup: soft brooms, conductive & nonsparking scoops, brushes with natural fiber bristles
- Use of vacuum cleaners to collect dust
- Prohibition of compressed air for cleaning in some industries while others permit this type of cleaning under very specific conditions
- Some standards establish an order for cleaning, i.e., brushed or swept first and then vacuumed
- Water cleaning requirements
- Inspection, testing and maintenance program requirements
- Employee training requirements

Sidebar 2-01.

with Class I, Class II and Class III location materials. Since dusts and fibers and flyings are solid materials rather than gas, they may be easier to contain by separation. Where separation of smaller hazardous areas within a larger facility is used as a method of protection, extreme caution should be used to completely close off the classified spaces. All openings and penetrations though the separation must be considered for possible releases of the combustible materials. Figure 2-06 shows an example where an unpierced wall on one side of a structure that contains a Class I point of release ends the classified space. The opposite wall of the structure has openings that require the classified area to extend outside the structure.

Figure 2-07 shows an example of a structure containing a Class II point of release. Walls on two sides of a structure are unpierced and an additional wall has an infrequently used self-closing door. The classified space does not extend beyond any of these walls. The other wall of the structure has a frequently opened door that requires the classified area to extend outside the structure.

When any means to contain combustible material is used as a method of protection, the goal is to remove the fuel side of the fire triangle.

Ventilation

Ventilation is the next method of protection for facilities that include flammable and combustible materials. *NEC* 500.5 recognizes the affect of ventilation in the area classification process. Adequate ventilation is defined in Section 1-3 of NFPA 497 as "a ventilation rate that affords either 6 air changes per hour, or 1 cubic feet per minute (cfm) per square foot of floor area, or other similar criteria that prevent the accumulation of significant quantities of vapor-air concentrations from exceeding 25 percent of the lower flammable limit." It should be recognized that the air change information included in this definition is not very specific. If the air changes noted do not limit the concentration of vapors to 25 percent of the lower flammable limit, the area classification should not be adjusted. In many cases where limited releases are occurring, those air change rates will likely provide adequate ventilation. In other cases where larger releases are expected, it may be determined that those air change rates are not sufficient to change the area classification. A review of the specific occupancy code, standard or recommended practice is advised prior to adjusting the area classification based on 6 air changes per hour. Some standards are very specific about the location of the exhaust and supply ducts, depending on the vapor density of the material involved. Some require product shutdown upon failure of ventilation. Others require gas detection systems to be interconnected with shutdown of a process. In every case, the code, standard, or recommended practice for the facility should be considered prior to adjusting area classification based on ventilation.

Section 3-3.2 of NFPA 497 also indicates that outside installations and installations within open or

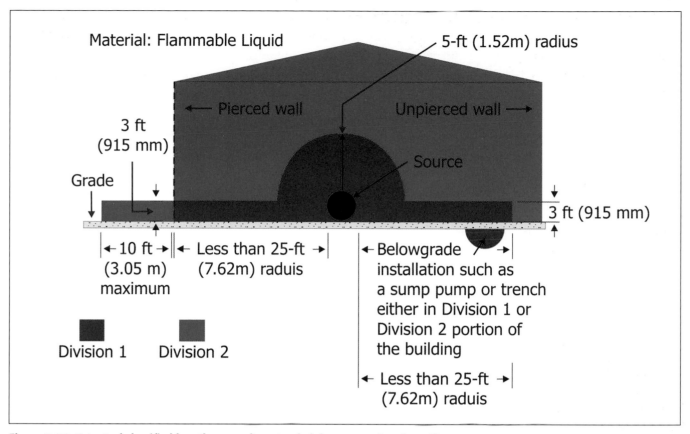

Figure 2-06. Extent of classified locations can be extended due to openings in walls or structures

partially open structures may be considered to have adequate ventilation and be classed "unclassified." A review of many of the occupancy documents will result in those spaces being classified. Section 1-2.3 of NFPA 497 indicates the document is a recommended practice and is intended as a guide that should be applied with sound engineering judgment. This is an excellent example of that statement. When the information is used within its context and all of the parameters are considered, some outside installations will result in unclassified areas and others will result in classified areas. When it is determined that adequate ventilation has been provided, the specific standard for the industry or material involved will provide the guideline for the

impact of ventilation on the area classification.

Great care should be used when the classification of a space and type of electrical equipment is changed based on the fact that ventilation is provided. Ventilation is required and may be provided in many facilities for reasons other than reducing the area

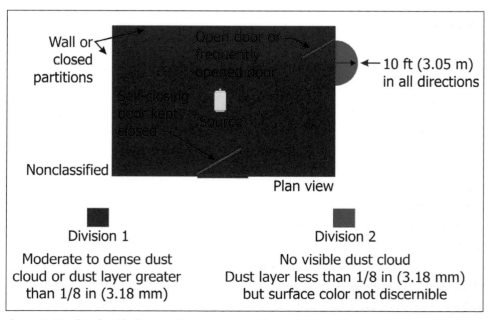

Figure 2-07. The classified space does not extend beyond the walls.

classification. NFPA 5000, Section 38.7 addresses attic ventilation; Section 54.4 requires ventilation of elevator machine rooms to maintain required temperatures during fire fighter service operations; Chapter 49 requires all rooms and occupied spaces in buildings to be ventilated; Section 49.2.2.1 requires various types of occupancies to conform to ASHRAE 62, *Ventilation for Acceptable Air Quality*. ASHRAE Standards provide ventilation requirements for spaces intended for human occupancy and specify minimum and recommended ventilation air quantities for the preservation of the occupant's health, safety, and well-being. That document defines *ventilation* as "the process of supplying and removing air by natural or mechanical means to and from any space." These requirements could certainly be met and have no impact on area classification.

NFPA 91, *Standard for Exhaust Systems for Air Conveying of Vapors, Gases, Mists and Noncombustible Particulate Solids* provides some general requirements for design and construction of exhaust systems which may be modified by other applicable standards. Systems that comply with this standard are limited to conveying flammables that are not more than 25 percent of the lower flammable limit unless they also meet the requirements of NFPA 69, *Standard on Explosion Prevention Systems*. Under normal conditions, fire detection and alarm systems are not permitted to shut down these air-moving devices.

Ventilation requirements for some codes and standards are shown in sidebar 2-02. These examples will provide some indication of the affects of ventilation on the electrical systems installed in hazardous (classified) locations.

Grounding and Bonding Requirements

The processes of grounding and bonding are the building of safety circuits associated with and that must work together with the electrical circuits and systems. The *NEC* covers the subject of grounding and bonding. Grounding is required for the protection of electrical installations, which, in turn, protect the buildings or structures in which the electrical systems are installed. Persons and even animals that may come into contact with the electrical system, or are in these buildings or

structures, are also protected if the grounding system is installed and maintained properly. The *Code* does not imply here that grounding is the only method that can be used for the protection of electrical installations, people or animals. Insulation, isolation and guarding are also suitable alternatives under certain conditions. Grounding of specific equipment is covered in several other articles of the *NEC*.

Scope and Purpose of Grounding and Bonding

The scope and general requirements for grounding and bonding are contained in *NEC* 250.4. Included are the grounding and bonding performance requirements for grounded systems and ungrounded systems as follows:

A. Grounded System
1. Electrical System Grounding
2. Grounding of Electrical Equipment
3. Bonding of Electrical Equipment
4. Bonding of Electrically Conductive Materials and Other Equipment
5. Effective Ground-Fault Current Path
B. Ungrounded Systems
1. Grounding of Electrical Equipment
2. Bonding of Electrical Equipment
3. Bonding of Electrically Conductive Materials and Other Equipment
4. Path for Fault Current

Grounding Fundamentals

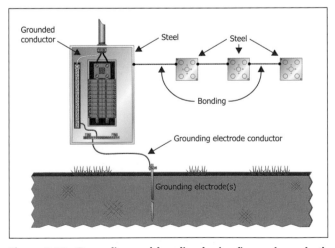

Figure 2-08. Grounding and bonding basics figure shows both grounding (connection to the earth) and bonding (electrically conductive materials connected together) for electrical systems

Electrical systems are solidly grounded to limit the voltage to ground during normal operation, and to prevent excessive voltages due to lightning, line surges or unintentional contact with higher voltage lines, and to stabilize the voltage to ground during normal operation [*NEC*, 250.4(A)]. Several methods of grounding electrical systems are used depending on *Code* requirements and system design and function. Methods of grounding electrical systems sometimes vary based on specific conditions, but generally systems are solidly grounded. *Solidly grounded* means the system has a conductor that is intentionally grounded with no intentional impedance between the earth and the grounded conductor of the system.

Definitions

Grounding Electrode. A device that establishes an electrical connection to the earth.[1] Grounding electrodes provide the essential function of connecting the electrical system or electrical equipment to the earth, which is considered to be at zero potential. In some cases, the grounding electrode serves to ground the electrical system. In other instances, the electrode is used to connect the normally non-current-carrying metallic portions of electrical equipment to the earth. In both situations, the primary purpose of the grounding electrode is to maintain the electrical equipment at the earth potential present at the grounding electrode.

Another essential function of the grounding electrode is to dissipate overvoltages into the earth. These overvoltages can be caused by high-voltage conductors being accidentally connected to the lower-voltage system, such as by a failure in a transformer or by an overhead conductor dropping on the lower-voltage conductor. Overvoltages can also be caused from lightning. A more complete discussion on lightning protection systems is provided later in this chapter. For complete information about lightning protection systems refer to NFPA 780, *Standard for the Installation of Lightning Protection Systems.*

Conductive materials enclosing electrical conductors or equipment, or that are part of the equipment, are grounded to limit the voltage to ground on these materials and bonded to facilitate the

Ventilation requirements for codes & standards

NFPA 30, Flammable & Combustible Liquids Code requires all atmospheric storage tanks that contain flammable or combustible liquids to be adequately vented to prevent the development of vacuum or pressure conditions that might distort the tank or exceed the design pressure of the tank. This adequate vent of the tank is not going to provide ventilation that is adequate to prevent the accumulation of vapor-air concentrations from exceeding 25 percent of the lower flammable limit. This code includes ventilation requirements in sections 2.2.7.5 for vaults that contain tanks storing Class I liquids; 2.3.4.4 for tank buildings; 4.4.2.7 for inside liquid storage areas; 4.6.3.4 for hazardous materials storage lockers; and 5.3.4.1 for enclosed processing areas handling or using Class I, Class II or Class III liquids above their flash point. With the ventilation requirements met, some of these spaces are Class I Division or Zone 1 and others are Class I, Division or Zone 2.

NFPA 57, Liquefied Natural Gas (LNG) Vehicular Fuel Systems Code requires buildings with indoor fueling to provide continuous mechanical ventilation or a mechanical ventilation system that is activated by a continuous gas monitoring system, which activates the ventilation system when a gas concentration of one-fifth of the lower flammable limit is present. Both of these ventilation options are required to shut down the fuel system if the ventilation system fails. The ventilation rate shall not be less than one cubic foot per minute per 12 cubic feet of room volume. When adequate ventilation is provided, some locations are classed Class I, Group D, Division or Zone 1 and others Class I, Group D, Division or Zone 2.

Additional requirements are provided for commercial marine vessels operating on LNG.

NFPA 120, Standard for Coal Preparation Plants allows adequate ventilation to reduce area classification from Class I, Division 2 where methane can reach ignitible concentrations to unclassified. Any equipment that is needed to restore the facility to a safe condition such as lighting, ventilation, and sump pumps must be installed based on Class I, Division 1 requirements. Additional gas monitoring and shutdown provisions are also required when area classification is reduced because of ventilation.

NFPA 409, Standard on Aircraft Hangars permits mechanical ventilation for vapor removal in accordance with NFPA 91, Standard for Exhaust Systems for Air Conveying of materials.

NFPA 651, Standard for the Machining and Finishing of Aluminum and the Production and Handling of Aluminum Powders includes a reference to the ventilation requirements in NFPA 30, where aluminum dusts or powders are present in the same area with flammable or combustible solvents.

Sidebar 2-02.

Ventilation requirements for codes & standards

NFPA 820, Standard for Fire Protection in Wastewater Treatment and Collection Facilities indicates that ventilation rates used in that standard are based on air changes per hour and are calculated by using 100 percent outside air for the supply air that is exhausted. Air changes are calculated using the maximum aggregate volume of the space to be ventilated under normal conditions. Ventilation is not required, but is permitted if designers and owners desire area classification reduction. Ventilation systems used to reduce area classification in this standard are required to have both supply and exhaust fans, a means to provide power from an alternate power source, a power loss alarm on the primary power source, and include a variety of ventilation rates depending on what location or function in the collection and treatment process is involved and area classification that is desired to be achieved. All continuous ventilation systems installed for these facilities are required to include flow detection devices which are connected to an alarm signaling system and include both visual and audible alarms located in specific locations.

NFPA 853, Standard for Installation of Stationary Fuel Cell Power Plants requires mechanical ventilation of rooms where fuel cell power plants are located. The exhaust rate must be at least 1 cfm per square foot of floor area for the room and not less than 150 cfm of total floor area. That standard also requires the ventilation to be interlocked so that the unit will be shut down upon loss of ventilation.

Sidebar 2-02 continued.

operation of overcurrent devices under ground-fault conditions [*NEC*, 250.4(A)]. Where the electrical system is grounded, the equipment grounding conductor is connected to the grounded system conductor (often a neutral) at the service or the source of a separately derived system. Where the electrical system is not grounded, the electrical equipment is connected to earth at the service to maintain the equipment at or near earth potential, and the equipment is bonded together to provide a path for fault current. This occurs where a second ground fault occurs before the first one is cleared.

Grounding and Equipment Grounding Conductor

As used in Article 250 and the other articles of the *Code*, grounding is a process that is ongoing. That is true for the equipment grounding conductors. The

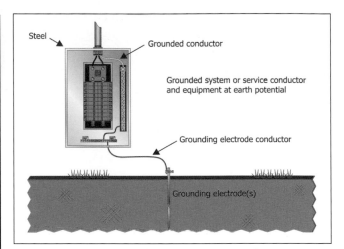

Figure 2-09. Grounding electrode fundamentals

action is ongoing; through every electrical enclosure, it is connected to all the way to the last outlet on the branch circuit. The equipment grounding conductor puts all metal enclosures at earth potential along the way, and also provides a low-impedance path for fault current to flow on if a ground fault should occur in the system.

So it is important that the equipment grounding conductor of the circuit make a complete and reliable circuit back to the source or service, where it and the grounded (neutral) conductor are required to be connected together through a main bonding jumper. The *main bonding jumper* is defined in the *Code* as "the connection between the grounded conductor and the equipment grounding conductor at the service." In a separately derived system, this connection is made with a system bonding jumper installed between the grounded conductor and the equipment grounding conductor. These bonding jumpers complete the

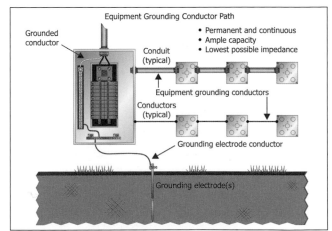

Figure 2-10. Equipment grounding conductor basic location and path in the safety circuit

fault-current circuit back to the source.

Grounding as Compared to Bonding

Both of these terms are well defined in *NEC* 100. Both of these functions are essential for the complete safety anticipated by the rules in Article 250, Grounding and Bonding. These are two separate functions with two different purposes. It is important that a clear understanding of the grounding (earthing) circuit and its purpose as compared to the equipment grounding conductors and bonding circuits be established. Section 250.4 has been broken down into grounded systems and ungrounded systems. The requirements in this section have been expanded and revised to include more descriptive performance requirements and to establish the purposes served by each of these actions.

Bonding Fundamentals

The *Code* provides requirements for bonding of electrically conductive materials and other equipment. Electrically conductive materials, such as metal water piping, metal gas piping and structural steel members, that are likely to become energized must be bonded to provide a low-impedance path for clearing ground faults that otherwise would energize the equipment at a level above earth potential. For systems that are grounded, the equipment is bonded to the grounded system conductor (often a neutral) at the service or source of a separately derived system. Where an electrical system is provided ungrounded, the electrical equipment is connected to earth (grounded) at the service or system to maintain the equipment at or near earth potential, and the equipment is bonded together to provide a path for fault current. Again, this occurs where a second ground fault occurs before the first one is cleared.

Effective Ground-Fault Current Path

Grounding and bonding must be effective and must include the following characteristics:

1. Be permanent and continuous path
2. Have adequate capacity for fault currents likely to be imposed
3. Have lowest possible impedance of current flow in the fault-current path

The *Code* is silent on specifying the maximum

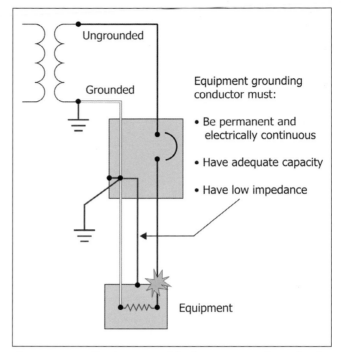

Figure 2-11. Effective ground-fault current path and principles of overcurrent device operation

impedance acceptable for the effective ground-fault path, except to say that the path must have impedance low enough to assure effective operation of the overcurrent protective devices. Every circuit has different characteristics associated with it that contribute to the impedance of the particular circuit, and, thus, the impedance value of the grounding circuit will vary but must be kept as low as possible in all grounding circuits. The goal of good design of the effective ground-fault path is to provide a permanent and adequate path of low impedance so enough current will flow in the circuit to cause a circuit breaker to trip or a fuse to open under fault conditions. If the opening of the breaker or fuse on the line side of the faulted circuit does not take place rapidly, thus taking the faulted equipment or circuit offline, the protective bonding and grounding system will have failed to perform its critically important function. This failure may result in greater equipment damage, and possibly fires or injury to personnel.

Grounding and Bonding Requirements in Hazardous Locations

The *Code* places some special requirements for grounding and bonding in hazardous (classified) locations. These requirements can be found in

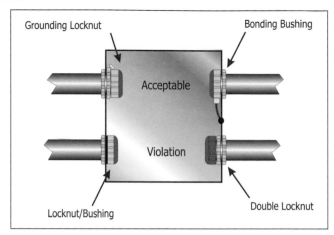

Figure 2-12. Both acceptable and unacceptable bonding means for hazardous locations wiring

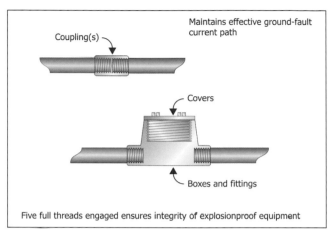

Figure 2-13. Threads fully engaged at couplings, fittings, boxes, etc.

Section 501.30 for Class I locations, Section 502.30 for Class II locations, and Section 503.30 for Class III locations. For Class I, Zone 0, 1 and 2 hazardous (classified) locations, see Section 505.25 that requires compliance with Section 501.30.

Grounding and bonding are essential for electrical safety in nonhazardous as well as in hazardous locations. In hazardous locations it is vital to have effective grounding and bonding to prevent an explosion. Under fault-current conditions when heavy currents are flowing through metal conduit, every connection point in the raceway system is a potential source of sparks and ignition. If there is an arcing fault to a metal enclosure in a hazardous (classified) location, the external surface temperature of the metal enclosure at the point of the arcing fault will start to rise to temperatures that could cause ignition of the flammable vapors or accumulations of combustible dust. Under these fault conditions, it is essential that the overcurrent device be caused to operate as quickly as possible to prevent a hot spot on the enclosure or even arcs that may burn through the enclosure from igniting the atmosphere, dust, or fibers and flyings on the outside of the enclosure. It is extremely important that all threaded joints be made up wrenchtight to prevent sparking at those threaded joints. If joints are other than the threaded type, such as locknuts and bushings or double locknuts and bushings at boxes, enclosures, cabinets, and panelboards, it is essential that bonding be assured around those joints in the fault-current bonding path to prevent sparking and assure a low-impedance path

for the fault current.

General bonding requirements are found in Part V of Article 250 of the *NEC*. Section 250.90 requires bonding "where necessary to ensure electrical continuity and the capacity to conduct safely any fault current likely to be imposed." Section 250.100 also includes bonding requirements for hazardous locations and indicates that regardless of the voltage, the electrical continuity of non-current-carrying metal parts of equipment, raceways, and other enclosures in any hazardous (classified) location as defined in Article 500 shall be ensured by any of the methods specified for services in Section 250.92(B) that are approved for the wiring method used.

During ground-fault conditions there are heavy currents flowing through metal conduits in the effective ground-fault current path. Every joint or connection point, such as couplings, locknuts, hubs and other fittings, can be a potential source of ignition from arcing or sparks and therefore a potential source of ignition. It is extremely imperative that all threaded fittings and joints be made up wrenchtight to prevent arcing from these threaded joints for the duration of time it takes the overcurrent device to clear the fault event. Fittings suitable for the bonding required must be used. The types of methods acceptable to meet these requirements are provided in 250.92(B).

By these special requirements, an effort is made to provide assured grounding and bonding to reduce the likelihood that a line-to-ground fault will cause arcing and sparking at connection points of metallic raceways and boxes or other enclosures. If such

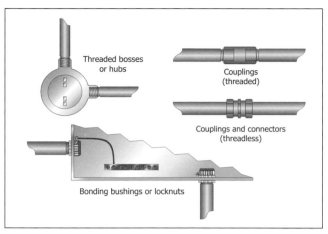

Figure 2-14. Acceptable bonding methods identified in Section 250.92(B)

arcing or sparking were to occur in a hazardous (classified) location while a flammable gas is present in its explosive range, it is likely that the flammable atmosphere would be ignited.

Generally, locknuts on each side of the enclosure, or a locknut on the outside and a bushing on the inside, cannot be used for bonding. Bonding locknuts or bonding bushings with bonding jumpers must be used to ensure the integrity of the bond and its capability of carrying the fault current that may be imposed, without arcing or sparking at the connections.

The bonding means required here must, generally, be installed from the hazardous (classified) location to the service equipment or point of grounding of a separately derived system that is the source of the circuit. This includes all raceways, fittings, junction boxes, enclosures, controllers and panelboards between the hazardous location and the service or separately derived system. The goal is to ensure a substantial flame path for ground-fault currents and to facilitate fast operation of overcurrent protective devices supplying the circuit in the hazardous locations. Hot temperatures on electrical enclosures can ignite hazardous atmospheres. If a ground fault should occur inside an explosionproof enclosure, a hot spot at the point of fault on the enclosure could develop if the overcurrent device does not clear quickly. These more restrictive bonding rules in chapter 5 of the *Code* are in place for these reasons. Bonding in hazardous locations is applicable to all metal raceways and enclosures in the hazardous location and to all intervening metal raceways and enclosures of the circuit extending back

to the applicable service or derived system where the grounding connections are established. Since current and fault current seek the source, this method of bonding must be accomplished from point of a ground fault in the circuit all the way back to the source or service grounding point, where the main bonding jumper or system bonding jumper is installed.

An exception to this general requirement clarifies that the bonding is required to be taken no further than the point where the grounded circuit conductor (may be a neutral) and the grounding electrode conductor are connected together on the line side of the building or structure disconnecting means that is grounded in accordance with Section 250.32(A), (B) or (C), and that branch-circuit overcurrent protection is located on the load side of the disconnecting means.

Section 250.32 provides grounding requirements where more than one building or structure are on the same premises and are supplied from a common service. Where the grounded circuit conductor is not grounded at the building or structure, the rule in Sections 501.30(A), 502.30(A) and 503.30(A) requires that the bonding extend from the hazardous location back to the service, even if it is in another building. This requires that the feeder raceway system be bonded if it is metallic.

Grounding in Hazardous Locations

Where flexible metal conduit or liquidtight flexible metal conduit is permitted and used in Class I, Division 2 hazardous (classified) locations, there must

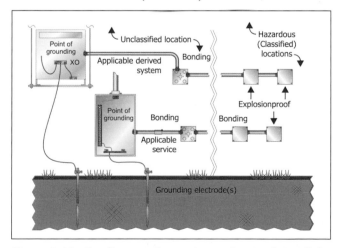

Figure 2-15. Bonding requirements must extend to all intervening metal raceways back to the applicable service or source of separately derived system grounding point.

be an internal or external bonding jumper installed to supplement the conduit. If installed outside the conduit, the bonding jumper is limited to 1.8 m (6 ft) in length by Section 250.102(E) [see *NEC*, 501.30(B)].

In these Class I, Division 2 areas, the bonding jumper is permitted to be omitted by exception under the following conditions:

1. Listed liquidtight flexible metal conduit not more than 1.8 m (6 ft) long with fittings listed for grounding is used.

2. Overcurrent protection of the circuit in the raceway does not exceed 10 amperes.

3. The load is not a power utilization load. (See Section 502.30(B) for similar rules for Class II areas and Section 503.30(B) for Class III locations).

Intrinsically Safe Systems and Circuits

Article 504 includes the requirements for intrinsically safe systems. Sections 504.50 and 504.60 include the grounding and bonding requirements for these systems.

Section 504.50(A) requires intrinsically safe

apparatus, associated apparatus, cable shields, enclosures, and raceways, if of metal, to be grounded. This covers the metal raceways and enclosures for such systems. A control drawing is required for these systems to provide specific information and instructions. These control drawings include grounding and bonding information that is critical to the integrity of the intrinsically safe system or circuit(s). Supplementary bonding to the grounding electrode may be needed for some associated apparatus, e.g., zener diode barriers, if specified in the control drawing. Additional information relative to these systems can be found in *Wiring Practices for Hazardous (Classified) Locations Instrumentation Part 1: Intrinsic Safety,* ANSI/ISA RP 12.6-1995.

Branch circuits that include an equipment grounding conductor as covered in 250.118 must supply intrinsically safe systems. The equipment grounding conductor is for grounding the metal enclosure(s) and other metal parts and equipment of the system.

It is not uncommon for the required control drawing(s) to specify a grounding electrode con-

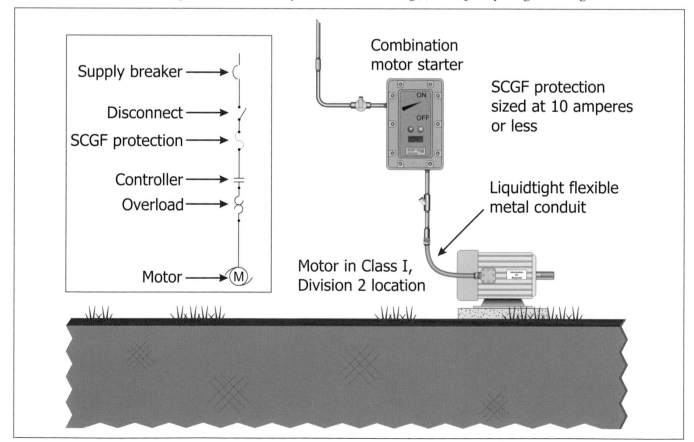

Figure 2-16. Liquidtight flexible metal conduit in Class I, Division II locations for circuits where the overcurrent protective device does not exceed 10 amperes

Photo 2-05. Typical intrinsically safe system control panel

ductor connection for these systems in addition to connection to an equipment grounding conductor. Usually, terminals for both of these conductors are located within the system enclosure or control panel. If a grounding electrode is required, then one of the electrodes in 250.50 must be used. The choice of grounding electrode to be used is governed by the same means specified in 250.30(A)(7) for separately derived systems: "The grounding electrode shall be as near as practicable to and preferably in the same area as the grounding electrode conductor connection to the system." It also must be the nearest of either of the following electrodes:

1. A structural metal grounding electrode as specified in 250.52(A)(2)

2. A metal water pipe electrode as specified in 250.52(A)(1) within 1.5 m (5 ft) of entry to the building or structure

3. Any other grounding electrode specified by 250.52(A)—if either of the above grounding electrodes is not available. Other electrodes might include concrete-encased electrodes, ground rings, rod, pipe and plate electrodes[*NEC,* 250.30(A)(7)].

If the intrinsically safe system requires a connection to a grounding electrode, usually the grounding electrode for the IS system will be one of the electrodes used for the service or separately derived systems installed in or at that building or structure. Installed electrodes such as rods, pipes, or plate types must only be used where the electrodes specified in 250.30(A)(7)(1) or (2) are not present. An example of that particular situation would include a system that is installed remote from a building or structure and supplied by a branch circuit.

The size of this grounding conductor is usually specified by the manufacturer's control drawing. Where shielded cables are used, the shields of such cables are required to be grounded, unless the shield conductor is itself part of the intrinsically safe circuit [see *NEC,* 504.50(C) Exception]. Bonding requirements for metallic enclosures and raceways

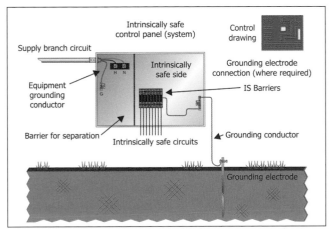

Figure 2-17. Intrinsically safe system control panel with the equipment grounding conductor of the branch circuit connected and also a connected grounding electrode conductor to the appropriate terminal on the circuit board as required by the control drawing

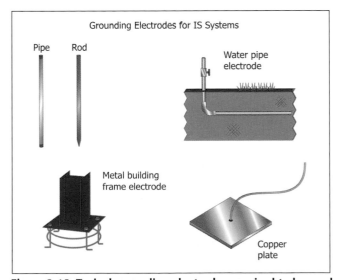

Figure 2-18. Typical grounding electrodes required to be used for the intrinsically safe system

enclosing intrinsically safe systems or circuits in hazardous locations must be in accordance with any of the methods suitable for the bonding on the line side of a service as specified in 250.92(B). Section 250.100 indicates that regardless of the voltage of the contained circuit or system, bonding must be assured by these methods.

Sections 501.30, 502.30, and 503.30 also provide specific requirements relative to these more restrictive and robust bonding requirements in hazardous locations, which include the metal raceways containing intrinsically safe circuit or system wiring. Bonding for these metal raceways or enclosures must also be extended and maintained for all intervening raceways and enclosures from the hazardous location all the way to the applicable service or separately derived system. This is intended to assure effective operation of the entire system.

In addition to providing protection from arcs and sparks or overheated enclosures, and so forth, due to ground-fault events, grounding is necessary to prevent the buildup of static electrical charges. The requirements for providing a low-impedance path in the metallic bonding circuit as previously discussed is not essential for static grounding and bonding protection methods. The following provides basic fundamentals about static electricity and methods of providing suitable protection from those ignition sources in hazardous locations.

Effective grounding is necessary to prevent the buildup of static electrical charges.

Static Protection through Bonding and Grounding

Effective grounding and bonding are important components in the overall electrical safety scheme. As previously discussed, properly grounded and bonded systems and conductive parts provide protection for persons and property. Protection against electrical shock and equalizing potential to earth are accomplished by grounding conductive parts. Fast and sure operation of overcurrent protective devices if a fault occurs is assured by creating an effective ground-fault current path back to the source, either the applicable service or source of separately derived system. Grounding and bonding

requirements in the *Code* for electrical installations in hazardous locations provide protection from such events.

In hazardous locations, electrical wiring and the grounding and bonding circuits are extremely important for safety. Because sources of ignition are a primary concern in explosive atmospheres, it is often necessary to provide a more enhanced protection system of handling static electricity in hazardous locations.

Humidity

Protection against static electricity is a requirement of a number of industries and establishments. The grounding of equipment is not necessarily a solution to static problems. Each static problem requires its own study and solution. Humidity plays an important part in the degree of concern. The higher the humidity is, the less chance there is of a static discharge occurring. In some industries, increasing humidity in the area of a static discharge has been found to be effective. One example is in the printing industry.

While humidification does increase surface conductivity of the material, the charge will dissipate only if there is a conductive path to ground. Surface resistivity of many materials can be controlled by the humidity of the surroundings. At a humidity of 65 percent and higher, the surface of most materials will absorb enough moisture to ensure a surface conductivity that is sufficient to prevent accumulation of static electricity. When the humidity falls below about 30 percent, these same materials could become good insulators, in which case accumulation of charge will increase. It should be emphasized that humidification is a not a solution for all static electricity problems encountered. Some insulating materials do not absorb moisture from the air and high humidity will not noticeably decrease their surface resistivity. Examples of such insulating materials are uncontaminated surfaces of some polymeric materials, such as plastic piping, containers, and the surface of most petroleum liquids [NFPA 77, 6.4.2.3].

Concerns of Static Electricity as Ignition Source

This chapter takes the reader beyond the requirements of the electrical *Code* and looks at means of protection from static electricity and sources of ignition related thereto. It should be clearly understood that the primary goal in providing static protection is to eliminate the ignition source of the fire triangle. Careful consideration and planning are necessary to evaluate all known possibilities of static ignition sources relative to providing this type of protection in hazardous locations. The degree of additional protection needed is specific to each condition encountered. There are no mandatory electrical *Code* requirements to provide such protection; however, hazards exist and providing protection must be considered for safety. Generally, the type of installation, type of explosive or flammable atmosphere (dust or gases), and the natural environment are all contributing factors to the degree or extent of static electricity as an ignition source. For a static electricity discharge to be a source of ignition, the following four conditions must exist simultaneously:

1. An effective means of separating charge must be present.
2. A means of accumulating the separated charges and maintaining a difference of electrical potential must be available.
3. A discharge of the static electricity of adequate energy must occur.
4. The discharge must occur in an ignitible mixture [NFPA 77, 4.3.1].

Sparks from ungrounded charged conductors, including the human body, are responsible for most fires and explosions ignited by static electricity. Sparks are typically intense capacitive discharges that occur in the gap between two charged conducting bodies, usually metal. The ability of a discharge spark to produce ignition or explosion is directly related to its energy, which will be some fraction of the total energy stored in the conductive object.

Beyond the NEC

The *NEC* provides a reference through a fine print note (FPN) to the recommended practice on protection from static electricity. The referenced document is titled *Recommended Practice on Static Electricity,* NFPA 77-2000. Lightning protection systems are also important considerations and provide reasonable planned protection for those natural events in the weather that produces lightning. An industry standard for these types of protection systems is the *Standard for the Installation of Lightning Protection Systems,* NFPA 780-2004. The American Petroleum Institute (API) also has produced a document that addresses protection techniques used to address both of these concerns and is titled, *Protection Against Ignitions Arising Out of Static Lightning and Stray Currents* API RP 2003-1998 [*NEC,* 500.4(B) FPN No. 3]. As previously discussed, the fine print notes in the *NEC* are explanatory in nature and are not mandatory requirements of the *Code* based on its structure and style [*NEC,* 90.5(C)]. However, these references provide clear direction to resources that provide specific criteria and guidelines for this enhanced protection. It is important to emphasize that these methods of protection from static electricity and static ignition sources must overlay the requirements of the *Code* and are in addition to those requirements and are never intended to substitute for those requirements.

Definitions

Static Electric Discharge. A release of static electricity in the form of a spark, corona discharge, brush discharge, or propagating brush discharge that might be capable of causing ignition under appropriate circumstances [NFPA 77, 3.1.16].

Static Electricity. An electric charge that is significant only for the effects of its electrical field component and that manifests no significant magnetic field component [NFPA 77, 3.1.17].

Static Electricity Fundamentals

All matter (materials), whether liquid or solid, is made up of various arrangements of atoms. Atoms are made up of positively charged nuclear components that give them mass and are then surrounded by negatively charged electrons. Atoms are considered to be electrically neutral in their normal state. Basically, this means there are equal amounts of positive and negative charge present. Atoms can become *charged*

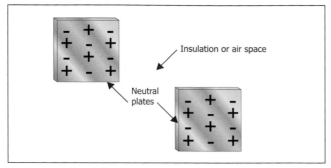

Figure 2-19. Two conductive plates each with like charges

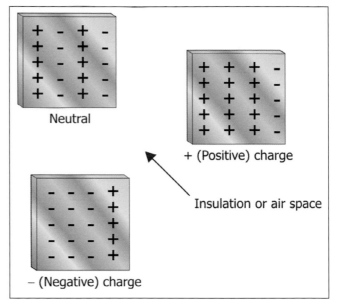

Figure 2-20. Two conductive plates with unlike charges

when there is excess or a deficiency of electrons relative to the neutral state (see figures 2-19 and 2-20).

In electrically conductive materials, such as metals of the ferrous and nonferrous types, electrons move freely. In materials made up of insulating material, such as plastic, glass, motor oil, etc., electrons are bonded more tightly to the nucleus of the atom and are not free to move. Some examples of electrically conductive materials are wire, metallic enclosures, busbars, etc.; while insulating materials include such items as glass, petroleum-based products, paper, rubber, etc.

In insulating materials in the form of fluids, an electron can separate from one atom and move freely or attach to another atom to form a negative ion. The atom losing the electron then becomes a positive ion. Ions are charged atoms and molecules.

Elimination or separation of the charge cannot be prevented absolutely because the origin of the charge lies at the interface of materials. When materials are placed in contact, some electrons move from one material to the other until a balance (equilibrium condition) in energy is reached. This charge separation is most noticeable in liquids that are in contact with solid surfaces, and in solids in contact with other solids. The flow of clean gas over a solid surface produces negligible charging [NFPA 77, 4.1.8].

This is the primary reason for the gasoline dispensing hazard warnings at motor fuel dispensers. It is important to observe and adhere to all warnings and directions relative to the transfer of gasoline to a motor vehicle or portable container. Always place portable gasoline containers on the ground when filling them; otherwise, the charging currents allow static charges to build without a path to dissipate.

Possibilities of ignition or explosion of gasoline vapors during these types of operations are increased when all appropriate safety procedures are not followed. Elimination of differences of potential (voltage) between objects reduces these hazards

Static Discharge and Separation

A *capacitor* is described basically as "two conductors that are separated by an insulating material." In static electric phenomena, the charge is generally separated by a resistive barrier, such as an air gap or form of insulation between the conductors, or by the insulating property of the materials being handled or processed. In many applications, particularly those where the materials being processed are nonconductive (charged insulators), measuring their potential differences is challenging to say the least.

One is probably most familiar with the common static charge built up by walking or scuffing the feet on carpet fibers. People are conductors of electricity and thus are capable of holding a static charge. The release of such static charges is also a familiar experience for most individuals. Children often are amused and entertained when this phenomenon is first realized. Electrical static charging results from rubbing materials together and is known as *triboelectric charging*. It is the result of exposing surface electrons to a broad variety of energies in an adjacent material, so that charge separation

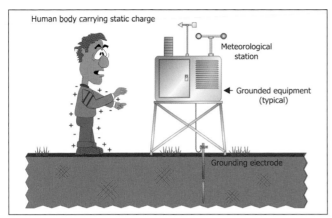

Figure 2-21. A charged person can be discharged to a grounded object by contact

(discharge) is likely to take place. The breakup of liquids by splashing and misting, or even flow in some instances, results in a similar charge release. It is only necessary to transfer about one electron for each 500,000 atoms to produce a condition that can lead to a static electric discharge. Surface contaminants at very low concentrations can play a significant role in charge separation at the interface of materials.

Electrically conductive materials can become charged when they are in the vicinity of another highly charged surface. Electrons in the conductive material are either drawn toward or forced away from the region of closest approach to the charged surface, depending on the nature of the charge on that surface. Like charges will repel and unlike charges will attract. If the electrically conductive material that is charged is connected to ground or bonded to another object, additional electrons can pass to or from ground or the object. If contact is then broken and the conductive material and charged surface are separated, the charge on the isolated conductive object changes. The net charge that is transferred is called an *induced charge*.

The basic objective when dealing with concerns and hazards of static electricity and stray voltages is to try to eliminate or at least minimize any differences of potential between electrically conductive objects and other objects and the ground. The potential difference, that is, the voltage, between any two points is the work per unit charge that would have to be done to move the charges from one point to the other. Work must be accomplished to separate charges, and

there is a tendency for the charges to return to a neutral (uncharged) condition. The separation of electric charge might not, in itself, be a potential fire or explosion hazard. There must be a discharge or sudden recombination of the separated charges to create arcing to pose an ignition hazard. One of the best methods of providing protection from static electric discharge is constructing an electrically conductive or semiconductive path that will allow the controlled recombination of the charges and dissipation of charges (usually to earth). The two terms used most often when providing protection from static electricity and lightning are: *grounding* or one of its derivatives, and *bonding* or one of its derivatives. Derivatives of these terms are in the following examples:

Grounding – Ground or Grounded

Bonding – Bond or Bonded

Definitions from NFPA 70 and NFPA 77

Grounded. "Connected to earth or to some conducting body that serves in place of the earth."

Bonding (Bonded). "The permanent joining of metallic parts to form an electrically conductive path that ensures electrical continuity and the capacity to conduct safely any current likely to be imposed" (see Article 100).

Grounding. "The process of bonding one or more conductive objects to the ground, so that all objects are at zero (0) electrical potential"; also referred to as 'earthing' [NFPA 77, 3.1.10]. Keep in mind that the term *earthing* is not currently a defined term.

Bonding. "The process of connecting two or more conductive objects together by means of a conductor so that they are at the same electrical potential, but not necessarily at the same potential as the earth" [NFPA 77, 3.1.2].

So for all practical purposes, when the term *grounding* is used, it should be thought of as including a connection or path to the earth to put electrically conductive materials at the same potential as the earth. When the term *bonding* is used, it should be thought of as connecting electrically conductive materials together to eliminate differences of potential between them and form one conductive mass. Note that bonding generally includes a path to the earth, but the earth is not referred to in the definitions. Figures 2-22, 2-23, 2-24, and 2-25 graphically demonstrate the differences between the two concepts and also show the two working together to provide desired protection. So it can be

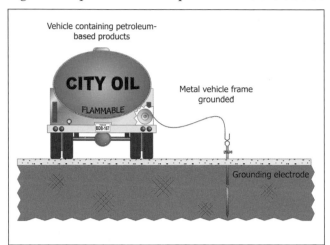

Figure 2-22. Vehicle is connected to the earth (grounded).

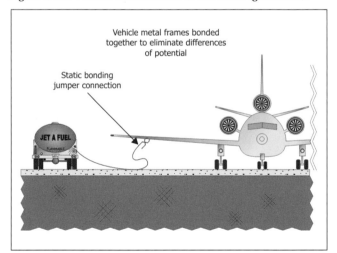

Figure 2-23. Vehicles are connected together (bonded).

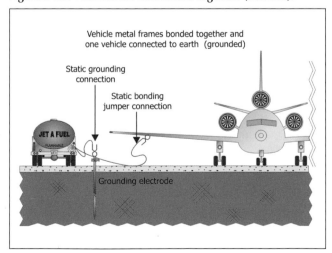

Figure 2-24. Two vehicles connected together (bonded), and one vehicle also connected to the earth

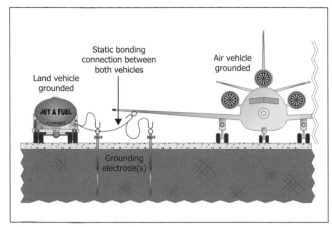

Figure 2-25. Two vehicles connected together (bonded) and, also, each vehicle is connected to the earth separately (grounded)

concluded that bonding conductive parts together minimizes the potential differences between them, even when the resulting system is not grounded. Grounding (earthing), on the other hand, equalizes the potential differences between the objects and the earth. The relationship between bonding and grounding is shown in the following illustrations:

Controlling Static Electricity Ignition Hazards

Ignition hazards from static electricity can be controlled by the following methods:

1. Removing the ignitible mixture from the area where static electricity could cause an ignition-capable discharge

2. Reducing charge generation, charge accumulation, or both by means of process or product modifications

3. Neutralizing the charges. Grounding isolated conductors and air ionization are primary methods of neutralizing charges.

Resistance in the Path to Ground

To prevent the accumulation of static electricity in conductive equipment, the total resistance of the ground path to earth should be sufficient to dissipate charges that are otherwise likely to be present. The basic goal here is to create a path of dissipation that will not be subject to any effects of pressure piling of electrons. A resistance of 1 megohm (10^6 ohms) or less is generally considered adequate. Where the bonding/

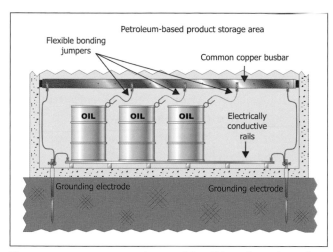

Figure 2-26. Drum containers with oil-based products in a storage room with a static grounding and bonding system employed at that location.

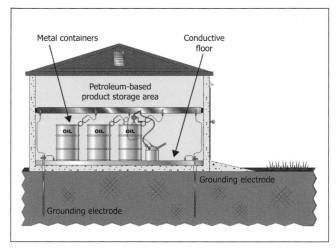

Figure 2-27. Conductive floor, containers and bonding jumpers for handling static charges

grounding system is all metal, resistance in continuous ground paths will typically be less than 10 ohms. Such systems include multiple component systems. Greater resistance usually indicates the metal path is not continuous, more often than not because of loose connections or the effects of corrosion. A grounding system that is acceptable for power circuits or for lightning protection is more than adequate for a static electricity grounding system.

Where electrical conductors of the wire-type are used, the minimum size of the bonding or grounding wire is dictated by mechanical strength, not by its current-carrying capacity. Stranded or braided wires should be used for bonding wires that will be connected and disconnected frequently [NFPA 77, 6.4.1.3]. Grounding conductors can be insulated (e.g., a jacketed or plastic-coated cable) or uninsulated (i.e., bare conductors). Uninsulated electrical conductors (wires) are recommended, because it is easier to detect defects in them.

Where static problems are present, workers in the area should be grounded. Workers should only be grounded through a resistance that limits the current to ground to less than 3 mA for the range of voltages experienced in the area. This method is called *soft grounding* and is used to prevent injury from an electric shock from line voltages or stray currents. In areas where static is a safety concern, rooms are often constructed with floors that are conductive or semi-conductive and connected to the electrode system. These rooms also generally include an electrical busbar connected to the grounding electrode system and the floor through a conductive plate or plates embedded within the conductive cure on the floor surface, which is applied during the floor finishing process. Portable jumpers connect portable containers and the busbar to assure a bond between the containers as well as a connection to the earth.

Liquids Flowing through Pipes

Charge separation occurs when liquids flow through pipes, hoses, and filters, when splashing occurs during transfer operations, or when liquids are stirred or agitated. The greater the area of interface is between liquid and surfaces and the higher the flow velocity, the greater the rate of charging. Charges become mixed with the liquid and are carried to receiving vessels where they can accumulate. The charge is often characterized by its bulk charge density and its flow as a streaming current to the vessel.

In the petroleum industry, for tank loading and distribution operations involving petroleum middle distillates, liquids in the semiconductive category are handled as conductive liquids. Such procedures are possible because regulations prohibit use of nonconductive plastic hoses and tanks, and multiphase mixtures and end-of-line polishing filters are not involved.

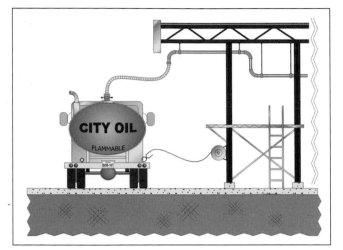

Figure 2-28. Basic flow of petroleum product through metallic piping and electron movement that results in charging of the metallic piping if not properly bonded and grounded for such operations. Reproduction of a figure from NFPA 77

Metallic Piping Systems

It is desirable that all parts of continuous metal piping systems have a resistance to ground that does not exceed ten ohms. Higher resistance could indicate poor electrical contact or connections, although this will depend on the overall system and can be affected by length and size of the system, which relate directly to the value of resistance. For flanged couplings, coatings such as paint on the flange faces or thin plastic coatings used on nuts and bolts will not normally prevent bonding across the coupling after proper tightening torque has been applied. Jumper cables and star washers are not usually

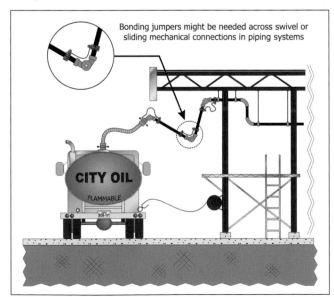

Figure 2-29. A wire bonding jumper across a fuel hose fitting from loading equipment to vessel.

needed at flanges. Star washers could even interfere with achieving proper tightening torque. Electrical continuity of the bonding and ground path should be confirmed after the system is completely assembled and periodically verified through testing thereafter to verify the integrity in the long term.

Additional bonding wires (jumpers) might be needed around flexible, swivel, or sliding mechanical connections or piping joints. Experience has shown that resistance in these joints is normally below the 10-ohm value, which is low enough to prevent accumulation of any static charges.

There are static bonding and grounding systems and equipment manufactured specifically for providing this type of protection. These systems are often interlocked with pumping operations to not allow fuel or oil flow in the piping systems until they have been connected. Other types of protection involve only a mechanical connection between the bulk storage tank and smaller vessel, without an electrical interlocking system. These types of operations are often observed at an airport where aircraft is being fueled by mobile vehicles.

Grounding Storage Tanks for Nonconductive Liquids

Storage tanks for nonconductive liquids should be grounded properly. Storage tanks on foundations constructed on the earth are considered inherently grounded, regardless of the type of foundation (e.g., concrete, sand, or asphalt). For tanks on elevated foundations or supports, the resistance to ground could be as high as 100 ohms and still be considered adequately grounded for purposes of dissipation of static electric charges, but the resistance should be verified in these cases for assurance that an adequate path to ground is achieved. The addition of grounding rods and similar grounding systems will not reduce the hazard associated with static electrical charges apparent in the liquid [NFPA 77, 7.5.2.2].

Basic Static Concerns with Combustible Dust

Combustible dust is defined as any finely divided solid material 420 µm or smaller in diameter (i.e., material that will pass through a U.S. No. 40 standard sieve)

Hazardous Locations

Photo 2-8. Static grounding and bonding equipment with operational indicator lights

Photo 2-10. A helicopter during the refueling process bonded to the mobile fuel vehicle. There is a bonding connection between the aircraft and also the ground to a rod driven at the landing location.

that can present a fire or deflagration hazard. For a static electrical discharge to ignite a combustible dust, the following four conditions need to be met:

1. An effective means of separating charge must be present.

2. A means of accumulating the separated charges and maintaining a difference of electrical potential must be available.

3. A discharge of the static electricity of adequate energy must be possible.

4. The discharge must occur in an ignitible mixture of the dust.

A sufficient amount of dust suspended in air needs to be present in order for an ignition to achieve sustained combustion. This minimum amount is called the *minimum explosive concentration* (MEC). It is the smallest concentration, expressed in mass per unit volume, for a given particle size that will support a deflagration when uniformly suspended in air.

For historical reasons, the ability of a solid to transmit electric charges is characterized by its volume resistivity. For liquids, this ability is characterized by its conductivity.

Powders are divided into the following three groups:

• Low-resistivity powders having volume resistivity in bulk of up to 10^8 ohm-m. Examples include metals, coal dust, and carbon black.

• Medium-resistivity powders having volume resistivity between 10^8 and 10^{10} ohm-m. Examples include many

Photo 2-9. Static grounding and bonding equipment in use at a tank loading facility

Photo 2-11. Static bonding and grounding connection for a smaller bulk storage tank

organic powders and agricultural products.

• High-resistivity powders having volume resistivity above 10^{10} ohm-m. Examples include organic powders, synthetic polymers, and quartz [NFPA 77, 8.4.2.1].

Figure 2-30 shows the resistivity measurements of electrically conductive combustible dusts and is now primarily of historical interest. This diagram is a reproduction of a diagram developed from data in the Instrument Society of America's Standard ISA-S12.10–1973 (Revised ANSI/ISA–1988) entitled *Area Classification in Hazardous (Classified) Dust Locations*. The figure shows the resistivity measurements of various electrically conductive combustible dusts. The lower the resistivity is (in ohm-centimeters), the greater the electrical conductivity of the dust. Group E dusts are considered to be metallic dusts that are electrically conductive in addition to being abrasive.

Powders with lower resistivity are prone to effects of static charges and can become charged during flow. The charge rapidly dissipates when the powder is conveyed into a storage device or container that is grounded. However, if conveyed into a nonconductive container, the accumulated charge can result in a spark as the charge in the dust and powder attempts to equalize potential differences during this process.

By applying many of the same fundamentals and principles related to bonding and grounding concerns,

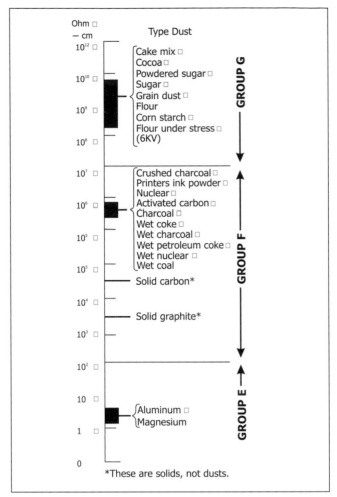

Figure 2-30. Resistivity measurements of electrically conductive combustible dust. Concept courtesy of Appleton EGS Electrical Group

hazards associated with static electrical charges created by handling of dusts can be minimized. It is common to use bonding jumpers across nonconductive flexible joints in ducted systems, because isolated portions of electrically conductive ductwork can become charged due to static and be an ignition source. In addition to bonding the isolated sections of conductive duct together, there is also a connection to a grounding electrode. It should be emphasized that this protection is not complete without an effective connection to the equipment grounding conductor of the branch circuit supplying the equipment (motors, etc.) associated with the duct system. Minimizing charging effects and differences of potential is critical for safety from fire and explosions related to these types of operations. The *Code* addresses bonding of metal duct systems only by a reference from a fine print note (see Section 250.104(B) FPN). Although it is clear that this type of bonding is not a requirement of the *NEC* in accordance with 90.5(C), it may well be a requirement contained in other NFPA standards that may be applicable to particular installations or special occupancies. Even if this type of protection is only a recommended practice, experience has shown that these practices are the best and most common, and are usually implemented.

Lightning Protection System Basics

Lightning protection systems are generally installed as a means of providing protection for property (buildings or structures) from damage that can be caused by these events. These systems are installed to divert lightning on a constructed path to the earth for dissipation, and they also provide a degree of protection against fire from lightning strikes because of bonding. Bonding minimizes differences of potential and thus minimizes arcs and flashover that can occur between electrically conductive objects when lightning events occur. Because protection in hazardous locations involves eliminating one or more components of the fire triangle, lightning protection systems are often installed to assist in providing that type of protection. It should be emphasized that providing a lightning protection system is not a guarantee that damage will not occur during a lightning strike. Providing lightning protection is an attempt to put a best plan (system) in place for protection against the damage that can be caused by these types of natural events.

Lightning protection is an important factor when considering protective systems at buildings or structures generally. Hazards associated with lightning become more of a concern for structures that are built at great heights above ground level. Basically, structures that are very tall also act as good air terminals for lightning. Lightning protection is an important consideration at outdoor electrical substations and at locations where thunderstorms are prevalent. Lightning discharges usually consist of very large voltages and currents of extremely short duration. Protection is accomplished by deliberately providing a path of low resistance to earth, compared to other paths. There is no guarantee that lightning will necessarily follow the lower resistance path that has been provided, but at least the low resistance path will reduce the likelihood of damage.

The steel fence around an outdoor substation, when properly grounded, offers good lightning protection for the equipment, especially if the fence is higher than the equipment within the station. Lightning rods (air terminals) should project at least one foot above any part of the structure and equipment, and the path to ground should be as direct as possible.

Each air terminal should have at least two connections to ground, with air terminals placed on each side of the structure. Surge arresters also should be used on the power lines and the equipment. The lightning down conductor system should be connected to earth through driven electrodes (ground terminals) and bonded to the station ground bus. Lightning conductors should not be smaller than 4 AWG, increasing in size as the primary voltage of the system increases.

Bonding of Lightning Protection Systems to Power System Electrodes

Ground terminals (grounding electrodes) for lightning protection systems are required to be bonded to the building or structure grounding electrode system (see 250.106). This section no longer requires metallic parts of an electrical wiring system to be bonded to the lightning protection system conductors where there are less than six feet of separation. However, specific requirements for bonding the systems together are found in NFPA 780, *Standard for Installation of Lightning Protection Systems*.

Lightning protection systems are also necessary at various hazardous (classified) locations. Properly installed lightning protection systems provide a path to the earth for these events. Basic fundamental objectives of lightning protection systems provide similar protection as that afforded by static protection systems. Similar concepts are considered when constructing each of these systems. For lightning protection systems, a connection to the earth is established and there are also requirements for bonding electrically conductive parts and equipment. Although the *NEC* is silent on the requirements contained in NFPA 780, there are important references to this standard provided in the *Code*.

Limited energy system grounding and bonding requirements in the *NEC* serve a few very important purposes. The systems and circuits covered in chapter 8 of the *Code* are required to be grounded to earth and to be bonded to the electrical power distribution systems for the building or structure. By providing the connection to a grounding electrode, the systems and circuits are afforded reasonable protection from spike and surge currents and also from brief elevated potentials due to lightning strikes. Bonding the electrodes of the systems in chapter 8 of the *NEC* to the grounding electrode system for the electrical system(s) for the building or structure limits the potential differences during normal operation and during surge or spike events and the effects of lightning discharges into the earth at close proximities. Bonding the grounding electrodes of the two systems together limits potential differences and shock hazards that could result from isolated grounding (earthing) connections. Bonding together all separate electrodes at the premises will limit the potential differences between them and between their associated wiring systems. Where lightning protection systems are installed, associated bonding requirements are essential for protection against both shock and flashover during lightning strikes. When lightning strikes happen, they force the potential on electrically conductive parts to rise to the potential (voltage) of the strike for the duration of the event. Even lightning strikes in the vicinity of a building or structure will cause the potential to rise on all electrodes or metal structures in the earth. Bonding all grounding electrodes of all power systems and lightning protection systems together as required by the *NEC* and NFPA 780 helps provide protection during the rise in potential across conductive parts; because, the potential should rise at the same rate, which minimizes shock hazards and flashover (including arcs) during these events. Eliminating the ignition source is an important objective where lightning protection systems are installed; these systems also provide the same benefits for hazardous (classified) locations because they serve to minimize the ignition component of the fire triangle.

Grounding and bonding are important elements of electrical safety in any electrical installation. For hazardous (classified) locations, there are additional concerns addressed by more specific and restrictive grounding and bonding requirements in the *Code*.

Static grounding, bonding and lightning systems and lightning protection systems are often installed and must overlay the grounding and bonding requirements of the *NEC*. When static systems are installed, they should be installed in accordance with NFPA 77, which contains the recommended practices for installing and maintaining such systems. Lightning protection systems are required to meet the applicable provisions of NFPA 780, where such systems are installed. Specific and detailed information about each of these types of protective systems is beyond the scope of this text and the reader is strongly encouraged to refer to those applicable standards for specific information when incorporating this type of protection method into any design. [See NFPA 780-2004, *Standard for the Installation of Lightning Protection Systems* and NFPA 77-2000, *Recommended Practice on Static Electricity*].

Other Electrical Systems

In addition to the electrical requirements found in the *National Electrical Code*, other electrical systems are required by occupancy codes, standards and recommended practices. Like fire alarm requirements in building codes, these documents normally refer to the *NEC* for installation requirements related to these systems. Although the intent of this document is not to completely cover all information related to these requirements, the intent of this section is to make persons involved in the electrical installation aware that additional electrical systems may be required and covered in other documents. Some of those systems include: fire alarms, gas monitoring systems, cathodic protection, power shutdown requirements, fuel shutdown requirements, and standby power requirements. A review of the requirements will reveal that each type of occupancy has unique requirements determined by the individual technical committees to be necessary for safety of the facilities within the scope of the documents.

Some of the other electrical system requirements found in occupancy documents are shown in sidebar 2-03. These examples will provide some indication of the types of systems and the specific requirements that may be required to protect these hazardous location occupancies.

System Shutdown and Alarms

Methods of protection for hazardous locations often include engineered designs that incorporate specific ventilation systems, interlocks, and alarms. The basic objective of these systems is to minimize or remove one or more of the components of the fire triangle, as discussed in the beginning of this chapter. Where movement of air is applied, the possibility of ignitible concentrations of hazardous atmospheres is reduced. This is a common method of protection applied in various hazardous locations. A couple of common examples are found in *NEC* Article 511. Section 511.3(A)(5) indicates that the area 450 mm (18 in.) above the floor in a commercial garage is unclassified if there is mechanical ventilation that provides a minimum of four air changes per hour or one cubic foot per minute of exchanged air across the entire floor area, and the exhausted air is taken from a point within 0.3 m (12 in.) of the floor. Section 511.3(A)(4) also indicates that lubrication service facilities are unclassified where there is no transfer of any Class 1 liquids, pits or work areas below grade level that are provided with not less than 0.3 m³/minute/m² (1 cfm/ft²) of exhaust ventilation. The exhausted air must be taken from a point within 300 mm (12 in.) of the floor level of the pit or subfloor work area. Note that there are no requirements for interlocks or alarms in these *Code* rules; however, the *Code* does require that the exhaust ventilation for the pit or below grade work areas be operational at all times when the building is occupied or when vehicles are parked over the pit or below grade work area(s). A mechanical engineer can usually provide a design and documentation verifying to approving authorities that the required air movement or exhaust has been provided to allow the area to be considered unclassified. It is important that the occupant and operators of the facility understand the importance of these ventilation systems as they relate to building and personnel safety.

Another method of protection can be provided by a combination of gas detection system and air changes. These types of engineered designs are generally project or location specific. An example of this type of design

Other Electrical System Requirements

NFPA 30, Flammable & Combustible Liquids Code requires metal underground fuel tanks to be protected from corrosion by a properly engineered, installed and maintained cathodic protection system. Photos 2-12, and 2-13 show cathodic protection equipment provided on a gas pipeline supplying a bulk storage facility. Vaults that house aboveground fuel tanks are required to have vapor and liquid detection systems that include on-site audible and visual warning devices with battery backup. Secondary containment tanks installed with aboveground fuel tanks are required to have means to prevent overfilling. That means must sound an alarm if the liquid level reaches 90 percent of capacity and automatically stop delivery to the tank when the liquid level reaches 95 percent of capacity. If the ventilation provided for tank buildings is not continuous, a gas monitoring system that alarms constantly at an attended location and starts the mechanical ventilation is required. Tank buildings are also required to have a means to notify both personnel at the plant and a public or mutual aid fire department in the event of a fire or other emergency. Ventilation systems for storage lockers are required to be interlocked so that an audible alarm is provided upon failure of the ventilation. Emergency system shutdown for vapor recovery and vapor processing systems are required to fail to a safe position in the event of loss of normal power or equipment malfunction.

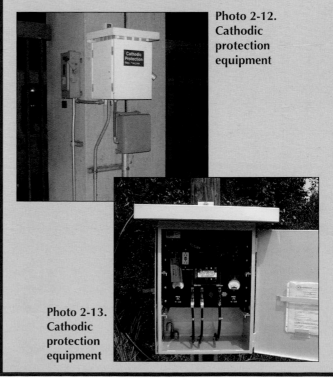

Photo 2-12. Cathodic protection equipment

Photo 2-13. Cathodic protection equipment

Sidebar 2-03.

Other Electrical System Requirements

NFPA 120, Standard for Coal Preparation Plants permits the use of ordinary location electrical systems for some equipment in Class I, Division 2 locations when adequate ventilation is provided. In order to take advantage of the reduced area classification, gas monitoring equipment must be provided. Gas monitors must provide audible alarms at 20 percent of lower explosive limit (LEL) and process equipment and power shutdown at 40 percent of LEL.

NFPA 655, Standard for Prevention of Sulfur Fires and Explosions requires a combustible gas detection system to measure the concentration of hydrogen sulfide when systems are handling liquid sulfur at normal handling temperatures. Operations are required to discontinue when combustible gas concentrations reach 35 percent of the lower explosive limit in the gas space of liquid sulfur containers. Operations are not permitted to resume until the concentration reaches 15 percent or less of the lower explosive limit.

NFPA 820, Standard for Fire Protection in Wastewater Treatment and Collection Facilities requirements include a variety of fire protection measures depending on what location or function in the collection and treatment process is involved. Some functions are required to have combustible gas detection systems, some require fire alarms systems, some require fire suppression systems and others require fire detection systems. Where combustible gas detection systems are required, they must be set to alarm at 10 percent of the lower flammable limit and be connected to the alarm signaling system.

NFPA 853, Standard for Installation of Stationary Fuel Cell Power Plants requires a fire suppression system that includes an automatic safety shutoff valve that will shut off fuel supply when the sprinkler system is activated. The standard also requires the installation of a combustible gas detection system that will alarm at 25 percent of the lower flammable limit and shut down the plant at 60 percent of the lower flammable limit.

Sidebar 2-03 continued.

might include an exhaust system that provides a minimum number of air changes in the appropriate location, depending on the properties (vapor density) of the gas involved. If the gas is heavier-than-air, exhausted air will generally be taken from locations close to the floor or grade level. If the gas is lighter-than-air, exhausted air is usually taken from locations near the highest point of the facility or location. Interlock systems are often used to provide warnings by audible and visual alarms, or both in combination, to warn qualified operators that the method of protection is not operational. In addition to interlocks for personnel warning systems, there could be a shutdown interlock system that removes power from the electrical system in the area where the exhaust or ventilation system has failed or is not operating. This can be accomplished by using shunt-trip breakers and contactors that are interlocked with the specific exhaust or ventilation system. Usually any necessary electrical circuits or systems, such as emergency lighting equipment of exit lighting, are provided in these areas, but they are installed using the appropriate protection technique for the area so they remain operational.

Sometimes gas detection systems are used as the primary protection method and are part of a system design that includes not only detection of ignitible concentrations but also works cooperatively with an exhaust or ventilation system and a shunt-trip interlocking system for system shutdown. These systems are usually equipped with early warning audible and visual alarms to warn facility personnel or operators of ventilation or exhaust systems failure and ignitible mixture accumulations that are increasing to hazardous (explosive) levels. These types of engineered systems or designs are generally limited to applications in industrial facilities or installations where there are qualified persons that are familiar with the operation and servicing of these safety systems. Even where these multilevel methods of protection are employed, safety depends on qualified persons that can respond appropriately if any necessary component of the designed system were to fail or become inoperative. The *Code* requires documentation of areas designated as hazardous (classified) locations as provided in 500.4(A). Although this section only calls for the hazardous areas to be designated, often the documentation provided by engineering and design teams includes how the area was classified, together with information about associated exhaust or ventilation systems and interlocked systems that allow for definitive delimitation of the hazardous locations. The documentation should also include the hazardous area classification that can result from ventilation system failure. As indicated in Section 500.4(A), the documentation is required to be available to those authorized to design, install, inspect, maintain, or operate electrical equipment at those locations. Chapter one clearly described the process of classifying hazardous locations. Once the area is classified, methods of protection for the building and personnel (operators) are designed and installed. It is important that an adequately designed protection system be properly operated and monitored to maintain minimum levels of safety in these hazardous locations.

As discussed earlier in this chapter, there are NFPA standards that provide general requirements for these types of exhaust and ventilation systems and explosion prevention systems.

NFPA 91 provides some general requirements for design and construction of exhaust systems, which may be modified by other applicable standards. Systems that comply with this standard are limited to conveying flammables that are not more than 25 percent of the lower flammable limit unless they also meet the requirements of NFPA 69, *Standard on Explosion Prevention Systems*. Under normal operating conditions, fire detection and alarm systems are not permitted to shut down these air-moving devices for the obvious safety reasons.

NEC Protection Techniques for Electrical Systems

In addition to the various protection methods and system designs described above, the *Code* provides a number of protection techniques that safeguard against electrical systems installed within hazardous (classified) locations becoming ignition sources. Those protection techniques are defined and described in *NEC* 500.2; 500.7; 505.2; and 505.8. At this point no zone protection techniques are included in Article 506, which provides a Zone system of classification in dust, fiber and flying atmospheres. These techniques include both the traditional *NEC* Division system techniques and also the traditional IEC Zone system techniques with the U.S. deviations. At this point, the *NEC* allows both sets of techniques to be installed on projects classified using the Division system and the Zone system. A project could have part of the electrical equipment protected by division techniques and the remainder protected by zone techniques. Unlike the classification process, which allows Division 2 and Zone 2 to abut but not overlap, no separation of protection techniques is required. Some small and simple projects may include only a single protection technique for electrical equipment installed in the classified areas, while others may include many different techniques for the electrical equipment. Information about the various protection techniques and their application is provided in chapter 3.

---

1 This was the definition accepted by CMP-1 for the 2005 *NEC* cycle.

Review Questions

1. Acceptable protection can be provided in hazardous (classified) locations when _____ component(s) of the fire triangle is removed from the location.

    a. all three
    b. one or more
    c. two
    d. explosionproof equipment eliminates the ignition

2. Explosionproof electrical equipment is available for electrical functions in all classes, divisions, zones, and groups of hazardous (classified) locations.

    a. True
    b. False

3. Although environmental regulations are not developed to address control of ignition, the control of the release of flammable and/or combustible materials can have an impact on the area classification of a facility that works with those materials.

    a. True
    b. False

4. For Class II and Class III locations both _____can impact the area classification of the facility.

    a. dust-ignitionproof and dusttight equipment
    b. intrinsically safe and nonincendive systems
    c. Class 2 and Class 3 circuits
    d. dust collection and housekeeping

5. For dust collection and housekeeping to effectively be used as a method of protection in hazardous (classified) locations, the building designers, the facilities maintenance department, and the facilities _____ must be aware of what is required and be responsible for addressing those requirements.

    a. operations department
    b. electrical equipment manufacturers
    c. stockholders
    d. fire protection team

6. In most indoor locations where flammables or combustibles are handled or processed, the hazardous (classified) area can be limited by _____ within the building into smaller spaces used for specific functions.

    a. cooling the space
    b. heating the space
    c. adding additional doors and windows
    d. partitioning the space

7. Adequate ventilation is achieved where the ventilation rate is able to prevent the accumulation of vapor-air concentrations from exceeding _____of the flammable material.

    a. 25 percent of the UFL
    b. 50 percent of the LFL
    c. 25 percent of the LFL
    d. 100 percent of the LFL

8. Some occupancy standards or recommended practices that allow area classification to be reduced as a result of mechanical ventilation, require the electrical equipment to be interlocked with the ventilation in such a way that the electrical equipment can no be energized until the ventilation is operable.

    a. True
    b. False

9. Only mechanical ventilation is permitted to reduce area classification where flammable materials can be released.

    a. True
    b. False

10. The *NEC* addresses protection from ignition by static electricity is addressed for hazardous locations _____.

    a. in the .30 sections of Articles 501, 502, & 503.

b. in Article 250
c. in Annex F
d. in an FPN located in 500.4(B)

11. Static electricity is only a concern in Class I locations.

a. True
b. False

12. Protection from static electricity and lightning are addressed in two different NFPA standards.

a. True
b. False

13. Although other electrically operated systems like fire alarms, cathodic protection of piping and tanks, and fuel shutdown systems provide protection in facilities that involve hazardous locations, the requirements to install those systems are not part of the *NEC*.

a. True
b. False

14. In many facilities that include hazardous locations, _____ methods of protection are provided.

a. two
b. three
c. multiple
d. no

15. Complete protection of a facility that includes hazardous locations will likely involve design from _____ engineers.

a. mechanical
b. electrical
c. process
d. all of the above

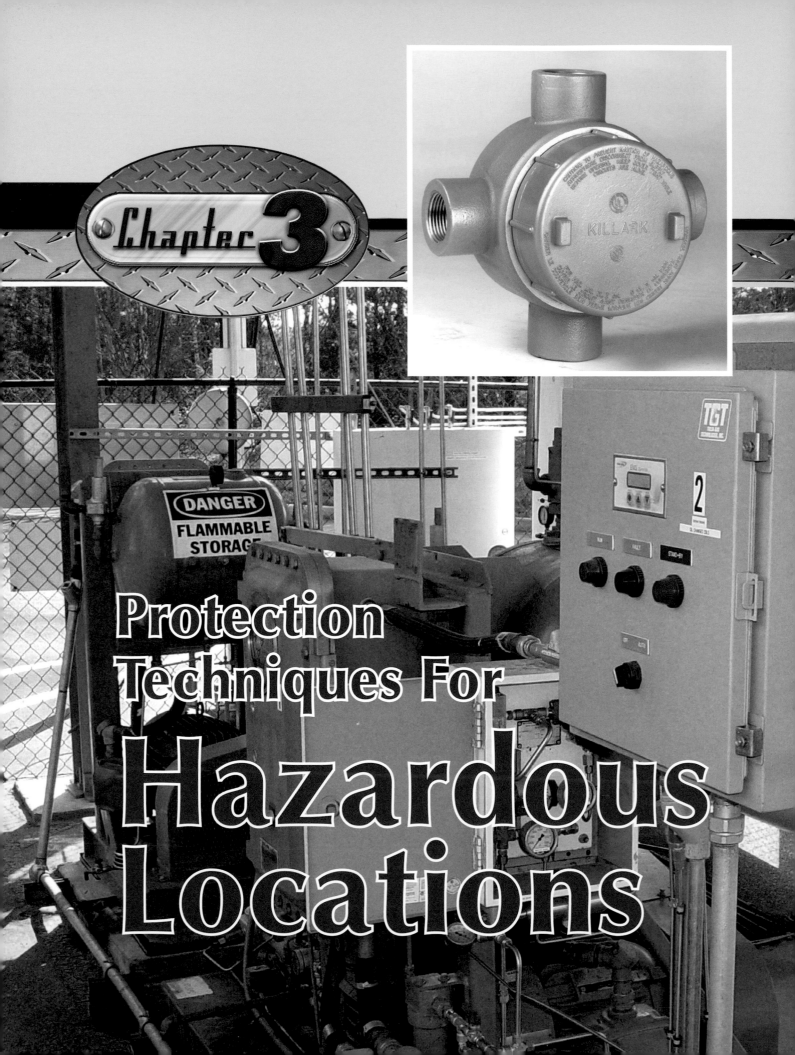

Chapter 3

Protection Techniques For Hazardous Locations

A fter the classification of a location is known and methods of protection are considered and included in a design for a hazardous location, appropriate protection tech-niques for the equipment must be selected. Whether the area is classified under the Division System or the Zone System, the *NEC* provides acceptable protection techniques suitable for each system of classification. Protection techniques suitable for the Division System are provided in Section 500.7, and the techniques for the Zone system are found in 505.8. This chapter provides a more detailed discussion of the various types of protection techniques, their applications, and includes descriptive information about each.

The type of protection permitted in a particular location depends on the class of location encountered. Many industries and facilities will have either Class I, or Class II, or Class III locations, or there could be various combinations of hazardous locations in the same facility. Where industries or facilities include a combination of more than one class of location, the electrical equipment installed must be suitable for each hazardous (classified) environment determined and anticipated.

Equipment Listing, Identification, and Approval

Equipment for use in hazardous locations can be evaluated and listed for single or multiple classifications and use. Electrical and electronic equip-ment manufacturers who have products for hazardous locations evaluated and listed often find it beneficial to have the equipment evaluated for more than one class. The markings on the equipment are required to identify the hazardous locations (class and group) for which it is suitable (see photo 3-01).

Likewise, electrical and electronic products for hazardous locations are often initially evaluated and listed for use in more than one classified location. The *NEC* also indicates that equipment identified for one location is also suitable for another if certain conditions are met. For example, Section 500.8(A)(2) indicates that equipment identified for a Division 1 location is permitted in a Division 2 location of the same class, group, and temperature class, within the limits of the conditions provided in 500.8(A)(2)(a) and (b). Luminaires (lighting fixtures) as well as many other types of equipment bearing such identification marks are suitable for use in either location, but are not suitable for exposure to both gases and dusts simultaneously (see photo 3-02).

Manufacturers of equipment for hazardous locations can also have products evaluated and listed for use where exposed to gases and dust environments simultaneously.

Selecting electrical and electronic equipment for use in a hazardous (classified) location involves verifying that the product is suitable for the application. The most common methods of determining product suitability are either *identification* or *listing* and often a combination of both. It is vital that the designers, installers and authority having jurisdiction work together in the field at the time of installation to confirm that the equipment provided is suitable for the environment shown in the classification documentation for the particular classified location. As discussed in the previous chapter, often the best approach is to locate as much of the equipment outside the hazardous (classified) area wherever possible; but when the equipment must be located in these areas, it must definitely be suitable for the use.

Photo 3-02. A luminaire (light fixture) that is listed for use in a Class I or Class II locations. Courtesy of Thomas and Betts

Equipment Suitability

The suitability of identified equipment is required to be determined by any of the following means:

• Equipment listing or labeling

• Evidence of equipment evaluation from a qualified testing laboratory or inspection agency concerned with product evaluation

Photo 3-01. Listing mark and data plate for emergency lighting equipment listed for use in Class I locations.
Courtesy of Thomas and Betts

Photo 3-03. Luminaire (light fixture) with a data plate and listing mark that indicates suitability for environments that include Class I and Class II locations Courtesy of Thomas and Betts

Photo 3-04. Luminaire (light fixture) with a data plate and listing mark that indicates suitability for environments that include Class I and Class II locations Courtesy of Thomas and Betts

• Evidence acceptable to the authority having jurisdiction such as a manufacturer's self-evaluation or an owner's engineering judgment [*NEC*, 500.8(A)(2)].

The term *approved* was used throughout Article 500 and was intended to apply to equipment suitability as used in those rules. However, the term has been changed to either *listed* or *identified* to provide needed clarification in most places. *Approved* still remains defined in Article 100 as "acceptable to the authority having jurisdiction." Its use in the hazardous (classified) location rules in the *NEC* is more consistent with its definition. Of the equipment protected under Division system protection techniques, some is required to be listed; some, identified; and some, only approved. All three of these terms are specifically defined in Article 100. Most equipment protected under Zone system protection techniques is required to be listed types. Purged and pressurized equipment, for either Division or zone applications, is required to be identified.

It is important to understand each method of determining suitability of identified equipment that is needed or permitted for a particular hazardous location.

Listing or Labeling

Method one consists of product listing or labeling. This method will, generally, be the most common

Approved, Identified or Listed

Prior to *NEC*–1996, most equipment required or permitted for use in hazardous (classified) locations was to be approved for the location. In *NEC*–1996, Article 505, Class I, Zones 0, 1, and 2 locations were included for the first time. Section 505-20 included a requirement for equipment to be listed where protected by Zone protection techniques. Most other equipment (protected by Division System techniques) was still required to be approved for the location. In *NEC*–2002, code-making panel (CMP) -14 reviewed the use of the terms *approved, identified*, and *listed* as defined in Article 100. New text was accepted in 500.8 (A)(1) and 505.9(A), which provides methods for approval of equipment used in hazardous (classified) locations.

Sidebar 3.01.

and the most desired way of identifying equipment, particularly by authorities having jurisdiction and responsibility for approvals. Usually, the AHJ will base approvals on the use of listed and labeled equipment, particularly for equipment in hazardous locations, where the approval process is even more critical. Using listing as a basis for approval assures that an independent, qualified electrical testing laboratory acceptable to the authority having jurisdiction has evaluated the equipment in a laboratory setting using a recognized product safety standard as a basis for listing the equipment. During the evaluation process in the testing environment (laboratory), products are often tested to the point of destruction, in order to determine the limitation of the equipment. The equipment is then subject to periodic follow-up inspections in the manufacturer's facility to ensure that the equipment that was successfully evaluated continues to be produced. That equipment would then bear a *listing mark* authorized by the applicable qualified electrical testing laboratory. With evidence of suitability indicated by listing marks on the equipment,

Photo 3-05. An increased safety "e" termination box, listed by Factory Mutual (FM)

designers, installers, and inspectors would need only to verify that (1) installation instructions supplied with the equipment are adhered to, and (2) applicable installation requirements in the *Code* are followed to ensure a safe installation. Photos 3-05 through 3-08 show examples of identified equipment determined by the first method. It should be understood that various qualified electrical testing organizations provide the services of product evaluation, testing, and listing.

Equipment Evaluation

Method two consists of evidence of equipment evaluation from a qualified testing laboratory or inspection agency concerned with product evaluation. In some cases, skid-type equipment (package units) is built off-site in a remote location and shipped to a user's site where it is connected to a source of power. Since this type of situation or product application includes both equipment and a partial installation that cannot be easily field-inspected for acceptability at the site, the authority having jurisdiction may require a field evaluation to serve as a basis for approval of this pre-wired skid.

In some cases, it is not possible to see everything necessary once the installation is completed. Identification labels necessary to determine suit-ability on certain parts of the installation may be enclosed or turned to a position where they are not visible to the inspector responsible for final approval of the equipment and the installation. In those cases, the approving authority often requires a field evaluation to be provided by a qualified, third party testing or inspection agency concerned with product evaluations.

These field evaluations are not listings since the

Photo 3-06. A luminaire (light fixture) listed by Underwriters Laboratories Courtesy of Thomas and Betts

Photo 3-07. A visual signaling appliance listed by Underwriters Laboratories Courtesy Cooper Crouse Hinds

Photo 3-08. An enclosed control panel relating to hazardous locations with intrinsically safe circuit extensions listed by Underwriters Laboratories

labeled equipment might include multiple pieces and the specific skid may be produced only one time. In which case, there would be no periodic follow-up inspections of the manufacturing facility and the skid would not be included in a published list by the testing agency. This type of evaluation would not include destructive testing that might be included on a listed product. Field evaluations are location specific and apply only to the particular equipment evaluated at that site. Field evaluation marks applied by the evaluating agency indicate the date and location the evaluation applies to. If this particular equipment were relocated to another site, the field evaluation would no longer be valid and should not be used as an approval basis (see photos 3-09 and 3-10).

Manufacturer's Evaluation or Owner's Engineering Judgment

Method three consists of evidence acceptable to the authority having jurisdiction, such as a manufacturer's self-evaluation or an owner's engineering judgment. Designers and installers must understand that this method should only be considered after consultation with the inspecting authority, and that most inspection jurisdictions would consider this method only under extremely special or limited circumstances or conditions.

It should also be emphasized that this is often the most practical and desired method, especially for installations of unique equipment for which *Code* rules or product standards have not yet been developed. These situations, although rare, present challenges for approving authorities. Consequently, the alternative of a manufacturer's self-evaluation or an owner's engineering judgment is included in the *Code* for this type of situation. Each authority

Crossover Use of Protection Techniques

When NEC–1996 first included Article 505 for the Zone System, protection techniques developed through the Zone System were limited for use in areas classified by the system. However, equipment developed and recognized for use in Division 1 locations was permitted in Zone 1 areas if the gas group and temperature ratings were the same. It was determined that equipment considered to be adequately protected for a Division 1 area would also protect a Zone 1 area, which excluded areas that included ignitible concentrations for long periods of time. The same was true regarding use of Division 2 equipment in Zone 2.

In *NEC–1999*, permission was provided for the use of Zone 0, Zone 1, and Zone 2 equipment in Division 2 locations where the same gas group and temperature requirements applied. Zone 0 and Zone 1 equipment was not permitted in Division 1 locations.

Sidebar 3.02.

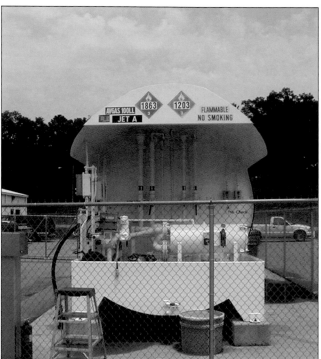

Photo 3-09. A jet fuel dispenser that was field evaluated by Intertek Testing Service (ITS)

Photo 3-10. ETL field evaluation label that was applied to the equipment upon completion of the field evaluation

having jurisdiction will have a different level of comfort, based on his or her level of experience with the application in question. In some cases, where governmental inspections are not in place, the AHJ may be the facilities safety engineer or electrical engineer and be very familiar with the specific hazards and standards that cover the installation. [See the FPN to the definition of *authority having jurisdiction* in Article 100].

AHJs with that particular experience may be much more comfortable using method three as a basis for equipment approval. An example of using an owner's engineering judgment as an approving basis would be a large petroleum and/or chemical facility where a pressurized enclosure might be an entire building or multiple buildings (see photo 3-11). In this case, the building or buildings might be constructed over a period of months by multiple crafts, and listing would not be practical since it is unlikely that any of the buildings would be the same. In that case, the owner's on-site engineering judgment may provide the evaluation of the product that is needed.

In other rare occasions, a listed product may have to be modified by the manufacturer for a specific application. That modification might prevent the manufacturer from labeling the equipment if their listing did not include the modification as a normal option. Therefore, the manufacturer may perform a self-evaluation to determine if the modification alters the performance of the product. In those cases, as long as it is acceptable to the authority having jurisdiction, this method would allow the product to be accepted as identified. As mentioned earlier, the manufacturer, designer and installer would certainly need to confirm that the AHJ would be willing to accept the self-evaluation prior to installing such a product in anticipation of required approvals.

Ordinary Equipment

A solenoid valve includes no arcing parts because it is a coil. Solenoid valves that are listed for ordinary locations may also be suitable for hazardous Division 2 locations because there are normally no temperature issues. It meets the Division 2 requirements, although it is not listed for Division 2 locations. The AHJ, who might be a governmental inspector, an insurance inspector or a facilities safety or electrical engineer, has the ability to approve this equipment as identified, based on the manufacturer's test results. Again, the manufacturer, designer and installer would certainly need to confirm that the AHJ would be willing to

Photo 3-11. This building serves as a pressurized enclosure for a unit substation at an oil refinery. The pressurized enclosure was approved by the AHJ based on the facilities engineers' (structural, mechanical and electrical) evaluations of the building as constructed.

accept the self-evaluation prior to installing such a product.

An authority having jurisdiction who is not intimately involved on a regular basis with this type of equipment and testing is not likely to be comfortable with this method of determining identified equipment. Yet, other inspection authorities may be completely comfortable approving this type of equipment in a Division 2 location (see photo 3-12).

Division and Zone System Protection Techniques

A variable related to the selection and use of protection techniques in hazardous (classified) locations has evolved since *NEC*–1996. Now there are two options: to use equipment protected by a technique (1) developed with the conventional U.S. Division System; or (2) one developed with the conventional IEC Zone system.

Division System Evolution

As the Division system evolved in the *NEC*, two levels of risk were established. Division 1 locations were those where ignitible conditions were assumed to be likely under *normal* operating conditions. Division 2 locations were those where ignitible conditions were assumed to be likely only under *abnormal* conditions. When the two levels of risk were established, two levels of protection techniques were developed to address that risk.

Zone System Evolution

As the Zone system of classifying hazardous locations evolved in the IEC, three levels of risk were established. Zone 2 included, for all practical purposes, the same level of risk as Division 2, ignitible conditions were assumed to be likely only under abnormal conditions.

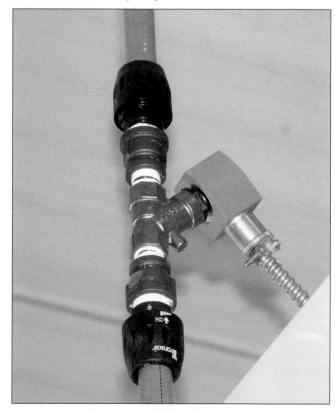

Photo 3-12. A solenoid valve that includes no arcing parts is suitable for use in a Class I, Division 2 location.

Division 1 areas were further divided into Zone 0 and Zone 1, based on the amount of time ignitible conditions exist under normal conditions. With three levels of risk established, that system developed three levels of protection techniques to address that risk.

Currently, the *Code* permits Zone 0, Zone 1 and Zone 2 equipment to be installed in Division 2 locations, and Zone 0 equipment to be installed in Division 1 locations where the same gas group and temperature requirements apply [*NEC*, 501.5]. Section 505.20 also permits the use of division equipment in locations classed as Zone 0, Zone 1, and Zone 2. In both systems, permission is provided to use equipment protected at a higher level than the location is classed if the equipment is suitable for the same material grouping and temperature rating.

While a variety of protection techniques evolved from the two completely different classification systems, the equipment is permitted in either a Zone or Division location, but the marking requirements for the equipment are different. The *Code* requires equipment for use in hazardous (classified) locations to bear certain identification marks that help installers apply the equipment properly in the field and inspectors endorse it during the approval process.

Equipment Markings

Equipment suitable for use under the Division system must meet the marking requirements provided in Section 500.8(B). These specific marking requirements include the class, the division if the equipment is only suitable for Division 2, applicable gas classification groups in accordance with 500.6, the temperature class or operating temperature at a 40°C ambient temperature. If the equipment is rated for use outside the normal ambient temperature range (-25°C to +40°C), the special range of temperatures must be marked and include the symbol "Ta" or "Tamb." These are general marking requirements, and they do not include exceptions for specific items and conditions.

Equipment suitable for use under the Zone system must meet marking requirements provided in 505.9(C). These specific marking requirements include: Class, Zone, the symbol "Aex," the protection technique(s), applicable gas group(s) in ac-

cordance with Table 505.9(C), and the temperature classification. If the equipment is suitable for use outside the normal ambient temperature range (-20°C to +40°C), the special range of temperatures must be marked and include the symbol "Ta" or "Tamb."

Users, designers, installers and inspectors should be aware that the: (1) two systems have differences in the gas groups and in "normal ambient temperatures;" and (2) Zone classified areas for Class II and Class III materials do not have protection techniques other than those that have been used in the Division system. Under the Division system marking requirements, it is not necessary for the protection technique to be identified in the markings; however, it is to be marked under the Zone system. A single piece of electrical equipment may include more than one protection technique in the markings. This is not the case on all equipment, but it is also not unusual either (see figure 3-01).

Protection Techniques

Because a fire or explosion will occur only when fuel, oxygen, and an ignition source are all present simultaneously in specific quantities, Class I protection techniques can be grouped into several practical principles that minimize the chance that the electrical equipment will ignite concentrations of flammable gases or vapors mixed with oxygen. It is always best to locate electrical equipment outside of the hazardous location, if possible. Since this is not possible for all equipment all the time, appropriate protection techniques must be used in the design and installation.

One practical method of protection involves the placement of electrical circuits and equipment within enclosures capable of containing an explosion and extinguishing the flame. This measure prevents kindling ignitible atmospheres surrounding the enclosure by sparks, flashes or an explosion within; and it controls the external temperature of the enclosure to a level below the autoignition temperature of the atmosphere. Ignition inside the enclosure might occur when contacts make and break, or when a ground fault or short circuit occurs inside the electrical enclosure. Elevated temperatures might occur from normal operating conditions or

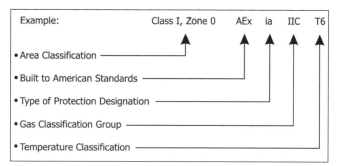

Figure 3-01. Zone equipment marking [reproduction of *NEC* 505.9(C)(2)]

overloaded equipment. Several protection techniques employ this method: explosionproof; flameproof; powder filled; and type of protection "n" and, specifically, "nC" or "enclosed break." The same practical protection is provided with all of these techniques.

Explosionproof Equipment

Explosionproof equipment is permitted to be utilized as a protection technique in Class I, Division 1, Division 2, Zone 1 or Zone 2 locations within the gas, group, and temperature limitations of the specific piece of equipment (see photo 3-13). Listed explosionproof enclosures would be evaluated to the requirements located in ANSI/UL 1203, *Explosion-Proof and Dust-Ignition-Proof Electrical Equipment for Use in Hazardous (Classified) Locations,* or FM 3615, or CSA 30.

Designers, users, installers, and inspectors should understand that although the primary purpose of all three of these product standards is the same, their content is not identical. In some cases, manufacturers will build products to comply with all three standards; in others, they may not. Or, the manufacturer may have some products listed to all three standards, and other products may not be. Manufacturers may also build a product to comply with all of three standards and choose not to list the product to any of the standards. A complete review of Article 501 and 505.9(C)(1) will reveal that most explosionproof equipment is required to be identified for Class I, Division 1 or 2 locations.

UL Standard 1203 includes prescriptive requirements for the enclosure material, the enclosure thickness, joints in the enclosures, shaft openings, holes in the enclosures, drain and breather fittings in the enclosures, supply connections to the enclosures for both fixed wiring and cord-connected portable

equipment, protection against corrosion, materials applied to joint surfaces, devices having coated threaded joint surfaces, and porosity in enclosure materials. In addition to the prescriptive requirements listed above, the standard also includes performance requirements that must be met.

This standard permits several types of joint construction, with each being governed by a number of variables. It should be realized that mixing and substituting components of an explosionproof enclosure could have a detrimental effect on the protection provided in the equipment design and evaluation. Those mating surfaces provide the vent path in the event that an explosion takes place inside the enclosure. Specific mating surfaces that meet both the prescriptive dimension and construction requirements, and pass the explosion test provide reasonable assurance that the exhaust from an internal explosion in an explosionproof enclosure will not ignite the atmosphere around the enclosure. The basic concept desired is that an explosion inside of equipment built as explosionproof will contain the exploding gases and flames and allow them to be released to the surrounding hazardous atmosphere, but only after the gases are cooled while passing across metallic joints. There are three basic types of joint construction in explosionproof equipment:

Photo 3-13. Typical equipment rated as explosionproof and suitable for Class I, Division 1 and 2 locations (cross-sectional view of a start-stop button manufactured by Hubbell/Killark)
Courtesy of Underwriters Laboratories Inc.

- Flat joint construction
- Threaded joint construction
- Labyrinth joint construction

These general principles for explosionproof enclosures will apply to many types of equipment including but not limited to: junction boxes, conduit fittings, luminaries, motors, generators, signaling devices, telephones, switches, control panels, electrically operated valves, receptacle-plug combinations, electric heaters, air conditioners, dispensers, and a multitude of other types of equipment used in Class I locations. In addition to the general principles found in UL Standard 1203, many of these types of equipment have more specific requirements related to the specific function of that equipment. Underwriters Laboratories has at least 13 different product standards that could apply to explosionproof equipment.

Flat Joint Construction

Flat joint construction involves two mating surfaces of metal. When an explosion happens inside the enclosure, hot gases are forced to pass through tightly joined flat metal surfaces and (in flame form) are cooled by the time they reach the outside of the enclosure. Explosionproof equipment with this type of joint construction depends heavily on all of the cover bolts being securely tightened for proper operation (see figures 3-02 and 3-03 and photos 3-14 and 3-15).

Threaded Joint Construction

Explosionproof equipment that utilizes threaded joint construction depends on a minimum of metallic threads for cooling of exploding gases inside the enclosure. As the exploding gases and flames pass over the metallic threads, they are moving in a back and forth motion and being cooled at the same time. It is important that these threads be made up wrenchtight, with five full threads fully engaged as required by Section 500.8(D). Figures 3-04 and 3-05 show the basic construction and operation of threaded joint construction in explosionproof equipment (see also photos 3-16 and 3-17).

The primary reasons for requiring five full threads fully engaged and wrenchtight is to prevent sparking when fault-current conditions occur and to ensure

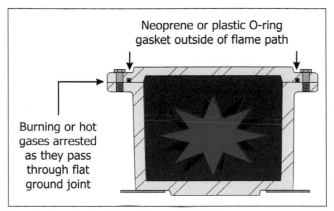

Figure 3-02. Flat joint construction in operation (cross-sectional views)

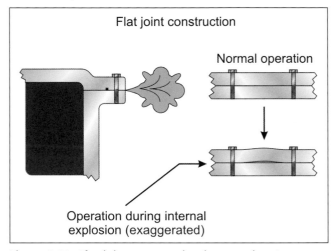

Figure 3-03. Flat joint construction in operation (cross-sectional views)

the integrity of the explosionproof enclosures and the conduit system, where applicable. An exception to this requirement allows only 4½ full threads fully engaged for listed explosionproof equipment for factory NPT [National (American) Standard Pipe Taper thread that provides a taper of 1 in 16 (3/4 in. per foot)] threads (see figure 3-06). This exception applies only to the explosionproof enclosure. Conduits that are installed and connected to the listed enclosure must all be made up at couplings, fittings, boxes, etc., with five full threads fully engaged [*NEC*, 500.8(D) and Exception]. Requirements for wiring methods and sealing fittings are covered in chapter 7.

Labyrinth Joint Construction

Explosionproof equipment that utilizes labyrinth path joint construction depends on a minimum of metallic surfaces arranged in a tongue-and-groove construction

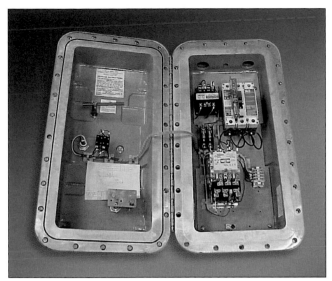

Photo 3-14. An explosionproof panelboard showing flat joint construction between enclosure and the cover Courtesy of Appleton EGS Electrical Group

for cooling of exploding gases inside the enclosure. As the exploding gases and flames pass over the metallic tongue and groove joined surfaces, they are moving in a back and forth motion and being cooled at the same time (see figure 3-07 and photo 3-18).

Flameproof Equipment

Flameproof equipment is permitted as a protection technique in Class I, Division 2, Zone 1 or Zone 2 locations within the gas group and temperature limitations of the specific piece of equipment. Requirements for listed flameproof enclosures are intended to provide the same practical protection as the explosionproof technique, which is providing reasonable assurance that the exhaust from an internal explosion will not ignite the atmosphere around the enclosure. A review of the standards reveals the major difference in the philosophies between standards development in North America ANSI/UL 60079-1 and other areas of the world. Zone standards provide similar performance requirements, but few prescriptive requirements. A comparison of requirements also shows that flameproof "d" equipment is only permitted in Zone 1, Zone 2 or Division 2 locations, not Division 1. *NEC* 505.20 requires flameproof equipment to be listed (see photos 3-19 and 3-20).

Flameproof enclosures could also be evaluated by a certification agency outside of North America using IEC 60079, or EN 50018, or some other country

Photo 3-15. An explosionproof switch enclosure showing flat joint construction between enclosure and the cover Courtesy of Cooper Crouse Hinds

specific version of the IEC 60079 standard. In many of those cases, the certification agency likely evaluated the product for explosion requirements and the manufacturer self-declared conformity to the ordinary location directives in the country where the evaluation took place.

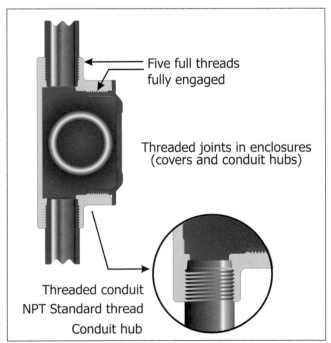

Five full threads fully engaged

Threaded joints in enclosures (covers and conduit hubs)

Threaded conduit NPT Standard thread

Conduit hub

Figure 3-04. An explosionproof enclosure showing threaded joint construction between enclosure and the cover

Industry Definitions

Understanding industry definitions always assists in proper applications in the field. The following are some unique and important definitions from NFPA 496 that are applicable to the use of purged and pressurized enclosures in Class I locations:

Alarm. A piece of equipment that generates a visual or audible signal that attracts attention

Analyzer Room or Building. A specific room or building containing analyzers, one or more of which is piped to the process

Enclosure Volume. The volume of the empty enclosure without internal equipment. The enclosure volume for motors, generators, and other rotating electric machinery is the volume within the enclosure minus the volume of the internal components, e.g., rotors, stators, and field coils.

Indicator. A piece of equipment that shows flows or pressure and is monitored periodically, consistent with the requirement of the application

Pressurization. The process of supplying an enclosure with a protective gas with or without continuous flow at sufficient pressure to prevent the entrance of a flammable gas or vapor.

Pressurizing System. A grouping of components used to pressurize and monitor a protected enclosure

Protected Enclosure. The enclosure pressurized by a protective gas

Protected Equipment. The electrical equipment internal to the protected enclosure

Protective Gas. The gas used to maintain pressurization or to dilute a flammable gas or vapor

Protective Gas Supply. The compressor, blower, or compressed gas container that provides the protective gas at a positive pressure. The supply includes inlet (suction) pipes or ducts, pressure regulators, outlet pipes or ducts, and any supply valves not adjacent to the pressurized enclosure.

Purging. The process of supplying an enclosure with a protective gas at a sufficient flow and positive pressure to reduce the concentration of any flammable gas or vapor initially present to an acceptable level.

Ventilated Equipment. Equipment, such as motors, that requires airflow for heat dissipation as well as pressurization to prevent entrance of flammable gases, vapors, or dusts.

Sidebar 3-03.

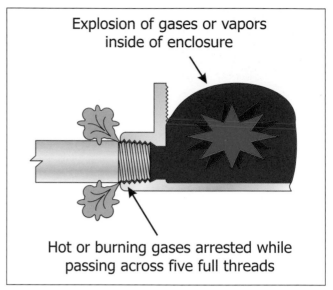

Explosion of gases or vapors inside of enclosure

Hot or burning gases arrested while passing across five full threads

Figure 3-05. An explosionproof enclosure showing threaded joint construction between enclosure and the cover (cross-sectional view)

The acceptability of that evaluation is to be determined by the local authority having jurisdiction. Everyone involved in the installation should realize that an evaluation by a certification agency outside of North America to a standard developed outside of North America is quite different than a North American listing. That product could be very similar or very different than a listed product.

Flameproof and explosionproof equipment will appear quite similar, except for the labeling. Designers, installers and inspectors need to realize that the differences will not always be obvious, but very slight. The identification marks on the equipment are important in proper application of this equipment within a classified location. The identification should clearly indicate the limits of use. Manufacturers of equipment can also provide additional information as needed.

Powder Filled "q"

Explosion protection afforded by this protection technique is accomplished by securing the electrical component capable of igniting a Class I atmosphere in place and completely surrounding that component with a glass or quartz filling material. This technique does not exclude the flammable atmosphere or ignition, but due to the combination of small free volumes in the filling material and the quenching of a flame that could pass

Photo 3-16. An explosionproof enclosure that uses threaded joint construction for the conduit entries and the cover of the enclosure Courtesy of Cooper Crouse Hinds

Photo 3-17. An explosionproof fitting that uses threaded joint construction for the conduit entries and the cover of the enclosure Courtesy of Cooper Crouse Hinds

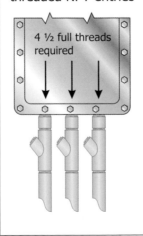

Explosionproof equipment

5 full threads required

Listed explosionproof equipment with factory threaded NPT entries

4 ½ full threads required

Figure 3-06. Explosionproof equipment requires 5 full threads, and listed explosionproof equipment is acceptable with 4½ full threads.

through the paths in the filling material, an external explosion can be prevented. This technique functions somewhat like a flame arrestor. Components that are listed for this protection technique will be evaluated to ANSI/UL 60079-5 *Electrical Apparatus for Explosive Atmospheres*. This protection technique is acceptable for Class I, Zone 1, Zone 2, and Division 2 locations. The prescriptive requirements of the standard address the: enclosure strength, filling procedure, means of closing the enclosure of the apparatus, filling material, spacing for conducting parts, cable entries, limitations of energy storing

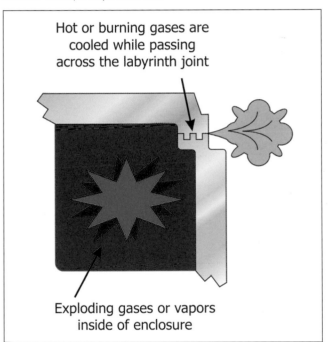

Hot or burning gases are cooled while passing across the labyrinth joint

Exploding gases or vapors inside of enclosure

Figure 3-07. Labyrinth joint construction (cross-sectional view)

devices, and temperature limitations. Powder-filled equipment is required to be listed [*NEC*, 505.20].

Type of protection "nC," Enclosed Break

This device incorporates both open and closed electrical contacts, and is able to withstand an internal explosion of the flammable material for which it is designed without suffering damage and without communicating that explosion to the external flammable atmosphere. This protection is acceptable in Class I, Zone 2 or Division 2 locations. The prescriptive requirements limit these devices to

Photo 3-18. Explosionproof enclosure that utilizes the labyrinth joint construction (enclosure and cover are shown)

Photo 3-19. Flameproof equipment certified to either IEC or CENELEC standards Courtesy of Cooper Crouse Hinds

use on a circuit having a rating of 660 volts and 15 amperes. The free internal volume is limited to 20 cm³. Gasket material and arrangement are addressed to ensure that they retain their sealing properties for the anticipated life of the device. Sealing or encapsulating materials are evaluated to determine that they are effective at temperatures exceeding the operating temperature of the device. Enclosed break equipment that includes type of protection "n" is required to be listed [*NEC*, 505.20].

The practical protection provided by these techniques does not prevent explosions from occurring in the enclosure by eliminating fuel, oxygen, or the ignition source. Instead, the protection contains explosions and controls temperatures so that the external atmospheres

around the electrical equipment are not ignited. When it is realized that containment of explosions is the principle of these techniques, it is easier to understand the sealing requirements associated with the wiring of the equipment. The seals actually complete the containment of the enclosure.

The more obvious method of protection would be to exclude the fuel from electrical components (ignition source). Several techniques use this principle to protect Class I atmospheres. The specific protection technique selected will be determined by the size (both physical and current-carrying capacity) of the electrical ignition source and the specific area classification of the locations. In some cases, the electrical ignition source may be a single set of contacts making and breaking a Class 2 control circuit; and in other cases, that source may be a 1000-horsepower, 4160-volt motor or an electrical control room. External temperatures of the electrical equipment must be controlled with these methods of protection as they were with the other practical methods of protection.

Several protection techniques using this principle can be grouped together, including: purged and pressurized equipment or type of protection "p" pressurization, hermetically sealed equipment or type of protection "nC" hermetically sealed, sealed devices, type of protection "nR" restricted breathing, type of protection "o" oil immersion, and type of protection "m" encapsulation. This section provides a short description and information about proper application of each.

Photo 3-20. Flameproof equipment certified to either IEC or CENELEC standards Courtesy of Cooper Crouse Hinds

Encapsulation "m"

The encapsulation "m" protection technique is permitted to be utilized in Class I, Division 2, Zone 1 and Zone 2 locations within the gas group and temperature limitations of the specific piece of equipment. In this technique, electrical parts that could ignite an explosive atmosphere by either sparking or heating are enclosed in a compound in such a way that the surrounding atmosphere cannot be ignited by an arc inside the encapsulation. This protection technique is likely to be utilized on smaller electrical components rather than on those using pressurization, but it applies the same principle. It excludes the fuel from the ignition source.

Hermetically Sealed Equipment or Type of Protection "nC"

Hermetically sealed equipment or type of protection "nC" hermetically sealed can be utilized as a protection technique in Class I, Division 2, or Zone 2 locations within the gas group and temperature limitations of the specific piece of equipment.

Requirements for this protection technique are included in standards developed in both the Division system and the Zone system. Protection is provided where the electrical component (in many cases, a set of contacts) is sealed against the entrance of a flammable atmosphere where the seal is made by fusion, for example, soldering, brazing, or the fusion of glass to metal. It should be realized that electrical components and equipment could include hermetically sealed contacts but not comply with the requirements in any of the hazardous location product standards. Components should be evaluated to the appropriate safety standard.

Oil Immersion "o"

Oil immersion (Division technique) or Oil immersion "o" (Zone technique) is permitted to be utilized as a protection technique in Class I, Division 2, Zone 1 and Zone 2 locations within the gas group and temperature limitations of the specific piece of equipment. With this protection, the electrical component is fixed in its operating position in such a way that it is immersed in a protective liquid so that flammable atmosphere located above the liquid or outside the enclosure will not be ignited.

Purged and Pressurized Enclosures

A review of NFPA 496 will assist in providing a basic understanding of the principles used with this protection technique. The purpose of the standard is to provide information on the methods for purging and pressurizing enclosures to prevent ignition of a flammable atmosphere. Such an atmosphere may be introduced into the enclosure by a surrounding external atmosphere or by an internal source. By use of this protection technique, electrical equipment not otherwise acceptable for a flammable atmosphere (ordinary location equipment) may be utilized (see figure 3-09).

The standard is permitted to apply to purging and pressurizing of electrical equipment installed in Class I locations; electrical equipment containing sources of flammable vapors or gases and located in either classified or unclassified areas; control rooms or buildings located in Class I locations; and analyzer rooms containing sources of flammable vapors or gases and located in Class I locations.

Type X pressurizing will reduce the classification within the protected enclosure from Class I, Division 1 or Zone 1 to unclassified.

Type Y pressurizing will reduce the classification within the protected enclosure from Class I, Division 1 to Class I, Division 2; or Class I, Zone 1 to Class I, Zone 2.

Type Z pressurizing will reduce the classification within the protected enclosure from Class I, Division 2 or Zone 2 to unclassified.

Purged and pressurized enclosures (equipment or complete buildings) may be listed or classified as a complete system, or they may include assemblies of listed or unlisted parts and components that may be factory or field assembled. Where systems are listed or classified, they would be evaluated to the requirements in NFPA 496, *Standard for Purged and Pressurized Enclosures for Electrical Equipment;* or FM 3620; or EN 50 016; or EN 50 021; or IEC 60079-2; or IEC 60079-15; or CSA 60079-2; or CSA 60079-15.

Designers, users, installers and code enforcement should understand that although the purpose of all of these standards is the same, the content is not identical. In many cases, because of job specific applications, systems that employ this protection technique will not be evaluated as a complete system. When manufacturers produce systems that can be used in multiple facilities with similar parameters, they may have the products evaluated to one or more of the standards. In some cases, manufacturers may build their products to comply with one or more of the standards, yet choose not to have third party evaluation. A complete review of Articles 500, 501 and 505 reveals that most pressurized equipment is required to be identified for the location where it is used.

This technique requires the protected enclosures

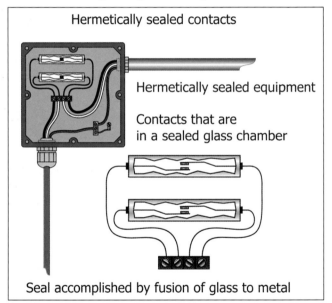

Figure 3-08. Hermetically sealed electrical contact (example)

to be constructed of material that is not likely to be damaged under the conditions to which it may be subjected. Precautions need to be taken to protect the enclosure from excessive pressure of the protective gas supply. Excess pressure-relieving devices that are required to protect in the case of a control failure must be designed to prevent the discharge of ignition-capable particles to a Division 1 location. In Division 1 locations, conduits that connect to pressurized enclosures are permitted but are not required to be pressurized. Where the conduit is not pressurized, an explosionproof seal is required as close as possible to the enclosure. The purpose for this seal, unlike those at explosionproof enclosures, is not to contain an explosion within the

pressurized enclosure but to contain any explosion that might occur within the conduit system rather than allowing it to propagate into the pressurized enclosure (see photos 3-21 through 3-26).

In Division 2 locations explosionproof conduit seals are not required at the pressurized enclosure. It is assumed that under normal operating conditions, a fault in the conduit system and a failure in the containment of the flammable or combustible material would not occur simultaneously. Therefore, explosions within the conduit system are not likely. A seal may be needed to maintain pressurization of the enclosure, but it would not be required to be explosionproof.

Protected enclosures are required to be constantly maintained at a positive pressure [25 Pa (0.1 in. water)] above the surrounding atmosphere during operation of the protected equipment. If positive pressure is not maintained in a protected enclosure, a suitable warning device is required to notify users or operators to take action or automatically de-energize power from ignition-capable equipment. The system must be protected by a protection technique acceptable for the location when components of the pressurized system can be energized while the system is not pressurized. Adequate instructions must be provided for the pressurization system to ensure that the system can be

Photo 3-21. Purged and pressurized enclosure used in a Class I, Division 1 location

Photo 3-22. Pressure indicator for pressurized enclosure

Photo 3-24. Pneumatic piping system shown connected to a purged and pressurized enclosure

Photo 3-23. Interior of purged and pressurized enclosure showing contained equipment suitable for use in unclassified locations

Photo 3-25. Closeup showing inert gas lines connected to the pressurized enclosure

used properly and that the enclosure will be protected from excessive pressure.

Protective Gas for Pressurized Enclosures

Specific requirements are provided to maximize the chance that the protective gas supply used to

Photo 3-26. Odorant injection system (suitable for use in unclassified locations) installed in a purged and pressurized enclosure

pressurize the protected enclosure(s) does not include flammable materials. Requirements are also provided to minimize the chance of power loss for the source of protective gas. When *double pressurization* is used (e.g., a Division I enclosed area pressurized to a Division 2 classification that contains ignition-capable equipment also protected by pressurization), the protective gas supplies are required to be independent.

Surface Temperature of Pressurized Enclosures

As with all electrical equipment installed in Class I locations, temperatures must be limited to prevent that equipment from reaching the autoignition temperature of the environment. In many cases, pressurized equipment will consist of ordinary location electrical devices within ordinary location enclosures that have been pressurized for use in Class I locations. In ordinary locations, those temperature issues do not exist and, therefore, that equipment will not likely leave the original manufacturer with adequate temperature

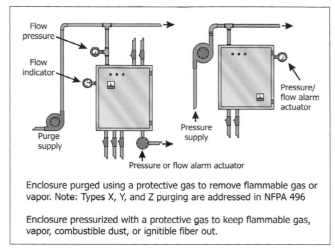

Figure 3-09. Purged and pressurized enclosures permitted as a protection technique

marking. Section 2-5 of NFPA 496 provides guidance for all of those involved in the pressurization process to determine the proper temperature marking of the equipment. It should be recognized that the temperature tests included in other product standards for equipment evaluated by certification agencies are quite complex. It should not be assumed that temperature evaluation for pressurized equipment would be less complex.

The protective gas supply is permitted to supply single or multiple pressurized enclosures. Where multiple enclosures are connected to a single protective supply, the piping for the protective gas is permitted to be series connected or manifold connected (see figures 3-10, 3-11, 3-12, and 3-13, which are reproductions of the concepts conveyed by Figure 2-8 in NFPA 496. Note: In figures 3-10 through 3-13, purge outlet devices that could be provided are not shown for clarity).

For Type Z pressurization (Division 2 or Zone 2 to unclassified), protected equipment is not required to be de-energized upon failure to maintain positive pressure; however, the failure is required to be detected

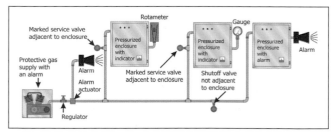

Figure 3-10. Indicators may be used if the protective gas supply has an alarm and the shutoff valve is adjacent to the enclosure.

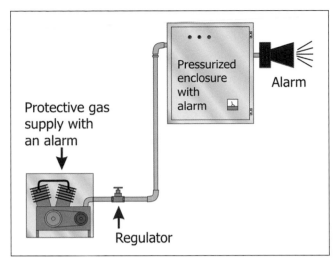

Figure 3-11. Enclosure alarm can also serve as the protective gas supply alarm.

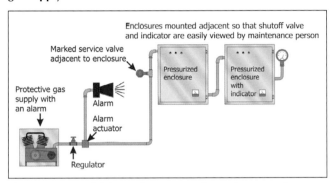

Figure 3-12. Multiple enclosures can be series purged.

by an alarm or indicator to notify those responsible for the operation that problems exist. For Division 2 or Zone 2 (areas that would only have an ignitable atmosphere under abnormal conditions), an alarm or indication that pressurization is not maintained provides a reasonable level of protection.

If an alarm is provided, it must be located at a constantly attended location; the alarm actuator must receive its signal from the protected enclosure and not be installed between the enclosure and the protective gas supply; the actuator must be mechanical, pneumatic, or electrical; the electrical alarms and electrical alarm actuators are required to be suitable for the environment in which they are installed; and no valves are permitted to be located between the alarm actuator and the enclosure.

If an indicator is provided, it is required to be located for convenient viewing; is not permitted to be installed between the enclosure and the protective gas supply; is required to indicate either pressure or flow; is not permitted to have valves located between the

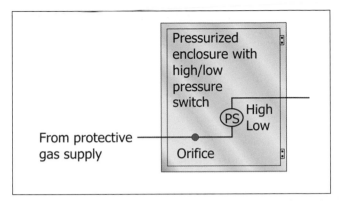

Figure 3-13. An enclosure with an internal fail-safe high-pressure switch arranged to alarm in an attended location as required

indicator and the enclosure; and is required to include an alarm for the protective gas supply that is located at a constantly attended location to indicate failure of the protective gas supply to maintain the required pressure.

Where Type Z pressurization is installed in Class I areas, the protected enclosures are required to be purged each time they are opened or have failed to maintain the required pressure, unless it can be confirmed that the atmosphere within the enclosure is nonflammable. That could be confirmed with gas detection equipment. Protected enclosures are not permitted to be energized until a minimum of ten (10) volumes of protective gas has been passed through the enclosure of rotating electrical equipment (e.g., motors, generators, etc.), or four (4) volumes through other enclosures while maintaining the required pressurization [25 Pa (0.1 in. water)] on the enclosure. Specific requirements are provided for multi-compartment enclosures, including compartments that enclose instruments or other devices that have vents and compartments that enclose devices or equipment that are additionally protected by other protection techniques.

For Type Y pressurization (Division 1 to Division 2 or Zone 1 to Zone 2), all of the requirements for Type Z pressurization are required to be met; and all of the equipment within the protected enclosure is required to be suitable for the Division 2 environment; and any ventilated equipment within the protected enclosure that is capable of reaching temperatures that exceed the marked T-Code rating if the ventilation fails is required to be de-energized

upon failure of the protected flow of protective gas.

Where Type Y pressurization is installed in Class I areas, chapter 3 of NFPA 496 includes the same purging requirements listed above for Type Z.

For Type X pressurization (Class I, Division 1 or Zone 1 to unclassified), a flow-actuated or pressure-actuated cutoff switch, suitable for the environment where it is installed, must be provided to de-energize all circuits and equipment within the protected enclosure upon failure of the protective gas supply to maintain positive pressure. In cases where immediate loss of power would result in a more hazardous condition, a limited delay can be introduced in the shutoff function where both audible and visual alarms are provided to a constantly attended location. In cases where circuits and/or equipment are suitable for the Division 1 or Zone 1 environment that exists, it is not necessary to de-energize those items. No valves are permitted between the cutoff switch and the protected enclosure. The cutoff switch shall take its signal from the protected enclosure and shall not be installed between the enclosure and the protective gas supply. Equipment, such as motors or transformers, that may be overloaded shall be provided with appropriate devices to detect any increase in temperature of the equipment beyond its design limits and shall de-energize the equipment automatically. In cases where immediate loss of power would result in a more hazardous condition, a limited delay can be introduced in the de-energizing of the overheated equipment where both audible and visual alarms are provided to a constantly attended location.

For ventilated equipment, the flow of protective gas shall provide sufficient cooling even during overload conditions or the equipment subject to overloading shall be provided with appropriate devices to detect any increase in temperature beyond its design limits and to de-energize that equipment automatically. In cases where immediate loss of power would result in a more hazardous condition, a limited delay can be introduced in the de-energizing of the overheated equipment where both audible and visual alarms are provided to a constantly attended location.

For Type X pressurization installed in Class I locations, chapter 3 of NFPA 496 includes all of the purging requirements stated above for Type Y or Z pressurization, with several additional safeguards. In addition to the specific number of air changes, a timing device is required to be installed to assure that the requisite is met prior to the equipment being energized. If the enclosure can be readily opened without the use of a key or tools, an interlock suitable for the Division 1 or Zone 1 environment is required to immediately de-energize all circuits within the enclosure that are not suitable for Class I, Division 1 or Class I, Zone 1 locations. Also, hot components installed within the enclosure that require a cool-down period are required to be opened with a tool or key.

There are some very specific warning and marking requirements for pressurized equipment. These markings or warnings must describe the type of pressurization used, the classification of the surrounding atmosphere, temperature limitations, and startup and operation warnings.

Pressurized Rooms or Buildings

In many facilities with Class I atmospheres, it is both cost effective and considered safer by some users to build pressurized control rooms or buildings to install much of the electrical equipment for the facility, rather than installing a large number of electrical devices throughout the classified areas of the facility and protecting those devices with various protection techniques. The principles for protection of these enclosures (rooms or buildings) are the same as for those of a smaller control panel or motor enclosure or other enclosure. However, since rooms and buildings normally include doors and other openings that may be operated on a more regular basis than the door of a control panel, specific requirements are provided to address those conditions. Also, since these rooms or buildings may include HVAC systems for the comfort of the occupants and air-consuming devices for operation of the facility (exhaust hoods, compressors, etc.), the relationship of those systems with the pressurization of the enclosure must be addressed. Types X, Y, or Z pressurization is utilized for such pressurized buildings or rooms under this protection technique. These techniques are often implemented under the design criteria of multiple designers or engineers from various associated disciplines.

Each separate pressurized building, room, or control room is unique and constructed for the specific application. It is not likely that any of these pressurized enclosures will be listed. Many of them will not be constructed in a manufacturing facility, but rather be constructed on site. That is the primary reason the *NEC* requires this protection technique be identified for approval rather than listed. All of the parties involved with these installations should be aware that suitability of *identified* equipment might still require third party evaluation of the installation. Another option for identified equipment involves a procedure commonly referred to as a *field evaluation* by most certification organizations. A final option involves approval of the equipment by the AHJ. Designers and installers should be aware that in situations where the owner's safety department is the AHJ, they might be comfortable evaluating the construction of the pressurization system without the assistance of a certification agency. That will depend on the experience, training and availability of the facilities engineering and safety department. This issue is one that should be considered and agreed upon by all involved in the planning and engineering design stages of the project.

Type of Protection "nR" Restricted Breathing

An enclosure that incorporates restricted breathing as a method of protection will rely on tight seals and gaskets to prevent diffusion of the ignitible atmosphere into the enclosure under normal operations. This protection is acceptable in Class I, Zone 2 or Division 2 locations. Gasket material and arrangement is addressed to ensure that they retain their sealing properties for the anticipated life of the device. Sealing or encapsulating materials are evaluated to determine that they are effective at temperatures exceeding the operating temperature of the device. Restricted breathing "nR" equipment is required to be listed [*NEC,* 505.20].

Other Common Protection Techniques

Limiting the energy in the electrical system is the next practical principle used to minimize the chance

that electrical systems will become an ignition source in Class I atmospheres. It is possible to limit the energy in the circuit and equipment to a point that arcs and sparks and surface temperatures are not ignition capable. Several protection techniques are included in the Division system and Zone system that operate on this principle including: intrinsically safe systems as described in *NEC* 500.7 and Article 504; nonincendive systems as described in *NEC* 500.2 and 500.7; intrinsically safe systems "ia" and ib" as described in *NEC* 505.2 and 505.8; and type of protection "nA" nonincendive. Although each of these protection techniques prevents the ignition of Class I atmospheres by limiting energy, the specific requirements of the systems are different, the product standards for each one is different, and the locations that each can be installed are different.

It is possible for these systems to be either a single piece of equipment or a self-contained circuit or system within a larger piece of equipment. One example of a self-contained system is an IS paging device. These devices are defined as *intrinsically safe apparatus* or *nonincendive equipment*. More often than self-contained systems, the intrinsically safe or nonincendive system will consist of multiple parts which are connected together in the field. Those cases will consist of a power supply, which limits the energy value, some interconnected field wiring, and field device(s). The power supply could be a battery, which is inherently energy limited, or it could be an associated apparatus supplied by a circuit that is not intrinsically safe or nonincendive. The IS circuit is then derived through a zener diode barrier or other type device which limits the output energy to a safe level (see photos 3-27 and 3-28). These systems can be evaluated by recognized laboratories as complete systems or as parts: e.g., associated apparatus, the associated nonincendive field wiring apparatus, the intrinsically safe or nonincendive field wiring apparatus, nonincendive components, or field devices can be evaluated and assigned parameters in which they can operate safely.

Intrinsically Safe Circuits and Systems "ia"

Intrinsically safe systems as described in *NEC* 504 or those described in 505.2, 505.8(C), and 505.9 as "ia"

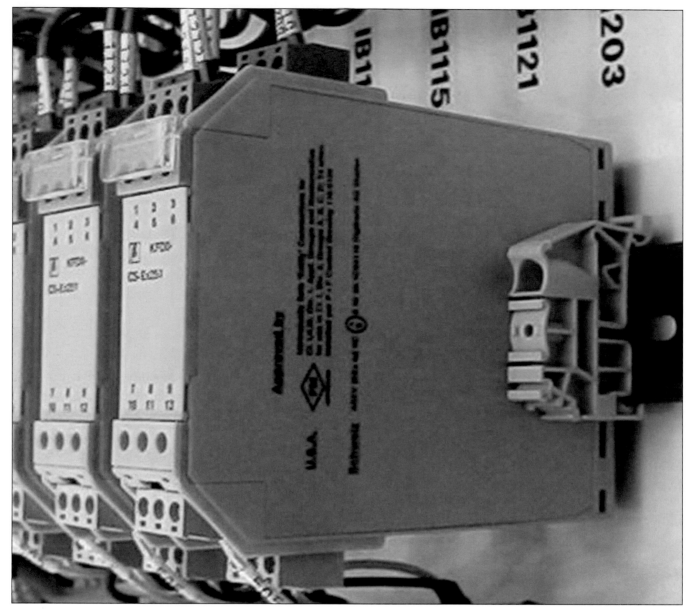

Photo 3-27. Listed zener diode barriers assembled in a control panel

are permitted in both Class I, Division 1 or Division 2 locations and also in Class I, Zone 0 or Zone 1 or Zone 2 locations within the gas group and temperature limitations of the specific piece of equipment (see photo 3-28). This technique has proven very effective for instrumentation work in areas that include ignitible concentrations for long periods of time. It is the only protection technique permitted in areas Classed Zone 0 (see figure 3-14).

For designers, installers and inspectors, the most important issue is that every IS system is required by 504.10 and the product standard to include a control drawing. Conforming to the specific requirements of the control drawing is the only way to ensure the integrity of

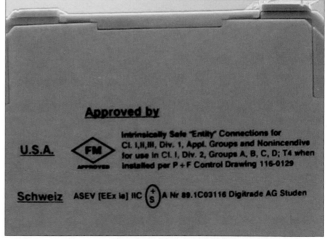

Photo 3-28. A typical listed zener diode barrier showing identification marks and reference to control drawing

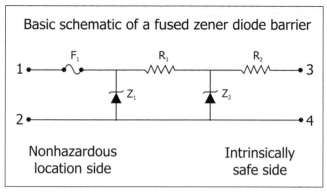

Basic schematic of a fused zener diode barrier

1 ●──〜F₁〜─────∿∿∿R₁──────∿∿∿R₂──────● 3

         ◥Z₁   ◥Z₂

2 ●──────────────────────────────────● 4

Nonhazardous   Intrinsically
location side   safe side

Figure 3-14. Basic diagram of a fused zener diode barrier [reproduction of Exhibit 504.2 from the NFPA 70, *NEC Handbook*]

the intrinsic safety of the system. It is also critical to use the exact components required by that control drawing. No installation or inspection of an IS system should begin without the control drawing. ISA-RP12.2.02 is a recommended practice for the preparation, content, and organization of intrinsic safety control drawings. This document promotes uniformity of control drawings in an effort to make them clear to those installing and inspecting this equipment.

Several options exist for control drawings. In some drawings, the manufacturers specify both associated apparatus and the intrinsically safe apparatus by specific model number. Control drawings often specify the intrinsically safe apparatus by model number. The associated apparatus is generally specified by entity parameters, such as current, voltage, capacitance and inductance values. Control drawings might also provide specific model numbers for the associated apparatus and provide entity parameters for the intrinsically safe apparatus, or limit the connection to simple apparatus. Control drawings will normally be provided on either 8 ½ x 11 or 11 x 17 inch paper (see examples of control drawings in the annex: figures A-04 through A-08).

The control drawing should contain a wiring diagram for interconnected wiring that must be installed. Model numbers or entity parameters for the various components that are connected to complete the system should be included. The control drawing should identify which components of the IS system are permitted to be located within the hazardous areas. The control drawings should include the manufacturer, an identification number of the drawing, the page number of the total pages, and a revision or date identifier. For associated apparatus,

a maximum unclassified location voltage level should be provided. The drawing should also reference Article 504 of the *NEC* or CE Code Part 1, Appendix F.

Many IS systems will include field devices known as *simple apparatus*. These might be contacts of switches, thermocouples, light emitting diodes (LEDs), or other devices not capable of storing or generating energy. These devices are not likely to be listed for use in hazardous locations (see figure 3-15). If the supply through which they are connected has an intrinsically safe output and these devices cannot store or generate any additional energy, there is no need for these devices to be evaluated for use in hazardous locations. Care should be taken to determine that these simple devices would operate within acceptable temperatures. Section 504.10(B) provides guidance for use of simple apparatus within acceptable temperatures.

Other IS systems will include devices that are not simple, such as transmitters, transducers, and relays. These and other types of devices have capacitive and/ or inductive characteristics that allow them to store and discharge or generate energy. These devices should be evaluated and listed for use in these systems and within the locations included in the product listing.

Intrinsically Safe System "ib"

Intrinsically safe systems as described in *NEC* 504 or those described in 505.2, 505.8(C), and 505.9 as "ib" are permitted in Class I, Division 2 locations and also

Photo 3-29. Listed intrinsically safe control panel that includes multiple zener diode barriers supplying various intrinsically safe circuits (note barriers)

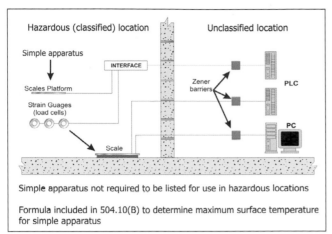

Figure 3-15. Simple apparatus is often used with intrinsically safe systems.

in Class I, Zone 1 or Zone 2 locations within the gas group and temperature limitations of the specific piece of equipment. Control drawings are required for installation and inspection. This type of intrinsically safe circuit offers only one level of protection as compared to the dual level of protection afforded by "ia" type of intrinsically safe circuit or system. For this reason, they are not permitted as a protection technique in Zone 0 or Division 1 applications.

Nonincendive Systems

Nonincendive systems are made up of various components, field wiring, equipment, and apparatus. The nonincendive protection technique is limited to use in Classes I and II, Division 2 and Class III, Divisions 1 and 2 locations [*NEC,* 500.7(F)].

A nonincendive circuit is one in which any arc or thermal effect produced under intended operating conditions of the equipment is not capable, under specified test conditions, of igniting the flammable gas–air, vapor–air, or dust–air mixture.

Nonincendive components have contacts for making or breaking an incendive circuit and the contacting mechanism is constructed so that the component is incapable of igniting the specified flammable gas–air or vapor–air mixture.

See UL Standard 1604-1994, *Electrical Equipment for Use in Class I and II, Division 2, and Class III Hazardous (Classified) Locations* for additional information.

Nonincendive equipment has electrical/electronic circuitry that is incapable, under normal operating conditions, of causing ignition of a specified

flammable gas–air, vapor–air, or dust–air mixture due to arcing or thermal means.

Nonincendive field wiring enters or leaves an equipment enclosure and, under normal operating conditions of the equipment, is not capable, due to arcing or thermal effects, of igniting the flammable gas–air, vapor–air, or dust–air mixture. Normal operation includes opening, shorting, or grounding the field wiring (see photo 3-30).

Nonincendive field wiring apparatus is intended to be connected to nonincendive field wiring (see photo 3-31).

For additional information about nonincendive electrical equipment and this protection technique,

Photo 3-30. Nonincendive field wiring connected to a sensing probe on a high-pressure gas line

see ANSI/ISA 12.12.01-2000, *Nonincendive Electrical Equipment for Use in Class I and II, Division 2, and Class III, Divisions 1 and 2 Hazardous (Classified) Locations.*

Type of Protection "n"

The protection technique "n" is where electrical equipment, in normal operation, is not capable of igniting a surrounding explosive gas atmosphere and a fault capable of causing ignition is unlikely to occur. This type of equipment generally has no arcing parts and the enclosure restricts the ingress of hazardous gases. This protection technique is permitted for equipment in Class I, Zone 2 locations.

Type of protection "n" is further subdivided into

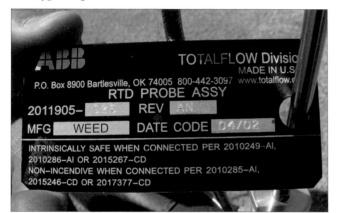

Photo 3-31. Nonincendive component (probe sensor assembly)

nA, nC, and nR. Type nA stands for nonsparking construction; type nC stands for hermetically sealed, nonincendive; and type nR stands for restricted breathing.

Combustible Gas Detection Systems

This protection technique utilizes stationary gas detectors and is limited in application to only industrial establishments with restricted public access and where the conditions of maintenance and supervision ensure that only qualified persons service the installation. Gas detection equipment shall be listed for detection of the specific gas or vapor to be encountered (see photo 3-32). Where such a system is installed, equipment specified in 500.7(K)(1), (2), or (3) shall be permitted.

Increased Safety "e"

Increased Safety "e" protection is applied to electrical equipment that does not produce arcs or sparks

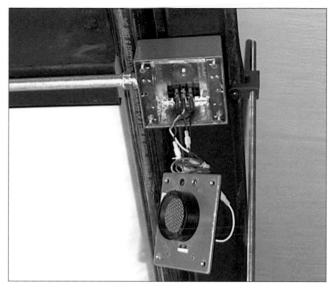

Photo 3-32. Listed combustible gas detector prior to circuit wiring being installed in conduit

in normal service and under specified abnormal conditions, in which additional measures are applied so as to give increased security against the possibility of excessive temperatures and of the occurrence of arcs and sparks. This protection technique must utilize high impact resistant materials FRP or GRP that will not hold a static charge and cannot produce any arcs or sparks. This type of equipment has special air line leakage and creep distances and must incorporate the IEC non-loosen connections. Also, this equipment must control internal and external temperatures, and the external temperature should not exceed T-6 (85° C) [see figures 3-16 and 3-17; photo 3-33].

Class I Location Protection Techniques Applications

The primary concerns in Class I locations center around fire or explosion hazards that may exist due to flammable gases or vapors or flammable liquids. Equipment installed in Class I locations must be suitable for the class, group and temperature class. Table 3-02 shows the acceptable protection techniques for Class I locations, including the divisions. Equipment suitable for use in Class I and II locations is required to be marked with the maximum safe operating temperature in accordance with *NEC* Table 500.8(B).

Class II Location Protection Techniques Applications

The primary concerns in Class II locations center

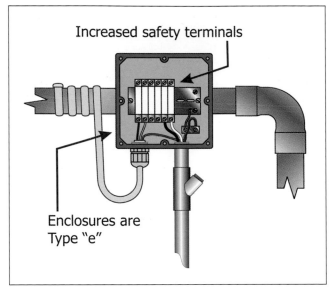

Figure 3-16. Increased safety "e" equipment depends on integrity of the terminations and enclosures with glands where cables are installed.

around fire or explosion hazards that may exist due to combustible dust in suspension in the air during operations or in accumulations as a result of such operations. Equipment installed in Class II locations must be able to function at full rating without developing surface temperatures that are high enough to cause excessive dehydration or gradual carbonization of any organic dust deposits

Table 2-5.2 Temperature Identification Numbers (T Codes)

Maximum Temperature		Temperature Class
°C	°F	(T Code)
450	842	T1
300	572	T2
280	536	T2A
260	500	T2B
230	446	T2C
215	419	T2D
200	392	T3
180	356	T3A
165	329	T3B
160	320	T3C
135	275	T4
120	248	T4A
100	212	T5
85	185	T6

Table 3-01. Classification of maximum surface temperature
[reproduction of *NEC* Table 500.8(B)]

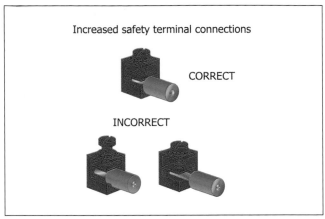

Figure 3-17. Terminals of increased "e" safety enclosures

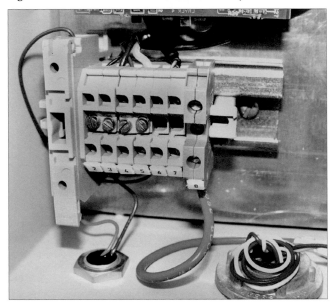

Photo 3-33. Increased safety terminals

or accumulations that may occur. Dust that is carbonized or excessively dry is highly susceptible to spontaneous ignition. Explosionproof equipment and wiring is not required and is generally not acceptable in Class II locations unless identified for such locations. Where Class II, Group E (combustible metallic) dusts are present in hazardous quantities, they are classified as only Division 1 locations. Table 3-03 shows the many acceptable protection techniques for Class II locations, including the divisions in which they are permitted to be used (see table 3-03).

Class III Location Protection Techniques Applications

Equipment installed in Class III locations must function at full rating without developing surface temperatures high enough to cause excessive dehydration or gradual carbonization of accumulated fibers or flyings. Organic material that is carbonized or excessively dry is highly susceptible to spontaneous ignition. Maximum surface temperatures dur-ing operation are not to exceed 165°C (329°F) for equipment that is not subject to overloading. For equipment such as motors or power transformers that may be overloaded at times, the maximum surface temperature is not to exceed 120°C (248°F).

Summary

The study of *NEC* protection techniques in this document includes descriptive information about each protection technique under both the Division and Zone Classification Systems. The type of protection permitted in a particular location depends on the class of location and particular Division or Zone encountered.

Each protection technique offers its own methods of removing one or more components of the fire triangle from the hazardous (classified) location equation. Each technique has suitable applications and limitations and must be used within those limits to ensure electrical safety.

The primary wiring method of the *NEC* continues to be conduit methods, while the primary wiring method for installations under the IEC rules is cable types. Both classification systems depend on proper application of protection techniques for safety. Various protection techniques under both classification systems offer more diversity in the wiring methods than

Division and Zone Protection Techniques Comparison

Protection Techniques for Class I Locations	
Technique	**Location**
Explosionproof Apparatus	Divisions 1 or 2
Purged and Pressurized	Divisions 1 or 2 (as identified)
Intrinsic Safety	Division 1 or 2
Nonincendive Circuit	Division 2
Nonincendive Equipment	Division 2
Nonincendive Component	Division 2
Oil Immersion	Division 2
Hermetically Sealed	Division 2
Combustible Gas Detection System	Divisions 1 or 2 (industrial)

Table 3-02. Protection techniques suitable for use in Class I locations

Protection Techniques for Class II Locations	
Technique	**Location**
Dustignitionproof Equipment	Divisions 1 or 2
Dusttight Equipment	Division 2
Pressurized	Divisions 1 or 2 (as identified)
Intrinsic Safety	Division 1 or 2
Nonincendive Circuit	Division 2
Nonincendive Equipment	Division 2
Nonincendive Component	Division 2
Hermetically Sealed	Division 2

Table 3-03. Acceptable protection techniques for Class II locations

Protection Techniques for Class III Locations	
Technique	**Location**
Dusttight Equipment	Divisions 1 and 2
Intrinsic Safety	Division 1 or 2
Nonincendive Circuit	Divisions 1 and 2
Nonincendive Equipment	Divisions 1 and 2
Nonincendive Component	Divisions 1 and 2
Hermetically Sealed	Divisions 1 and 2

Table 3-04. Acceptable protection techniques for Class III locations

Class II Group	Equipment Not Subject to Overloading		Equipment (Such as Motors or Power Transformers) That may be overloaded			
			Normal Operation		Abnormal Operation	
	°C	°F	°C	°F	°C	°F
E	200	392	200	392	200	392
F	200	392	150	302	200	392
G	165	329	120	248	165	329

Table 3-05. Class II temperatures [reproduction of *NEC* Table 500.8(C)(2)]

Protection Technique Designations for the Zone System

Symbol	Technique	Zone
d	Flameproof enclosure	1
e	Increased safety	1
ia	Intrinsic safety	0
ib	Intrinsic safety	1
[ia]	Associated apparatus	Unclassified
[ib]	Associated apparatus	Unclassified
m	Encapsulation	1
nA	Nonsparking equipment	2
n C	Sparking equipment in which the contacts are suitably protected other than by a restricted breathing enclosure	2
n R	Restricted breathing enclosure	1
o	Oil immersion	1
p	Purged and pressurized	1 or 2
q	Powder filled	1

Table 3-06. Protection techniques under the Zone System of classification

is allowed for electrical and electronic equipment in hazardous locations. The protection technique chosen in the design and how it is installed and used is directly related to electrical safety in any hazardous (classified) location.

Glossary

AEx is a symbol that designates equipment built to NEC standards for use in NEC Zone designated areas. Such products are not suitable for use in EEx or EX European Zone areas.

Cable Gland is a term used internationally to describe a variety of products used for cable ter-minating in IEC systems. Available for armored and unarmored cable, and for "d" and "e" protection methods

Cable Seal, Explosionproof is a terminator for cable that when used in Class I, Divisions 1 and 2 areas, is filled with compound or epoxy to contain or minimize the passage of vapors/gases through cable from one location to another. Traditionally a product for NEC applications

CEC. Canadian Electric Code

CENELEC. European Committee for Electrical Stand-ardization is a group of 19 European countries and 11 affiliated countries that have CENELEC standards based on the parallel working IEC/CENELEC.

"d" protection is similar to "explosionproof," contains explosion, external temperature limited.

"de" or "ed" protection is protection combining "d" and "e" techniques.

Divisions is a term used in U. S. NEC to describe condition, frequency or duration where an explosive or flammable substance is present.

"e" protection is control of internal and external temperatures. Normally sparking components excluded.

Sidebar 3.04.

PROTECTION TECHNIQUES RECOGNIZED BY IEC, NEC® AND CEC

Protection method	Identification letters	Permitted in division	Permitted in zone	Principle
Flameproof	d	2	1 or 2	Containment
Intrinsic safety (zone 0)	ia	1 or 2	0, 1, 2	Energy limited
Intrinsic safety (zone 1)	ib	2	1 or 2	Energy limited
Pressurization	p	1 or 2	1 or 2	Expels vapors
Increased safety	e	2	1 or 2	No arcs
Immersed in oil	o	1 or 2	1 or 2	Arc immersion
Filled powder/sand	q	2	1 or 2	Arc immersion
Encapsulated	m	2	1 or 2	Hermetic seal
Apparatus with "n"* protection	n	2	2	No sparking

Table 3-07. Various protection techniques recognized by the *NEC*, IEC, and the CE Code Part I.

EEx is a designation for equipment complying with EN standards.

Encapsulation—"m" protection. In this technique, parts that could ignite an explosive atmosphere are enclosed in an encapsulant preventing exposure to the explosive atmosphere.

EX is a designation for hazardous location equipment complying to IEC standards or non-CENELEC standards.

Flameproof is an IEC or European term using "containment" protection. Similar to, but not exactly the same as U. S. explosionproof.

Hazardous Location is an area where potentially explosive or combustible gases, dusts or flyings may occur.

Increase Safety—"e" protection is a explosion protection that does not produce arcs or sparks in normal service. Design gives security against excessive temperature and occurrence of sparks and arcs.

Intrinsic Safety is a method of protection that limits the energy passing into hazardous areas utilizing safety barriers. Regardless of fault in hazardous area, energy to ignite an explosive atmosphere cannot be released.

Intrinsic Safety—"I" protection. Refers to an electrical system that uses only intrinsically safe equipment (wiring, circuits, apparatus) that is incapable of causing ignition to a surrounding hazardous atmosphere.

IP. Ingress Protection System used by IEC and CENELEC. This system is similar to but not the same as U. S. NEMA enclosure ratings. Two numbers used: first number rates protections against solid bodies ingress; second number protection against liquid ingress.

NEC. National Electrical Code

Restricted Breathing—"nR" protection is used extensively on lighting fixtures in IEC systems. Components can be tightly closed to prevent access of flammable atmosphere into internal parts. Operating temperatures are taken externally thus allowing fixture use in areas having low gas ignition temperatures.

Subdivision is a Zone system grouping of various gas/vapors roughly equal to NEC "Group."

Zone defines conditions under which explosive gases are present in an area. Zones are similar to divisions, but are generally based on length of time hazardous materials may be present.

Used by permission of EGS Electrical Group, Appleton.

Sidebar 3.04. continued

Courtesy of Appleton EGS Electrical Group

Review Questions

1. The most common *NEC* protection technique used with power equipment installed in Class I, Division 1, locations is_____.

   a. increased safety
   b. hermetically sealed
   c. dust-ignitionproof
   d. explosionproof

2. Explosion protection is achieved with explosionproof equipment enclosures by excluding all flammable liquids, gases and vapors that eliminates the fuel side of the fire triangle.

   a. True
   b. False

3. Which protection technique permitted in Class I locations excludes the fuel side of the fire triangle?

   a. Intrinsic safety
   b. Dust ignitionproof
   c. Purged and pressurized
   d. Flameproof "d"

4. Which Class I protection technique is permitted in both Division 1 and Zone 0 locations?

   a. Intrinsic safety
   b. Explosionproof
   c. Purged and pressurized
   d. Increased safety

5. Which of the following protection techniques cannot be used all three classes of hazardous (classified) locations; Class I, Class II, and Class III?

   a. Intrinsic safety
   b. Hermetically sealed
   c. Explosionproof
   d. Nonincendive equipment

6. Nonincendive equipment is not permitted in Group ___ hazardous locations.

   a. B
   b. D
   c. E
   d. G

7. All equipment with a suitable temperature class that is identified for use in Class I, Division 2, locations is also permitted in Class I, Zone 2, locations with the same gas.

   a. True
   b. False

8. Dusttight enclosures are not permitted for use in _____ locations that include ignitible fibers and flyings.

   a. Class III, Division 1
   b. Class III, Division 2
   c. Zone 22
   d. Zone 20

9. A pressurized enclosure that is installed in a __ _____ hazardous (classified) location would not be purged.

   a. Class II, Division 2
   b. Class I, Zone 1
   c. Class I, Division 1
   d. Class I, Division 2

10. Increased safety equipment is permitted in Class I, Division 1, locations.

   a. True
   b. False

11. Powder filling is permitted as a protection technique in Class I, Zone 1, locations.

   a. True
   b. False

12. Flameproof equipment is permitted in Class I, Division 2, locations.

   a. True
   b. False

13. Equipment that is hermetically sealed is permitted in a Class I, Zone 1, location.

   a. True
   b. False

14. Intrinsic safety type "ib" equipment is permitted in a Class I, Division 1, location.

   a. True
   b. False

15. Intrinsic safety type "ia" equipment is permitted in a Class I, Division 1, location.

   a. True
   b. False

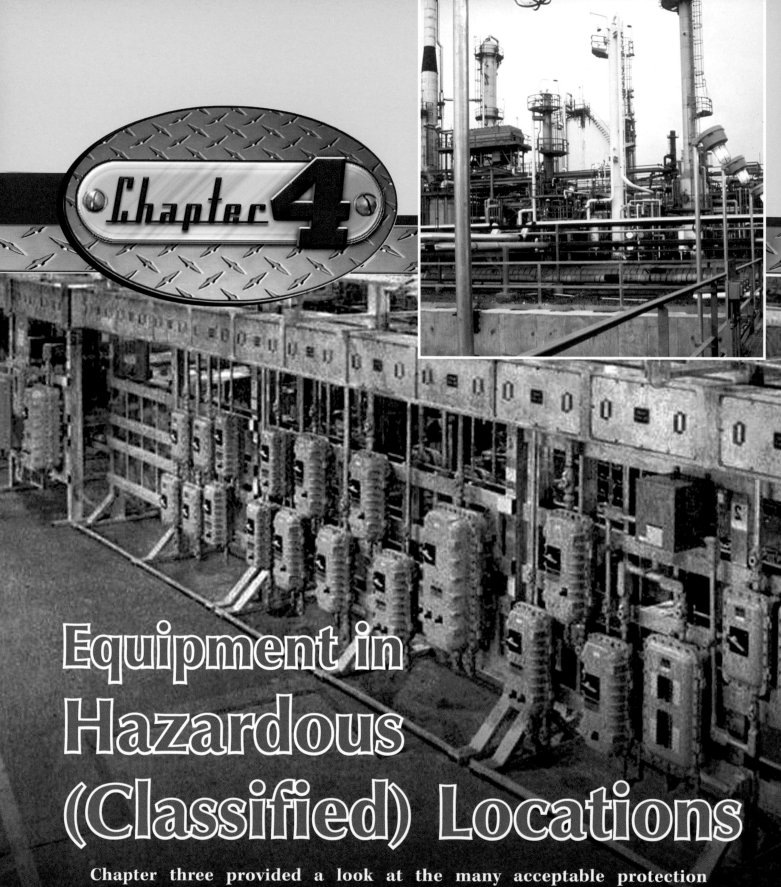

Chapter 4

Equipment in Hazardous (Classified) Locations

Chapter three provided a look at the many acceptable protection techniques used for electrical equipment installed in hazardous locations classified either under the Division system or the Zone system. Protection techniques for each classification scheme are similar for both systems, with a few differences.

As discussed in the previous chapter, wiring and equipment often utilized in locations classified under the Division system is explosionproof and suitable for such locations; while under the Zone system, cable wiring methods and protection techniques that limit energy levels are more common. Whether the design is under the Division system or the Zone system, a common objective should always be to locate as much electrical wiring and equipment outside of the hazardous locations as practical. Doing so is a function of good engineering design judgment and careful exercise of ingenuity; however, in many cases, this is not always possible. Where electrical wiring and equipment have to be located within hazardous (classified) locations, they are required to be suitable for the purpose and installed properly. The arc produced at the contacts of listed or labeled intrinsically safe equipment is not ignition-capable because the energy available is insufficient to cause ignition, and thus it is common to see intrinsically safe systems and circuits utilized for many control and limited energy systems installed in Class I, II, or III locations.

In chapter two, a review of various protection methods involved electrical equipment or products that incorporate multiple protection techniques. This is especially true with equipment that incorporates some of the protection techniques suitable for use under the Zone system of classification. An unwritten rule indicates that where conditions are such that two or more faults occur simultaneously in order for there to be an explosion, acceptable protection techniques must be provided.

Chapter three reviewed the various acceptable methods of protection that minimize the chance of the electrical equipment becoming an ignition source in atmospheres that include ignitible concentrations of flammable gases or vapors (Class I locations). Although nothing in the *Code* or product standards prohibits the use of any protection technique acceptable for the specific location, many types of electrical equipment, including utilization equipment, are not available for certain atmospheres. The excessive cost of manufacturing certain types of equipment and the ability to simply move or relocate many devices and equipment to a location less likely to include ignitible concentrations has resulted in no equipment being manufactured or available for certain applications. Often it is just a matter of practical economics.

Equipment for Use in Class I Locations

This chapter provides a review of the various types of electrical and electronic equipment, including utilization equipment, recognized by the *Code* for installation in Class I, II, or III locations. Suitability of the equipment for the intended use includes a few key characteristics that must be incorporated in the design of such equipment. One important consideration is whether normal operation produces arcing or sparking conditions, such as in switching or contact devices, motors, generators, and so forth. Another important factor is the surface temperature of the equipment, especially the likelihood of heat production in normal operation, such as in transformers, resistors, luminaires (light fixtures), etc. Equipment must not only be identified for the specific hazardous atmosphere anticipated, but must also operate at safe temperatures that are below the ignition temperatures of the hazardous gas, vapor, dust, fibers or flyings. Some equipment is identified as suitable for use in multiple classified locations, but may well have different limitations on use due to the marked operating temperature and the specific environment in which it is installed. For example, a luminaire installed in a Class I, Division 1 location is required to be identified for use in that location and clearly marked to indicate the maximum wattage of lamps for which it is identified [*NEC*, 501.130(A)(1); also see photo 4-01 and figure 4-01].

Class I Temperature

If the temperature class of electrical equipment is provided, it must be indicated on equipment nameplates using the temperature class (T Codes) shown in *NEC* Table 500.8(B) [see table 4-01] and be consistent with those values. Electrical equipment for use in Class I locations is required to be marked with the maximum safe operating temperature, as determined by simultaneous exposure to the combinations of Class I conditions. The temperature marking specified in *NEC* Table 500.8(B) must not exceed the ignition temperature of the specific gas or vapor encountered.

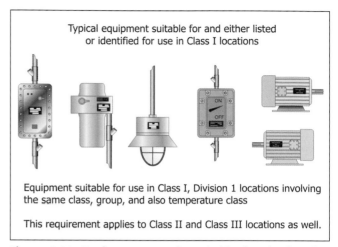

Typical equipment suitable for and either listed or identified for use in Class I locations

Equipment suitable for use in Class I, Division 1 locations involving the same class, group, and also temperature class

This requirement applies to Class II and Class III locations as well.

Figure 4-01. Equipment must be suitable for the location where it is installed and used.

Photo 4-01. Luminaires (light fixtures) are required to be identified for the use in Class I locations. Courtesy of Hubbell/Killark

The *Code* calls for mandatory identification marks and information on the products to assist in appropriate use for field installations. Manufacturers of equipment suitable for use in hazardous locations provide a lot of information so that products may be applied within their limitations of use, and they are more than willing to provide assistance when clarifications are needed. It is important to understand the required identification marks and to ask questions when there are doubts as to suitability of the electrical equipment for a particular application.

General Provisions

Under the Division System

Division 1 equipment is assumed to be operating in an

Temperature Identification Numbers (T Codes)		
Maximum Temperature		**Temperature Class**
°C	°F	T Code
450	842	T1
300	572	T2
280	536	T2A
260	500	T2B
230	446	T2C
215	419	T2D
200	392	T3
180	356	T3A
165	329	T3B
160	320	T3C
135	275	T4
120	248	T4A
100	212	T5
85	185	T6

Table 4-01. Classification of maximum surface temperature
[a reproduction of *NEC* Table 500.8(B)]

environment that can include ignitible concentrations during normal operations. No fault in the containment of the flammable material is required to develop this explosive atmosphere. A single fault in the electrical system is not permitted to cause ignition to the normally explosive atmosphere. Two failures of the electrical equipment must occur simultaneously before the equipment becomes ignition capable.

Division 2 equipment is assumed to be operating in an environment that does not include ignitible concentrations under normal conditions. A fault in the containment of the flammable or combustible material must occur before an explosive environment could exist and then an additional (second) fault must occur simultaneously in the electrical system before ignition could occur.

Under the Zone System

Zone 0 equipment, like Division 1, is assumed to be operating in an environment that includes ignitible concentrations under normal conditions; however, in Zone 0 locations these ignitible concentrations will be present for long periods (typically continuously). For this reason only "ia" (two-fault) intrinsically safe equipment is permitted in Zone 0 locations.

Zone 1 equipment is assumed to be operating in an environment that could include ignitible concentrations under normal operations, but not for long periods of time. For that reason, the requirements for Zone 1 equipment are somewhat less restrictive than those for Zone 0 or Division 1, but more restrictive than those for Division 2 or Zone 2.

Zone 2 equipment, like Division 2 equipment, is assumed to operate in an environment that does not include ignitible concentrations under normal conditions. Like Division 2, a fault in the containment of the flammable or combustible material must occur before an explosive environment could exist and then an additional (second) fault must occur simultaneously in the electrical system before ignition could occur.

Some equipment in hazardous locations is identified for use in either the Division system or the Zone system (see photo 4-02).

Specific Equipment

This chapter takes a more in-depth look at the specific requirements for electrical and electronic equipment installed in Class I, II, or Class III locations, respectively. Part III of Articles 501, 502, and 503 contains the general rules for various types of electrical equipment and some utilization equipment installed in hazardous locations. As reviewed in chapters two and three, various protection methods and protection techniques can be used to prevent equipment installed in these classified locations from becoming a source of ignition. This segment of chapter four reviews the requirements for specific equipment installed in Class

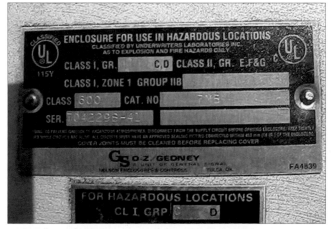

Photo 4-02. Both zone and division system use are identified on the equipment label. O-Z GEDNEY Equipment

I locations. Rules for specific electrical equipment installed in Class I locations are provided in Part III of Article 501, Equipment. Part III of Articles 502 and 503 also carries the title "Equipment."

Transformers and Capacitors

Requirements for transformers and capacitors installed in Class I locations are provided in *NEC* 501.100. Transformers and capacitors are natural sources of heat that is generated during normal operating conditions (see photo 4-03).

Class I, Division 1 Locations

In Class I, Division 1 locations, transformers or capacitors that contain liquid that will burn are to be installed in transformer vaults that comply with all of the requirements for vaults included in Part III of Article 450. Vaults are to be continuously ventilated to minimize the chances of allowing the explosive environment to enter. For transformers and capacitors that do not contain liquid that will burn, the same option for transformer vaults with special ventilation requirements is available, or the equipment is permitted to be approved for Class I locations. *Approved* is defined in the *Code* as "acceptable to the authority having jurisdiction."

Class I, Division 2 Locations

For Division 2 locations, transformers are to be installed in accordance with the ordinary location requirements in 450.21 through 450.27. Equipment requirements in 500.8 must also be met. A review of laboratory product directories reveals limited certifications for transformers evaluated for use in Class I locations and no certifications for capacitors. Under specific conditions in industrial establishments with restricted public access, and where the conditions of maintenance and supervision ensure that only qualified persons service the installation, a combustible gas detection system can be provided.

If a facility is classified using the Zone system, the rules in *NEC* 505.15(A) and 505.20(A) permit only intrinsically safe wiring and equipment for locations classified as Zone 0. This excludes the installation of power equipment, such as transformers and capacitors, in these areas. The most common practice

Photo 4-03. Equipment, including transformers, must be suitable for the location.

for protection of this equipment is to locate it either inside a pressurized control room or in an unclassified location. In Zone 1 locations, the *Code* permits many protection techniques for equipment, including those allowed for Division 1 locations; however, at this time, manufacturers of transformers and capacitors have chosen not to build products and have them evaluated and certified for use in Zone 1 locations [*NEC*, 505.20(B)]. A review of Part II in the UL Red Book reveals that currently there are no listings for transformers or capacitors (see photo 4-03).

Meters, Instruments, and Relays

Meters, instruments, and relays installed in Class I locations are covered by the requirements in 501.105 of the *Code*.

Class I, Division 1 Locations

In Class I, Division 1 locations, these electrical devices are required to be provided with enclosures that are either explosionproof or purged and pressurized (see photo 4-04). Equipment utilizing purged and pressurized protection would be evaluated to the requirements found in NFPA 496. Although not specifically mentioned in 501.105, the use of intrinsically safe systems is permitted in any classified location where the system has been evaluated for the atmosphere that is present. As mentioned above for transformers and capacitors, a combustible gas detection system can be provided in specific facilities under specific conditions and permit additional options for the installation of meters, instruments and relays.

Class I, Division 2 Locations

Because the degree of hazard is somewhat less in Class I, Division 2 locations, a variety of protection options are available for these types of equipment. The protection required will depend on the components of the overall device and the energy used. If the device includes make-and-break contacts and utilizes ignition capable energy, it may be required to utilize an enclosure suitable for Class I, Division 1 locations. If the make-and-break contacts are oil immersed or if the energy utilized is nonincendive, general-purpose enclosures may be permitted [*NEC*, 501.105(B)(1) and Exception].

If the equipment includes heat-producing components, like resistors, rectifiers, and so forth, that are capable of igniting a flammable atmosphere, it may be required to utilize an enclosure suitable for Class I, Division 1 locations. If the temperature of the components can be limited to 80 percent of the ignition temperature of the atmosphere, then general-purpose enclosures may be permitted [*NEC*, 501.105(B)(2) and Exception].

If the equipment includes components that are coil or winding type devices without sliding or make-and-break contacts, then general-purpose enclosures may be permitted. If the facility is classified using the Zone system, *NEC* 505.15(A) and 505.20(A) permit only intrinsically safe wiring and equipment for the Zone 0

Class I Enclosure Combinations

Additional information about circuit breaker and enclosure combinations listed for Class I, Division 1 locations is included in UL Red Book, CCN, DKAR and DKNZ.

Information about switches and enclosures is provided in CCN, WQNV, WRTB, WRPR, WSQX and WTEV. Equipment installed using purged and pressurized protection techniques would be evaluated to NFPA 496.

Sidebar 4-01.

areas. Intrinsically safe systems that include meters, instruments and relays are common and readily available for use. This equipment would be one of the more common types permitted for installation in Zone 0 areas. In Zone 1 locations, *NEC* 505.20(B) permits many protection techniques for equipment, including those allowed for Division 1 locations. For Zone 2 locations, the complete list of protection techniques discussed in chapter 3 is available for protection of the electrical equipment.

Switches, Circuit Breakers, Motor Controllers, and Fuses
Requirements for switches, circuit breakers, motor controllers, and fuses installed in Class I locations are provided in 501.115. These types of equipment generally include arcing functions and contacts that produce arcing during normal operation. The concern is that the arcs produced inside the enclosures for these types of equipment do not cause ignition and explosion of the surrounding hazardous atmosphere.

Class I, Division 1 Locations

In Class I, Division 1 locations, these types of equipment are required to be provided with enclosures identified for use in Class I locations. Evaluation of equipment using explosionproof protection includes the combination of the electrical component and the enclosure as an assembly (see photos 4-05 and 4-06). Changes of either the component or the enclosure could impact the safety of the equipment assembly. Explosionproof equipment is generally listed to UL 1203.

Photo 4-04. Instruments that are suitable for Class I locations

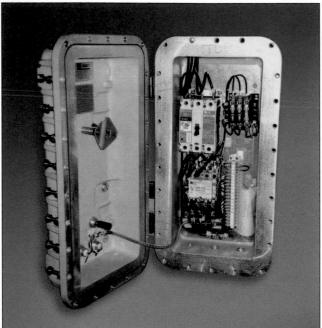

Photo 4-05. Explosionproof magnetic motor controller Courtesy of Hubbell/Killark

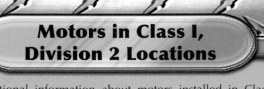

Motors in Class I, Division 2 Locations

Additional information about motors installed in Class I, Division 2 locations can be found in IEEE Std. 1349-2001 *Guide for the Application of Electric Motors in Class I, Division 2 Hazardous (Classified) Locations.*

Sidebar 4-02.

Class I, Division 2 Locations

Equipment that incorporates multiple protection techniques is available to perform the electrical functions covered in Class I, Division 2 locations. In some cases where switches, circuit breakers, and motor controllers are breaking circuits with ignition capable current under normal conditions, they are required to utilize a protection technique acceptable for use in Class I, Division 1 locations. General enclosures are also permitted if the interruption of current takes place within a hermetically sealed chamber or within a factory-sealed explosionproof chamber, contacts are immersed in oil, or the device is solid state (without switching contacts) as indicated in 501.115(B)(1)(1) through (4).

Control Transformers and Resistors

Specific requirements for control transformers and resistors installed in Class I locations are provided in 501.120. These types of electrical devices are often used in conjunction with motors, generators, and appliances.

Class I, Division 1 Locations

Heat-producing equipment presents challenges when it is required to be installed in hazardous locations. Where this type of equipment is installed in Class I, Division 1 locations, it must be identified for such use.

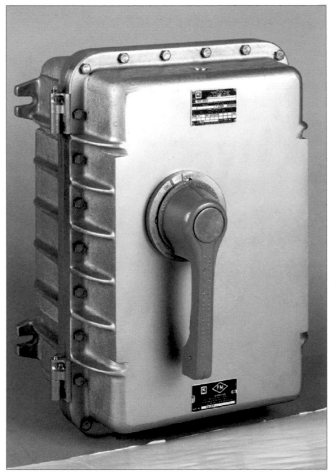

Photo 4-06. Explosionproof switch and enclosure Courtesy of Hubbell/Killark

Class I, Division 2 Locations

If this type of device or equipment is installed in a Division 2 location, it must meet the rules in 501.120(B)(1) through (3). Where it includes switching mechanisms, they must be in enclosures suitable for Class I, Division 1 locations. Solenoids, transformers, or impedance coils are permitted to be installed using general-purpose enclosures, and resistors are required to be provided with suitable enclosures in accordance with 501.120(3).

Motors and Generators

Class I, Division 1 Locations

Motors and generators installed in Class I locations are covered by the requirements provided in 501.125. It is fairly common to have electric motors and other rotating machinery installed within Class I, Division 1 locations. It is less common to see generators installed in these areas; but that is not to say it never happens, particularly since economics generally drives acceptablity (see figure 4-02).

Motors, generators, or other rotating machinery installed in Class I, Division 1 locations are required to meet one of the following criteria:

• Identified for use in Class I, Division 1 locations (see photos 4-07 through 4-09).

• Equipment is of the totally enclosed type and supplied with positive pressure ventilation.

• Equipment is of the totally enclosed inert gas type supplied with a reliable source of inert gas.

• Equipment is designed to be submerged in a liquid that is flammable only when vaporized and mixed with air (see photo 4-07).

It is important to verify that totally enclosed motors covered by the rules in 501.125(A)(2) and (A)(3) have no external surface temperature in excess of 80 percent of the ignition temperature of the gas or

Photo 4-07. Motor designed to be submerged in gasoline

Photo 4-08. Explosionproof motors used in Class I, Divisions 1 and 2 locations

vapor [see *NEC*, 501.125(A)(1) through (4) for all of the specific requirements].

Class I, Division 2 Locations

Motors, generators, or other rotating machinery that employ sliding contacts or other switching mechanisms, such as overload or overtemperature devices, and so forth, that operate while starting or running and are installed in Class I, Division 2 locations are generally required to be identified for use in Class I, Division 1 locations. Sliding contacts are acceptable when they are inside enclosures and are identified for use in Class I, Division 2 locations [*NEC*, 501.125(B)].

Luminaires (Light Fixtures)

NEC requirements for luminaires (light fixtures) installed in Class I locations are provided in 501.130,

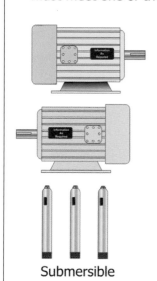

Motors installed in Class I, Division 1 locations must meet one of the following four criteria:

Identified for Class I, Division 1 locations

Totally enclosed and supplied with positive pressure ventilation

Totally enclosed inert gas type and supplied with a reliable source of inert gas

Submersible pump motors

Motor is designed to be submerged in a liquid that is flammable only when vaporized

Figure 4-02. Motors in Class I, Division 1 locations must meet one of four specific criteria.

Photo 4-09. Explosionproof motors used in Class I, Divisions 1 and 2 locations

and the rules for other utilization equipment are found in 501.135. As a general rule, luminaires are considered utilization equipment based on the definition of *equipment*, but when they are installed in Class I locations several specific requirements must be met.

Class I, Division 1 Locations

As with other equipment, luminaires (light fixtures) installed in Class I, Division 1 locations are required to be identified as a complete assembly for the Class I, Division 1 location (see photo 4-10). The maximum wattage of lamp permitted in the luminaire must be clearly marked on identification labels. Any portable luminaires are required to carry listings specifically for that use. Permanently installed or portable types of luminaires are required to be protected from physical damage either by suitable guards or by location.

The *Code* requires pendant luminaires (light fixtures) to be installed using pendants made of threaded rigid metal conduit or intermediate metal conduit and a set screw for thread locking purposes to prevent loosening. Where the stem (pendant) extends longer than 300 mm (12 in.), permanent and effective braces against lateral displacement are required. This bracing

must be adequate and meet the location provisions in 501.130(A)(3). Any box, box assembly, or fitting used to support luminaires in Class I locations is required to be identified for that use.

Class I, Division 2 Locations

Luminaires (light fixtures) installed in Class I, Division 2 locations must meet similar rules as those installed in Division 1 locations with a few

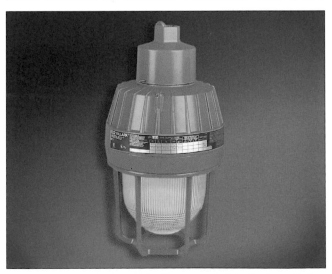

Photo 4-10. Luminaire (light fixture) suitable for installation and use in Class I, Division 1 locations Courtesy of Hubbell/Killark

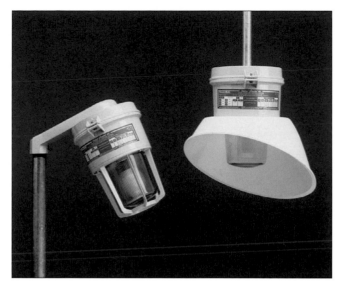

Photo 4-11. Luminaires (light fixtures) are required to be identified for the use in Class I, Division 2 locations. Courtesy of Thomas and Betts

small differences. First, where the lamp size and type operate under normal conditions at a temperature that exceeds 80 percent of the ignition temperature in degrees Celsius of the particular gas or vapor in which it is installed, it must be suitable for Class I, Division 1 locations as provided in 501.130(A)(1) or shall be of a type that has been tested to determine the marked operating temperature or temperature class (T Code). In other words, the luminaire in the Class I, Division 2 location generally is required to be suitable for Class I,

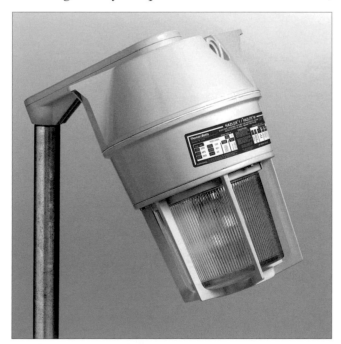

Photo 4-12. Luminaires (light fixtures) are required to be identified for the use in Class I, Division 2 locations. Courtesy of Thomas and Betts

Division 1 locations, unless specifically identified with a temperature class [*NEC*, 501.130(B)(1)]. Second, luminaires installed in Division 2 locations must meet the same requirements for protection from physical damage that luminaires installed in Division 1 locations must adhere to (see photos 4-11 and 4-12), except there is also a containment requirement where there is a danger of falling hot particles or sparks from lamps that could ignite flammable gases or vapors below them.

Pendants (stem-mounted units) are required to meet the same rules as those that apply to luminaires (lighting fixtures) installed in Class I, Division 1 locations as covered above. Portable lighting equipment is generally required to be identified as a complete assembly for use in Class I, Division 1 locations with an exception that allows for the use of flexible cord in accordance with 501.140. Any switches that are part of the assembled luminaire or of an individual lampholder must be enclosed to meet the requirements in 501.115.

Utilization Equipment

Class I, Division 1 Locations

Utilization equipment installed in Class I locations is governed by the requirements provided in 501.135. Any utilization equipment installed in a Class I, Division 1 location must be identified for use in the Division 1 location [*NEC*, 501.135(A)].

Class I, Division 2 Locations

Utilization equipment covered by the rules in 501.135(B) includes heaters, motors, switches, circuit breakers, and fuses. Usually, the operating temperature of the heater, when continuously operated, must not exceed 80 percent of the ignition temperature in degrees Celsius of the particular gas or vapor involved at the maximum rated ambient temperature as required by 501.135(B)(1); otherwise, it is required to be identified for Class I, Division 1 locations. An exception permits electrical resistance heat tracing identified for Class I, Division 2 locations. In Class I, Division 2 locations, motors of motor-driven utilization equipment are required to meet the rules in 501.125(B). Basically this means, if there are sliding contacts,

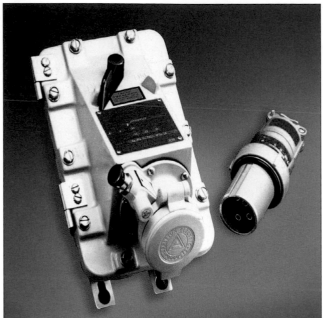

Photo 4-13. Receptacle suitable for use in Class I, Divisions 1 and 2 locations Courtesy of Appleton EGS Electric Group

centrifugal or other types of switching mechanisms, such as overtemperature devices, the motor must be identified for Class I, Division 1 locations. Any switches, circuit breakers or fuses must be installed in suitable enclosures, and the enclosure and apparatus must be identified as a complete assembly suitable for use in a Class I, Division 1 location.

Flexible Cords

Flexible cords installed in Class I locations are covered by requirements provided in 501.140. Flexible cords are permitted for use in Class I locations for both Divisions 1 and 2, but with several limitations. First, it should be determined that flexible cord is the best and most practical way to supply the equipment. Once this has been determined, then the cord is permitted for equipment such as portable lighting equipment, mobile electrical utilization equipment, submersible pumps and for electric mixers that require travel in and out of open mixing vats. For those types of equipment, the *Code* recognizes flexible cord as long as the specifics of the rules in 501.140(A)(1) through (4) are met. Second, the cords must also meet restrictive requirements in 501.140(B) such as being listed for extra hard usage, containing an equipment grounding conductor, and being connected to terminals or supply conductors in an approved manner. The cords are also

required to be in a continuous length, be provided with suitable tension take up provisions or other means to keep tension from the terminal connections, and be provided with sealing fittings of the explosionproof type where the cord enters a box, terminal housing, fitting, or other enclosure. The cord should not be subject to physical damage, even though it is listed as extra hard usage [see the requirements in 400.8(7)].

Receptacles and Attachment Plugs

The *Code* rules for receptacles and attachment plugs installed in Class I locations are provided in 501.145 and apply to both Divisions 1 and 2. Both the receptacles and the mating attachment plugs are required to be identified for the location and must include integral provisions for connection to the grounding conductor of the flexible cord, other than those flexible cords used specifically to facilitate replacements of process control instruments where all the requirements of 501.105(B)(6) items (1) through (5) are met.

Equipment for Signaling, Alarm, Remote-Control, and Communications Systems

Class I, Division 1 Locations

Signaling, alarm, remote-control, and communications systems installed in Class I locations are governed by the rules provided in 501.150. Since even

Photo 4-14. Audible signaling device (horn) for use in Class I, Division 1 locations Courtesy of Cooper Crouse Hinds

limited energy systems present ignition hazards in classified locations, the *Code* specifically requires this type of equipment to be suitable for Class I, Division 1 locations, regardless of the voltage. Field-installed wiring to such equipment must be in accordance with the requirements for power circuits installed in Class I, Division 1 locations, including the wiring method and the sealing and drainage rules [*NEC*, 501.150(A)].

Class I, Division 2 Locations

Rules for these types of equipment installed in Class I, Division 2 locations are less restrictive but still specific. Where devices or equipment includes make-and-break contacts, enclosures are required to be identified for Class I, Division 1 locations, unless one of the protection techniques below is provided:

- Oil immersed contacts
- Hermetically sealed contacts
- Nonincendive circuits
- Equipment is part of a nonincendive component

Any resistors or similar heat-producing equipment must meet the rules in 501.105(B)(2), which generally require an enclosure identified for Class I, Division 1 locations or enclosures that are purged and pressurized. Enclosures suitable for general use are permitted by exception where the equipment is without make-and-break or sliding contacts and if the maximum operating temperature of any exposed surface does not exceed 80 percent of the ignition temperature in degrees Celsius of the gas or vapor involved or has been tested and found to be incapable of igniting the gas or vapor, with the exception of thermionic tubes.

All conduit and cable sealing and drainage requirements must be in accordance with 501.15(B) and (C), and the field-installed wiring system must meet the specific applicable provisions of 501.10(B).

Equipment for Use in Class II Locations
General Provisions
Division 1 and 2 Locations
Division 1 equipment is assumed to be operating in an environment that includes airborne dust in quantities sufficient to produce explosions or ignitible mixtures; or combustible dust accumulations on

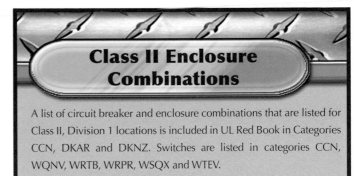

Class II Enclosure Combinations

A list of circuit breaker and enclosure combinations that are listed for Class II, Division 1 locations is included in UL Red Book in Categories CCN, DKAR and DKNZ. Switches are listed in categories CCN, WQNV, WRTB, WRPR, WSQX and WTEV.

Sidebar 4-03.

electrical equipment is greater than 1/8 inch thick, and the electrical equipment is capable of external temperatures high enough to reach the ignition temperature of the dust or dry the dust to a point that it would self-heat; or a Group E combustible metal dust is present in hazardous quantities. A single fault in the electrical system is not permitted to cause ignition to the normally explosive atmosphere. Two failures of the electrical equipment must occur simultaneously before the equipment becomes ignition capable.

Division 2 equipment is assumed to be operating in an environment that does not include ignitible concentrations under normal conditions. An abnormal operating condition must occur before an explosive environment could exist, and then an additional (second) fault must occur simultaneously in the electrical system before ignition could occur.

Zone 20, 21, and 22 Locations
Zone 20 equipment, like Division 1, is assumed to be operating in an environment that includes ignitible concentrations under normal conditions; but in Zone 20, these ignitible concentrations will be present continuously or for long periods of time. Equipment must be listed and suitable for the Zone 20 location or be "ia" intrinsically safe apparatus listed for use in Class II, Division 1 locations and have a suitable temperature class. Currently, the *NEC* does not recognize any Zone system protection techniques for dust or fibers and flyings.

Zone 21 equipment is assumed to be operating in an environment that could include ignitible concentrations under normal operations, but not for long periods of time. For that reason, the equipment is required to be listed and suitable for the Zone 21 location or be listed for use in Class II, Division 1 locations and have a suitable temperature class or pressurized equipment identified for use in Class II, Division 1 locations. Currently, the *NEC* does not recognize any Zone system protection techniques for dust or fibers and flyings.

Zone 22 equipment, like Division 2 equipment, is assumed to operate in an environment that does not include ignitible concentrations under normal conditions. Just as for Division 2, an abnormal operating condition must occur before an explosive environment could exist, and then an additional (second) fault must occur simultaneously in the electrical system before ignition could occur. For that reason, the equipment must be listed and suitable for the Zone 22 location or be listed for use in Class II, Division 2 locations and have a suitable temperature class or pressurized equipment identified for use in Class II, Division 2 locations. Currently, the *NEC* does not recognize any of the Zone system protection techniques for dust or fibers and flyings.

Class II Temperature

In Class II locations, as covered previously, the concerns are for conditions where combustible dust is suspended in the air in sufficient quantities to produce ignitible or explosive mixtures. There are also hazards associated with dust accumulations on electrical enclosures and equipment; and where conductive and abrasive dusts are involved, other hazards must be addressed. For Class II locations, one of the primary concerns is the ignition temperature of the specific dust involved. The temperature values in *NEC* Table 500.8(B) are required to be less than the ignition temperature of the dust. Specific restrictions are placed on locations where organic dusts that may dehydrate or carbonize are involved. For those cases, the temperature marking on equipment must not exceed the lower of either the ignition temperature of the dust or 165°C (329°F) [see Table 4-01]. The maximum ignition temperature of combustible dusts can be found in Table 2-5 of NFPA 499, a reproduction of which can be found in the Annex.

The ignition temperature for which equipment was approved is assumed to be as shown in *NEC*

Table 500.8(C)(2). Three conditions are addressed in this temperature table. The first condition is the operating temperature of equipment that is not subject to overloading conditions. The second and third conditions involve equipment, such as motors and power transformers, which may be overloaded. The two types of overload provided in the table are where the equipment is overloaded in normal operation or where it is overloaded in abnormal operation (see Table 4-02).

Table 500.8(C)(2) Class II Temperatures						
	Equipment Not Subject to Overloading		Equipment (Such as Motors or Power Transformers) That may be overloaded			
			Normal Operation		Abnormal Operation	
Class II Group	°C	°F	°C	°F	°C	°F
E	200	392	200	392	200	392
F	200	392	150	302	200	392
G	165	329	120	248	165	329

Table 4-02. Class II Temperatures [a reproduction of *NEC* Table 500.8(C)(2)]

Equipment used in dust environments (Class II locations) must not ignite the dust in the air and also must not have surface temperatures that can cause fires because of dust accumulations on enclosures.

The following segment of this chapter reviews the *Code* rules for specific electrical equipment installed in Class II locations provided in Part III of Article 502, Equipment.

Specific Equipment
Transformers and Capacitors

Transformers and capacitors are natural sources of heat generated through normal operation. The requirements for transformers and capacitors installed in Class II locations are provided in *NEC* 502.100.

Class II, Division 1 Locations

In Class II, Division 1 locations, transformers or capacitors that contain liquid that will burn are required to be installed in transformer vaults that comply with all of the requirements for vault construction as provided in Part III of Article 450 (see figure 4-03). These rules include special requirements

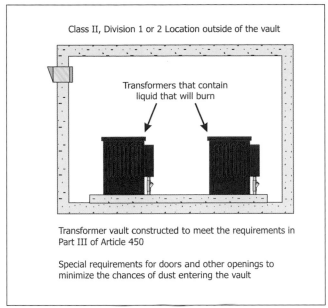

Class II, Division 1 or 2 Location outside of the vault

Transformers that contain liquid that will burn

Transformer vault constructed to meet the requirements in Part III of Article 450

Special requirements for doors and other openings to minimize the chances of dust entering the vault

Figure 4-03. Transformer vault constructed to meet the requirements of Part III of Article 450

for doors and other openings to minimize the chance of dust entering the vault.

For transformers and capacitors not containing liquid that will burn, the same option for transformer vaults is permitted or the complete equipment assembly, including terminal connections, is required to be identified for Class II locations. Transformers and/or capacitors are not permitted to be installed in Class II, Group E atmospheres where dust from magnesium, aluminum, aluminum bronze powders, or other metallic dusts with similar characteristics are present [*NEC*, 502.100(A)].

Class II, Division 2 Locations

In Class II, Division 2 locations, transformers or capacitors that contain liquid that will burn are to be installed in transformer vaults that comply with all of the requirements of Part III of Article 450.

Transformers that contain askarel and have a rating above 25 kVA must have pressure-relief vents and a means to absorb gases generated by arcing inside the case, or the pressure-relief vent must be extended to the outside of the building. The transformers must also be installed with a minimum of 150 mm (6 in.) of air space between the transformer case and any combustible material.

Dry-type transformers installed in Division 2 locations must be installed in vaults or be limited to 600

volts and have their windings and terminal connections enclosed in tight metal enclosures without ventilating or other openings. The most common practice for installation and protection of this equipment is to locate it inside a pressurized control room or in an unclassified location. [*NEC*, 502.100(B)]

Switches, Circuit Breakers, Motor Controllers, and Fuses

Class II, Division 1 Locations

Equipment or devices in this category typically include arcing functions in normal operation and must be installed in suitable enclosures. The rules for switches, circuit breakers, motor controllers, and fuses installed in Class II locations are provided in *NEC* 502.115.

In Class II, Division 1 locations, these electrical devices are required to be provided with dust-ignitionproof enclosures or pressurized enclosures where they are intended to interrupt current during normal operation. Isolating switches, not intended to interrupt current, and that do not contain fuses and are not installed in Group E locations are required to be installed in enclosures similar to those that are dusttight and have no openings through which sparks or burning material could escape, causing ignition of dust or adjacent combustible material external to the enclosure [*NEC*, 502.115(A)(2)]. Where metallic dusts may be present, enclosures for fuses, circuit breakers, motor controllers, and switches are required to be identified for Class II, Division 1 locations.

Equipment using pressurization for protection would be evaluated to NFPA 496.

Photo 4-15. Three phase enclosed switch suitable for use in Class II, Divisions 1 and 2 locations Courtesy of Hubbell/Killark

Class II, Division 2 Locations

Enclosures for switches, motor controllers, circuit breakers, and fuses installed in Class II, Division 2 locations are required to be of the dusttight types.

Control Transformers and Resistors

Class II, Division 1 Locations

Control transformers and resistors installed in Class II locations are required to meet the rules provided in 502.120. The equipment in this category includes solenoids, impedance coils, resistors, control transformers, overcurrent devices, and any switching mechanisms associated with circuit breakers.

Enclosures for this equipment installed in Class II, Division 1 locations are required to be dust-ignition-proof. Where metallic dusts from magnesium, aluminum, aluminum bronze powders, or other metals with similar hazardous characteristics may be present, the enclosures must be identified for the specific location. It is important that enclosures in metallic dust environments be suitable for this use since these dusts are generally highly conductive and abrasive.

Specific requirements for control transformers and resistors installed in Class II locations are provided in 501.120. These types of electrical devices are often used in conjunction with motors, generators, and appliances. Where installed in Class II, Division 1 locations, they must be in enclosures identified for the specific location.

Class II, Division 2 Locations

If these types of devices are installed in enclosures in a Division 2 location, they must meet the rules in 502.120(B)(1) through (3). Where they include switching mechanisms, they must be in enclosures that are dusttight. Enclosures for solenoids, transformers, or impedance coils must be provided with tight metal housings without ventilating openings. Any resistors or resistance devices installed in Class II locations are to be in dust-ignitionproof enclosures identified for Class II locations [*NEC*, 502.120(B)].

Motors and Generators

Class II, Division 1 Locations

Requirements for motors and generators installed in Class II, Division 1 locations are provided in 502.125

and give the option of meeting one of the following:
• Identified for Class II, Division 1 locations
• Totally enclosed and pipe-vented, meeting temperature limitations in 502.5

Class II, Division 2 Locations

Motors, generators, and other rotating electrical equipment installed in Class II, Division 2 locations are required to meet one of the following criteria:
• Totally enclosed and nonventilated
• Totally enclosed and pipe-ventilated
• Totally enclosed and water-cooled
• Totally enclosed and fan-cooled

Equipment can also be dust-ignitionproof for which maximum full-load temperature must meet the values in 500.8(C)(2) for normal operation in free air (free from dust blanketing) and the enclosure can have no external openings.

By exception, the authority having jurisdiction could accept this type of equipment if he or she believes accumulations of nonconductive or non-abrasive dust will be moderate. In which case, one of the following types of equipment is permitted.

• Standard open-type machines without sliding contacts, centrifugal or other types of switching mechanisms, such as motor overcurrent, overloading, and overtemperature devices, or integral resistance devices

• Standard open-type machines with such contacts or devices indicated above that are enclosed in dusttight housings without ventilating or other openings

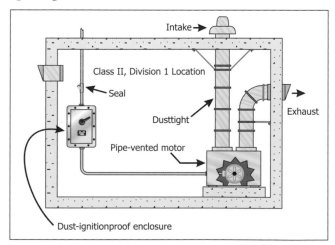

Figure 4-04. Pipe-vented motor enclosure routed to the exterior of a building

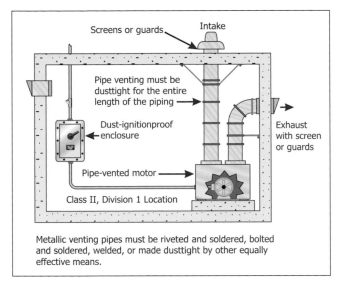

Figure 4-05. Pipe venting must be dusttight throughout its entire length.

- Self-cleaning textile squirrel-cage motors

Ventilating Piping for Motors, Generators, or Other Rotating Machines

Ventilating piping used for electric motors, generators or other rotating machines installed in Class II locations is governed by the rules provided in 502.128, which stipulate that it must be not less than 0.53 mm (0.021 in.) in thickness or of equivalent noncombustible material that also meets the following criteria:

- Venting leads directly to a source of clean air outside the building.
- It is secured at the outer ends with screens or similar means to prevent birds and other small animals from entering it.
- It must be protected from physical damage and against other influences, such as corrosion or deterioration (see figure 4-04).

Class II, Division 1 Locations

Pipe-venting for motors, generators, or other rotating electrical equipment in Class II, Division 1 locations must be dusttight throughout its entire length; and metallic venting pipes must also be either:

- Riveted and soldered
- Bolted and soldered
- Welded
- Rendered dusttight by some other equally effective means

Class II, Division 2 Locations

Ventilating piping and associated connections used in Class II, Division 2 locations are required to be sufficiently tight to prevent appreciable quantities of dust from entering the ventilated equipment or enclosure. For metal piping, locking seams and riveted or welded joints are permitted. Where flexibility is necessary, such as for connections to vibrating equipment like motors, generators and other equipment, tight-fitting slip joints are permitted [*NEC*, 502.128(B)].

Luminaires (Light Fixtures)

Requirements for luminaires (light fixtures) installed in Class II locations are provided in 502.130. As with other equipment installed in Class II locations and covered in this section, the primary concerns for luminaires are the maximum surface temperatures at which they operate and the locations where metallic dusts are encountered.

Class II, Division 1 Locations

Luminaires (light fixtures) installed in Class II locations are required to be identified for Class II locations and marked to indicate the maximum wattage of the lamp permitted. In locations that include metallic dusts, such as aluminum, magnesium or metallic dust, that present similar hazardous characteristics, luminaires must be specifically identified for the location. They must also be protected from physical damage either by a suitable guard or guards or by location (see photo 4-16).

Pendant luminaires (light fixtures) are permitted in Class II, Division 1 locations but must meet the same requirements for pendant types installed in Class I, Division 1 locations, which basically requires the use of rigid metal conduit or intermediate metal conduit to suspend the pendant and effective bracing against lateral displacement. In Class II, Division 1 locations, luminaires are also permitted to be installed as pendants using flexible cord listed for extra-hard usage. Suitable sealing fittings are required at the luminaire, and the cord is not to be used as the means of support for the luminaire [*NEC*, 502.130(A)(3)]. Any boxes, box assemblies, or fittings used for support of the luminaires are required to be identified for Class II locations.

Photo 4-16. Luminaire (light fixture) suitable for use in Class II, Division 1 and 2 locations Courtesy of Hubbell/Killark

Class II, Division 2 Locations

Fixed luminaires (light fixtures) installed in Class II, Division 2 locations are required to be designed to minimize the accumulations of dust on the lamps and prevent the escape of sparks, hot metal, or burning materials. Each luminaire is to be marked to indicate the maximum wattage of the lamp permitted without exceeding the exposed surface temperature values provided in 500.8(C)(2) under normal operating conditions. Portable luminaires must be identified for Class II, Division 2 locations and be marked with the maximum wattage of lamp that can be used. Both portable and fixed luminaires installed in Class II locations must be protected from physical damage either by location or by providing a suitable guard or guards [*NEC*, 502.130(B)].

Pendant luminaires (light fixtures) in Class II, Division 2 locations are to meet the same requirements as those installed in Class II, Division 1 locations. In Class II, Division 2 locations, luminaires are also permitted to be installed as pendants using flexible cord listed for extra-hard usage. Suitable sealing fittings are required at the luminaire, and flexible cord is not allowed to be used as the means of support [*NEC*, 502.130(A)(3)]. Any boxes, box assemblies, or fittings

used for support of the luminaires are required to be identified for Class II locations [*NEC*, 502.130(B)(4)]. Any starting and control equipment used in conjunction with electric discharge luminaires using switching mechanisms must be installed in dusttight enclosures. Coils and windings, such as ballasts, must utilize enclosures without ventilating openings; and resistors and resistance devices are to be provided with dust-ignitionproof enclosures.

Utilization Equipment

Rules for utilization equipment installed in Class II locations are provided in 502.135. As with other equipment installed in Class II locations and covered in this section, the primary concerns for luminaires (light fixtures) are the maximum surface temperatures at which they operate and the locations where metallic dusts are encountered.

Class II, Division 1 Locations

The basic requirement for all utilization equipment installed in Class II, Division 1 locations calls for the equipment to be identified for Class II locations. Where metallic dusts, such as aluminum, magnesium, aluminum bronze powders or other dusts with similar hazardous characteristics, may be present, the equipment is to be identified for these specific locations. The primary issues here are conductivity of the dust and the abrasive effects on equipment in these locations.

Class II, Division 2 Locations

Utilization equipment, such as motors, heaters, switches, circuit breakers, fuses, and equipment that incorporates windings or coils, such as transformers or solenoids, installed and utilized in Class II, Division 2 locations must meet the requirements provided in 502.135(B). Heaters must be identified for Class II locations. Motors and motor-driven utilization equipment must meet the same requirements for this type of equipment installed in Class II locations in accordance with 502.125(B).

Motors, generators, and other rotating electrical equipment installed in Class II, Division 2 locations are required to meet one of the following criteria:

• Totally enclosed and non-ventilated

118

- Totally enclosed and pipe-ventilated
- Totally enclosed and water-cooled
- Totally enclosed and fan-cooled

The equipment can also be dust-ignitionproof for which maximum full-load temperature must meet the values in 500.8(C)(2) for normal operation in free air (free from dust blanketing), and the enclosure can have no external openings. The exception to 502.125(B) lists additional permissions required to be under the judgment and acceptability of the authority having jurisdiction.

Enclosures for switches, fuses, and circuit breakers are required to be dusttight when this type of equipment is installed in Class II, Division 2 locations.

Any transformers, solenoids, impedance coils, or resistors installed in Class II, Division 2 locations are required to meet the rules in 502.120(B). Where the equipment includes switching mechanisms, it must be in enclosures that are dusttight. Enclosures for solenoids, transformers, or impedance coils must be provided with tight metal housings without any ventilating openings. Any resistors or resistance devices installed in Class II locations are generally to be installed in dust-ignitionproof enclosures identified for Class II locations.

Flexible Cords

Requirements for flexible cords installed in Class II locations are provided in 502.140. In Division 1 and Division 2 locations, cords are generally required to be (1) listed for extra-hard usage or hard usage for pendant luminaires (light fixtures), (2) contain an equipment grounding conductor, (3) be connected to terminals or supply conductors in an approved manner, (4) be supported in a manner that will eliminate tension on connections, and (5) be sealed where terminated to boxes and fittings in a manner that will prevent the entrance of dust. Where flexible cords are used, suitable seals must be provided to prevent the entrance of dust where the cord enters boxes, fittings, or enclosures required to be dust-ignitionproof. No additional restriction or permissions are placed on the use of cords in these locations, other than those provided in 400.7 and 400.8. As with any use of flexible cord or cable, the concern for physical

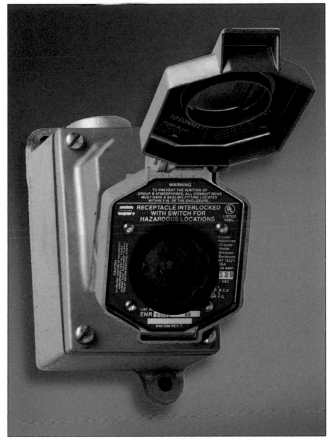

Photo 4-17. Receptacle for use in Class II, Division 1 locations
Courtesy of Cooper Crouse Hinds

protection must be a serious consideration even if the cord is listed as extra-hard usage type. Section 400.8(7) does not permit flexible cords or cables to be used where they are subject to physical damage. It is always the best practice to have the authority having jurisdiction involved in such determinations.

Receptacles and Attachment Plugs

Requirements for receptacles and attachment plugs installed in Class II locations are provided in 502.145 and include the rules for installations in both Division 1 and Division 2 locations.

Class II, Division 1 Locations

Attachment plugs and receptacles installed in Class II, Division 1 locations must provide for connection to the equipment grounding conductor of the flexible cord and be identified for use in Class II locations [*NEC*, 502.145(A) and see photo 4-17].

Class II, Division 2 Locations

Attachment plugs and receptacles installed in Class

II, Division 2 locations must provide for connection to the equipment grounding conductor of the flexible cord and be designed such that the connection to the supply circuit cannot be made or broken while any live parts are exposed [*NEC*, 502.145(B)].

Signaling, Alarm, Remote-Control, and Communications Systems

To emphasize it once again, even limited energy systems present ignition hazards in classified locations. The *Code* specifically requires this type of equipment to be suitable for Class II, Divisions 1 and 2 locations, regardless of the voltage.

Class II, Division 1 Locations

In Class II, Division 1 locations, field-installed wiring to this equipment is covered by 502.150 and is to be in accordance with the requirements for equipment installed in Class II, Division 1 locations as provided in 502.100(A) for transformers and capacitors. Any equipment that includes contacts, such as circuit breakers, relays, and so forth, and current-breaking contacts for items, such as bells, horns, sirens, and so forth, is to be provided with enclosures identified for use in Class II locations. There is an exception for equipment that includes contact devices immersed in oil or where the interruption of current occurs within a chamber sealed against the entrance of any dust.

Resistors and similar equipment are also to be provided with enclosures suitable for Class II locations, and the same exception for oil immersion can be applied for this type of equipment as well. Where any rotating equipment such as motors or generators are used in these circuits, the requirements of 502.125(A) must be applied; this rule stipulates that the rotating equipment either be identified for the Class II, Division 1 location or be totally enclosed pipe-ventilated and meet the temperature limitations of 502.5.

Where limited energy equipment is installed in Class II, Division 1 locations and the dust is combustible and electrically conductive in nature, the enclosures used must also be identified for Class II locations. Metallic dusts present concerns not only for

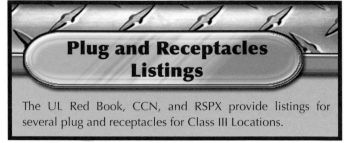

Plug and Receptacles Listings

The UL Red Book, CCN, and RSPX provide listings for several plug and receptacles for Class III Locations.

Sidebar 4-04.

conductivity but also for abrasion. Any of this type of equipment installed in locations that involve metallic dusts must be identified for the specific conditions.

Class II, Division 2 Locations

Where signaling, alarm, remote-control, and communications systems and similar equipment is installed in Class II, Division 2 locations, they must meet all of the applicable rules provided in 502.150(B)(1) through (5). Where contact devices are installed and used, enclosures must be tight metallic types designed to minimize the entrance of dust. Covers for these enclosures must be telescoping or tight fitting and have no openings that would allow sparks or burning metal to escape after installation and during use. Transformers and similar equipment are required to be provided with tight metal enclosures without any ventilating openings. Any resistors and resistance equipment must generally meet the rules in 502.130(A)(1) which include identification requirements for the specific location; however, thermionic tubes, nonadjustable resistors, or rectifiers with maximum operating temperatures that do not exceed 120°C (248°F) are permitted where installed in general-purpose enclosures.

Any rotating machines or equipment, such as motors or generators, are required to meet the rules in 502.125(B); and all wiring methods used for the circuits that supply or are supplied from this type of equipment covered by 502.150 must meet the applicable provisions of 502.10(B).

Equipment for Use in Class III Locations
General Provisions for Equipment
Divisions 1 and 2

Division 1 electrical equipment is assumed to be operating in an environment in which easily ignitible fibers and flyings are handled, manufactured or used. A single fault in the electrical system is not permitted to cause ignition to the normally ignitible atmosphere. Two failures or faults of the electrical equipment must occur simultaneously before the equipment becomes ignition capable.

Division 2 equipment is assumed to be operating in an environment in which easily ignitible fibers and flyings are stored or handled other than in the process of manufacture and does not include ignitible concentrations under normal conditions. An abnormal operating condition must occur before an explosive environment could exist, and then an additional (second) fault must occur simultaneously in the electrical system before ignition could occur.

Zones 20, 21, and 22

Currently, the *NEC* does not recognize any Zone system protection techniques for dust or fibers and flyings. The Zone system covered by Article 506, unlike the Division system, treats fibers and flyings as an equivalent hazard to those associated with combustible dusts. Equipment requirements for typical Class III locations would be much more restrictive if these locations were classified using the Zone system.

Zone 20 equipment is assumed to be operating in an environment that includes ignitible concentrations under normal conditions; but in Zone 20, these ignitible concentrations will be present continuously or for long periods of time. Equipment must be listed and suitable for the Zone 20 location or be apparatus listed for use in Class II, Division 1 locations and have a suitable temperature class.

Zone 21 equipment is assumed to be operating in an environment that could include ignitible concentrations under normal operations, but not for long periods of time. For that reason, the equipment must be listed and suitable for the Zone 21 location or be listed for use in Class II, Division 1 locations and have a suitable temperature class or pressurized equipment identified for use in Class II, Division 1 locations.

Zone 22 equipment, like Division 2 equipment, is assumed to operate in an environment that does not include ignitible concentrations under normal conditions. Just as for Division 2 locations, an abnormal

operating condition must occur before an explosive environment could exist and then an additional (second) fault must occur simultaneously in the electrical system before ignition could occur. For that reason, the equipment must be listed and suitable for the Zone 22 location or be listed for use in Class II, Division 2 locations and have a suitable temperature class or pressurized equipment identified for use in Class II, Division 2 locations.

Specific Equipment
Transformers and Capacitors

Requirements for transformers and capacitors installed in Class III locations are provided in 503.100. These types of equipment often produce heat and hot surfaces during normal operation.

In Class I, Divisions 1 and 2 locations, transformers or capacitors containing liquid that will burn are to be installed in transformer vaults that comply with all of the requirements located in Part III of Article 450. Transformers that contain askarel and have a rating above 25 kVA must have pressure-relief vents and a means of absorbing gases generated by arcing inside the case, or the pressure-relief vent must be extended to the outside of the building. Transformers must also be installed with a minimum of 150 mm (6 in.) air space between the transformer case and any adjacent combustible material. Dry-type transformers must be installed in vaults or be limited to 600 volts and have their windings and terminal connections enclosed in tight metal enclosures without ventilating or other openings. The requirements in 500.8 that cover equipment approval for class and properties must also be met. A review of applicable laboratory product directories reveals that there are currently no certifications for transformers nor are any capacitors evaluated for use in Class III locations. The most common practice for protection of this equipment, as with many other types of equipment, is to locate it in an unclassified location.

Switches, Circuit Breakers, Motor Controllers, and Fuses

Switches, circuit breakers, motor controllers, and fuses installed in Class III locations are governed by

requirements provided in 503.115. In Division 1 and Division 2 locations, equipment used to perform the electrical functions covered in this section is required to be dusttight (see photo 4-18).

Control Transformers and Resistors

Control transformers and resistors installed in Class III locations are covered by the rules in 503.120. In Division 1 and Division 2 locations, equipment used to perform the electrical functions covered in this section is required to be dusttight and have a maximum surface temperature not exceeding 165°C (329°F) while operating.

Motors and Generators

Motors and generators installed in Class III locations are covered by the rules in 503.125. In Division 1 and Division 2 locations, rotating machinery is required to be either totally enclosed nonventilated, or totally enclosed pipe-ventilated, or totally enclosed fan-cooled. Where the AHJ determines that the rotating machinery is located so that limited amounts of lint will collect on or near the machine and the machine is accessible for routine cleaning, an exception allows self-cleaning textile motors of the squirrel-cage type; or standard open-type machines without

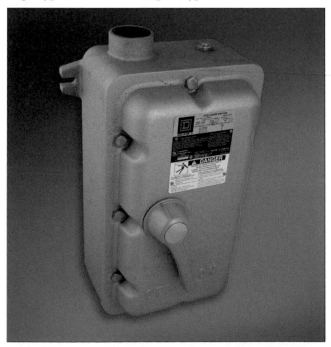

Photo 4-18. A dusttight, NEMA 7 & 9, 3-pole, 100-ampere, 600-volt, enclosed molded-case switch suitable for use in Class III locations. Courtesy of Schneider Electric / Square D Company

switching devices; or standard open-type machines with switches but with the switches enclosed in tight housings without openings.

Ventilating Piping Used for Motors, Generators or Other Rotating Machines

Ventilating piping used for motors, generators or other rotating machines installed in Class III locations is covered by the requirements in 503.128, which describes the vent piping used with totally enclosed pipe-ventilated motors or generators. This construction is important to minimizing the chance that lint and dust can collect within the vent and be ignited or cause overheating of the equipment.

Luminaires (Light Fixtures) Fixed and Portable Types

Luminaires installed in Class III locations are governed by the rules provided in 503.130. This type of equipment produces heat and can also produce arcs and hot particles in abnormal conditions, such as the premature rupturing of a lamp.

In Division 1 and Division 2 locations, luminaires (light fixtures) are required to include enclosures for the lamps that will minimize the entrance of fibers and flyings and the chance of hot filament escaping the lamp enclosure if the lamp breaks. If the luminaire is exposed to physical damage, it must be protected by a suitable guard. Requirements are also provided for bracing certain pendant luminaires and grounding portable lighting equipment. Portable lights are not permitted to be switched or to include receptacles for attachment plugs.

Utilization Equipment

Utilization equipment installed in Class III locations is covered by the rules in 503.135. In Division 1 and Division 2 locations, heaters must be identified for Class III locations and motor-driven appliances must be meet the Class III motor requirements.

Flexible Cords

Flexible cords installed in Class III locations are required to meet the rules in 503.140. In Division 1 and Division 2 locations, cords must be listed for extra-hard usage, contain an equipment grounding conductor, be connected to terminals or supply conductors in an approved manner, be supported in a manner that will eliminate tension on connections, and be terminated to boxes and fittings in a manner that will minimize the entrance of fibers and flyings. No additional restriction or permission, other than those located in 400.7 and 400.8, are included for flexible cords in Class III locations.

Receptacles and Attachment Plugs

Receptacles and attachment plugs installed in Class III locations are required to meet the rules found in 503.145. In Division 1 and Division 2 locations, receptacles and attachment plugs are required to be of the grounding type and to minimize the accumulation or entry of fibers and flyings. They must also prevent the escape of sparks or molten particles. If the AHJ determines that the receptacle is located so that limited amounts of lint will collect and it is accessible for routine cleaning, an exception allows general-purpose grounding type receptacles to be used.

Signaling, Alarm, Remote-Control, and Loudspeaker Intercommunications Systems

Requirements for signaling, alarm, remote-control, and loudspeaker intercommunications systems installed in Class III locations are provided in 503.150. In Division 1 and Division 2 locations, the components of the systems are required to comply with the applicable sections of Article 503 for motors, resistors, switches, and so forth.

Electric Cranes, Hoists, and Similar Equipment

Electric cranes, hoists, and similar equipment installed over or within Class III locations are covered by the requirements in 503.155. Power supplies to contact conductors are required to be: electrically isolated from all other systems; ungrounded; equipped with a ground detector that provides an alarm and also de-energizes the contact conductors in the event of a ground fault or provides a continuous visual and audible alarm as long as the fault exists. Contact conductors must be guarded or protected from accidental contact with foreign objects. Current collectors must be installed to prevent the escape of sparks or hot particles. Reliable means must be provided to prevent accumulation

of fibers and lint on contact conductors and current collectors. Crane controls must comply with applicable sections of Article 503.

Requirements for storage battery charging equipment installed in Class III locations are provided in Section 503.160. Storage battery charging equipment is not allowed in Class III, Division 1 and Division 2 locations. This equipment is required to be located in separate rooms built or lined with substantial noncombustible material and designed to prevent the entrance of ignitible flyings or lint. These rooms must also be well ventilated.

Summary

This chapter provided a fairly comprehensive overview of the requirements for specific equipment installed and used in hazardous (classified) locations. Similar rules are applicable to equipment in Class I, II, or Class III locations. A common thread between all of these locations is the requirement that the equipment in any location be suitable for that use. Product listing is often required in some of these rules, and identification of equipment for intended use is more often required.

An important point is to use equipment within its limitations in hazardous locations. Manufacturers of electrical and electronic equipment for use in these locations can provide information about how the product should be used and whether any important limitations or conditions must be followed.

As previously reviewed, it is always good design and engineering practice to locate much of the electrical and electronic equipment outside of the classified location, but it is not always possible. When equipment must be located within a Class I, II, or Class III location, it must meet all applicable *Code* rules as well as any requirements of the applicable product standard(s).

Once the appropriate equipment is selected and installed, the process of installing the electrical wiring circuits that supply the equipment or that is supplied from such equipment can begin. A detailed look at the requirements for wiring installations including the types of wiring methods permitted, types of conductors permitted, conduit sealing and drainage installation, and location rules for the various hazardous (classified) locations are provided in chapter five.

Review Questions

1. An instrument installed in a Class I location would be permitted to be enclosed in a general purpose enclosure if _____.

    a. connected to a Class 2 power supply and located in a Division 1 location
    b. it was nonincendive equipment and installed in a Zone 0 location
    c. it was intrinsically safe
    d. connected to a Class 2 power supply and located in a Zone 1 location

2. Squirrel cage motors that do not include arc-producing devices, and are installed in Class I, Zone 2, locations are required to be explosionproof.

    a. True
    b. False

3. Which protection technique is not likely to be used on a motor installed in a Class I, Zone 1, location?

    a. Intrinsic safety
    b. Increased safety
    c. Flameproof
    d. Explosionproof

4. Enclosures for lighting circuit breakers that are located in a Class II, Division 1, location are required to utilize _____ protection.

    a. dusttight
    b. dust ignitionproof
    c. increased safety
    d. nonincendive

5. Flexible cord used for pendant luminaires installed in Class II, Division 1, locations shall be _____ type.

    a. extra hard usage
    b. junior hard usage
    c. portable
    d. hard usage

6. Transformers are not permitted in Class II, Group E, hazardous (classified) locations.

    a. True
    b. False

7. Pushbuttons installed in Class II, Division 2, locations shall be dust ignitionproof.

    a. True
    b. False

8. The surface temperature for fixed luminaire installed in Class III location is limited to _____ degrees F under normal conditions.

    a. 165
    b. 392
    c. 302
    d. 329

9. All enclosures in Class I, Division 1, locations shall be explosionproof.

    a. True
    b. False

10. Luminaires for use in Class I locations are sometimes protected by a single protection technique and are also suitable for use where protected by multiple protection techniques.

    a. True
    b. False

11. Since explosionproof motors are not available for use in Group A hazardous locations, a process that involves a motor application can not be used.

    a. True
    b. False

12. The highest T Code permitted for a dust ignitionproof enclosure installed in Class II location where the combustible dust has an ignition temperature of 210°C would be _____.

    a. T4
    b. T3
    c. T2
    d. T1

13. The clearance between two terminals for connection of field wiring of different intrinsically safe circuits is permitted to be less than 2 inches where _____.

    a. the terminals are installed in an unclassified location
    b. the reduction is included in the control drawing
    c. the one of the circuits is connected to a simple apparatus
    d. both circuits are connected to simple apparatus

14. Flameproof and explosionproof luminaires are permitted to be interchanged in all applications.

    a. True
    b. False

15. Attachment plugs and receptacles installed in Class I, Division 2, locations are required to be identified for the location.

    a. True
    b. False

Chapter 5

Wiring Requirements

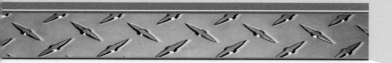

As reviewed in chapter two, one common way of minimizing possibilities of electrical wiring and equipment becoming an ignition source in hazardous (classified) locations is to locate the equipment and wiring outside of the hazardous location wherever possible. This is always a practical approach and a good exercise of ingenuity, although it is not always possible. Many times equipment and wiring installations have to be located within hazardous locations. Safe installations of electrical wiring in hazardous (classified) locations require a thorough understanding of generally more restrictive wiring rules than those presented in chapters 1 through 4 of the *Code*. A fairly comprehensive review of the various wiring methods permitted for use in classified locations, conduit and cable sealing requirements, and intrinsically safe systems are among the major topics covered in this chapter.

Sections 90.3, 500.3, and 505.3 provide clear direction that all general wiring requirements not modified in *NEC* chapter 5 are applicable to installations covered by chapter 5. In other words, the general requirements of chapters 1 through 4 apply to these installations unless modified or amended by the specific applicable rules in chapter 5. A failure in the wiring system in any location is never a desirable situation, but the risk of explosion that exists in hazardous locations provides urgent reasons to ensure that the general minimum requirements of the *Code* are met.

Although some of the issues covered in *NEC* 500.8, Equipment, apply to protection techniques for utilization equipment and devices, other requirements located in the section are applicable to wiring as well. Based on the definition of *equipment* located in Article 100, almost every component of an electrical circuit and every piece of utilization equipment connected to that circuit would qualify as equipment. In general, 500.8 limits the operating temperature of the circuit and equipment, provides for marking requirements, and establishes the threading requirements for conduit, fittings, and threaded entries into equipment. Within those threading requirements are provisions for adapting from National (American) Standard Pipe Taper (NPT) to metric threading. These general requirements apply to the wiring in Class I, Class II, and Class III locations. Similar requirements are covered in 505.9 for Class I, Zone installations and in 506.9 for Class II and Class III, Zone installations.

Class I Locations

Wiring Outside the Classified Area

Article 501 does not specifically address or restrict wiring requirements outside of classified locations. However, those involved with electrical installations should be aware that many occupancy standards and recommended practices do limit wiring methods or modify general wiring requirements in unclassified locations near classified spaces. In some situations, an electrical system (wiring and/or equipment) outside the classified space could provide ignition of a flammable atmosphere by releasing ignition capable particles that could communicate to the classified spaces. Since the details of these possible hazards vary greatly from process to process, and from material to material, and from electrical system to electrical system, specific occupancy standards address the issues and requirements rather than their being addressed in the wiring requirements in Part II of Article 501. Examples can be found in Section 7 of Articles 511 through 516. Additional examples can be found in documents such as NFPA 50B, *Liquefied Hydrogen Systems at Consumer Sites*, which prohibits the installation of hydrogen systems beneath electric power lines.

Wiring requirements within Class I hazardous areas using Division system are found in Part II of Article 501. The recognized acceptable wiring methods are included in 501.10, with (A) addressing Division 1 locations, and (B) addressing Division 2 locations.

Photo 5-01. Equipment, threaded metal conduit, and conduit seals installed in a Class I, Division 1 location

Division System

Since Class I, Division 1 locations are expected to include ignitible concentrations of flammable gases or vapors under normal operating conditions, the wiring requirements are more restrictive (see photo 5-01). Wiring methods permitted in these spaces include threaded rigid metal conduit, threaded steel intermediate metal conduit, Type MI cable, and

within specific industrial applications, Types MC-HL and ITC-HL cable systems. Although these wiring methods are not evaluated as explosionproof, it is anticipated that ground faults and/or short circuits could take place within them and they would be able to contain those faults. Since ignitible concentrations are expected under normal conditions, it is also anticipated that these faults could result in an explosion within the wiring method that must be contained. In many cases, these types of wiring methods are connected to explosionproof enclosures and, consequently, become an extension of that enclosure (see figure 5-01).

In addition to the more robust wiring methods described above, where the wiring is intrinsically safe, any wiring method permitted for unclassified locations and any wiring method or cabling system recognized in chapters 7 or 8 of the *NEC* is permitted [*NEC*, 504.20]. All of these systems provide acceptable protection of the electrical circuits and containment of possible faults to prevent ignition of surrounding ignitible atmospheres. It should be noted that additional wiring methods might be permitted where part of a pressurized system.

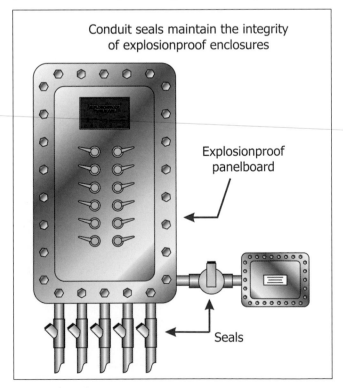

Figure 5-01. Explosionproof enclosures require proper connections of wiring methods and conduit seals to maintain the integrity and functionality of the enclosure.

Wiring Methods for Class I, Division 1 Locations

Rigid Metal Conduit and Intermediate Metal Conduit

The current wiring methods permitted in Class I, Division 1 locations are identified in Sections 501.10(A) and 504.20 and include threaded rigid metal or threaded steel intermediate conduit. The conduit must be threaded with a National (American) Standard Pipe Taper (NPT) thread that provides a 1 in 16 (¾ inch) taper per foot. It must be made up wrenchtight and have five threads fully engaged where connected to explosionproof enclosures. Some listed explosionproof enclosures may require only 4½ threads to fully engaged because of the factory provided NPT entries; these are recognized by exception to the general requirement. The requirement to be wrenchtight is one of the most important installation rules for conduit installed as a wiring method for hazardous locations. Installers and inspectors must assure that this requirement is met. In many cases, the integrity of explosionproof enclosures depends on this requirement being satisfied [see figure 5-02].

The *Code* requires electrical work to be installed in a neat and workmanlike manner, as provided in Section 110.12. Two characteristics of workmanlike installations in hazardous locations include tightness of fittings and suitable securing and supporting of

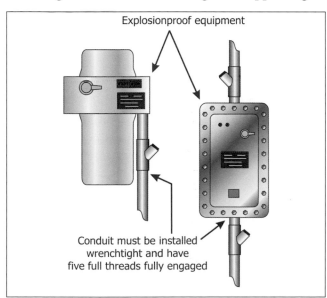

Explosionproof equipment

Conduit must be installed wrenchtight and have five full threads fully engaged

Figure 5-02. Rigid metal conduit and intermediate metal conduit installed in Class I, II, or III locations must be wrenchtight and have five full threads fully engaged.

In the 1920s electrical wiring for hazardous (classified) locations was primarily required to be installed in rigid metal conduit, which was an acceptable wiring method then, and may still be the most common wiring method utilized within Class I, Division 1 locations. Only limited use of hard usage flexible cord was permitted for connection of portable equipment in the late 1920s.

The *Code* recognized explosionproof flexible fittings for use in the 1930s. Interestingly, a 1932 handbook indicates that although explosionproof flexible fittings were permitted, none were available at that time.

The 1947 *NEC* included the Division system; and in Division 2 locations, electrical metallic tubing was recognized as a wiring method. Where flexibility was required in Division 2, flexible metal conduit was permitted.

Between 1947 and 1959, EMT was removed from the permitted wiring methods in Division 2 locations. Rigid metal conduit remained the only wiring method in Class I, Division 1 locations until 1959. The *Code* included Type MI cable as a wiring method in 1953 and, in 1959, recognized it for use in Class I, Division 1 and 2 locations. By 1959, the use of flexible cord was limited only to extra-hard usage type and to lengths necessary to connect to permanent wiring.

By 1965, metal-clad cable (Type MC) and aluminum-sheathed cable (Type ALS) were added to the *Code* as wiring methods suitable for use in Division 2 locations. Shielded nonmetallic-sheathed cable (SNM) was included in the 1971 *NEC,* and it was also recognized for use in Class I, Division 2 locations. Both flexible metal conduit and liquidtight flexible metal conduit were allowed in Division 2 locations but only where flexibility was necessary.

The 1975 *NEC* added new wiring methods for Division 2 locations, including, enclosed gasketed busways, tray cable (TC), and metallic-shielded high

Sidebar 5.01.

Evolution of Wiring Methods for Hazardous Locations

voltage cables installed in cable trays where properly protected from damage. This edition also permitted by exception the use of all of the wiring methods in *NEC* chapter 3 where electrical circuits were nonincendive, although the term *nonincendive* was not included or defined in the *Code* at that time.

Threaded steel intermediate metal conduit (IMC) was introduced and recognized as a wiring method in 1975; and in 1978, it became the first additional wiring method accepted for Class I, Division 1 locations since 1959. It was also recognized for use in Division 2, along with power-limited tray cable (PLTC) and medium voltage cable (MV). A more detailed recognition of cable tray use in hazardous locations was provided in the 1978 *NEC*. Type ALS cable was removed from the *Code* and, therefore, removed from the Division 2 list of wiring methods.

Enclosed gasketed wireways were included for use in Division 2 in 1984.

In the 1990 *NEC*, Article 504 covering intrinsically safe systems was added. Where intrinsically safe circuits or systems were used, any wiring method suitable for use in unclassified locations, including cable systems recognized in *NEC* chapters 7 and 8, were and still are permitted in Class I, Division 1 locations. The primary reason is, the energy levels used in these circuits are limited to a point that they are not ignition capable. Although the *NEC* did not include Article 504 until 1990, intrinsically safe systems had been used for many years prior. The 1990 *NEC* also expanded the list of wiring methods permitted where limited flexibility was necessary to include armored cable (Type AC) and liquidtight flexible nonmetallic conduit. AC cable was then removed in the 1993 *NEC*.

In 1996, two exceptions for wiring methods in Class I, Division 1 locations were added. The first permitted rigid nonmetallic conduit in underground spaces where encased in at least two inches of

Sidebar 5.01. continued

the rigid metal conduit as required. The *National Electrical Installation Standards* (NEIS) includes a family of publications that provide excellent guidelines and criteria for what constitutes good workmanship in electrical contracting. ANSI/NECA NESI-1 provides general requirements for good workmanship in electrical contracting, and NEIS 101 provides specific installation guidelines for rigid metal conduit, intermediate metal conduit, and coated rigid metal conduit.

Rigid Nonmetallic Conduit

Some raceways are installed in underground applications where flammable liquids are stored, handled or processed above those spaces. A risk always exists that this flammable material could be spilled and absorbed into the earth below, possibly entering the raceways and then communicating to ignition sources. Several sections of the *NEC* and some occupancy standards and/or recommended practices actually classify the space within the earth; others simply restrict the wiring in the underground spaces.

Since a Class I location is a space where flammable vapors exist in an ignitible concentration with oxygen, the possibility of appreciable amounts of oxygen would normally occur only in voids of underground spaces. The inside of the raceway itself could provide that oxygen and, certainly, where pipe chases or pits are in the ground, enough oxygen could be available to form a ignitible concentration. In an ideal and most conservative situation, the installation of underground raceways below these spaces should be avoided. However, ideal situations do not always exist. In many facilities or installations, raceways must be installed underground to electrical equipment located in the aboveground space.

Use of rigid nonmetallic conduit in underground installations evolved from permission for use in bulk storage facilities in the 1950s to an exception that permitted the use underground in any facility with Class I locations in 1996. The permission provided in several of the special occupancies requires that rigid nonmetallic conduit be installed below a minimum of two feet of cover and converted to threaded metal two feet prior to the point where the bend to emerge from

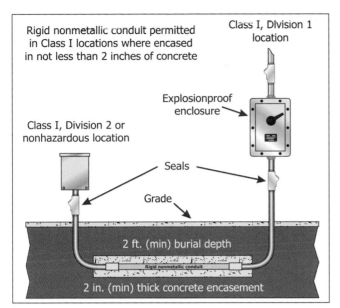

Figure 5-03. Rigid nonmetallic conduit is permitted to be installed in accordance with 501.10(A)(1) Exception (concrete-encasement is required).

the earth occurred. Provisions accepted in 1996 to include the current exception into Article 501 permit rigid nonmetallic conduit to be installed underground in any facility that includes Class I locations. That permission placed an additional restriction of two-inch concrete encasement on the underground installation of rigid nonmetallic conduit where it was installed in a location not already addressed in Articles 511 through 515. The concrete encasement provided some additional protection where normal activities within facilities are less predictable than those within the special occupancies (see figure 5-03).

Mineral-Insulated Cable (Type MI)

Type MI cable is a fairly unique wiring method. It is a factory assembly of one or more conductors insulated with a highly compressed refractory mineral insulation enclosed in a liquidtight and gastight continuous copper or alloy steel sheath. This type of cable is permitted to be used in Class I locations when the termination fittings are listed for this location. MI cable has multi-piece fittings that are threaded together when installed. The listing for the fittings ensures that these threaded connections result in an explosionproof assembly. Physical installation of the cable must be done in a manner to prevent tensile stress on these terminations (see figure 5-04 and photo 5-02).

Evolution of Wiring Methods for Hazardous Locations

concrete and converted to RMC or IMC at least two feet before turning up to emerge. The minimum depth for this underground installation is two feet. The second exception permitted a new metal-clad cable identified as MC-HL. This is a special metal-clad cable that includes specific prescriptive construction and testing requirements. It is limited to use in industrial establishments with restricted public access, where the conditions of maintenance and supervision ensure that only qualified persons service the installation. The 1996 *NEC* removed Type SNM cable as a permitted wiring method in Division 2. Article 337, covering Type SNM cable, was deleted from the *NEC*. Article 727, Instrumentation Tray Cable, was added to the *NEC* and to the list of methods permitted in Division 2 locations.

An extreme change to the text covering the use of flexible cords was recognized for use in the 1999 *NEC*. With evolving automation in industrial applications, and the need and/or desire to use mobile equipment to perform many functions within hazardous process locations, permission to use cord to supply this equipment was recognized. The 1999 *NEC* also included the use of ITC-HL cable in Division 1 locations.

In the 2002 *NEC*, the use of nonincendive wiring was recognized for use in Division 2 locations, and a new subsection titled "Nonincendive Field Wiring" provided a clearer description of what is permitted for nonincendive field wiring, circuits, components, and so forth.

Sidebar 5.01. continued

The product standard used to evaluate these is UL 886, *Outlet Boxes and Fittings for Use in Hazardous (Classified) Locations*. Fittings available in the market-place are either listed as explosionproof or not listed as explosionproof. Unless the marking is visible after installation, it may not be obvious whether the fittings meet the requirements of the product standard.

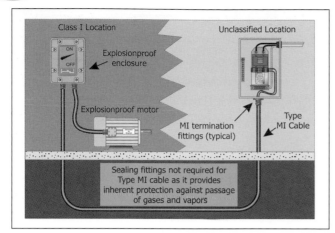

Figure 5-04. Type MI Cable is permitted as a wiring method for Class I locations.

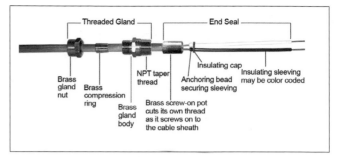

Photo 5-02. MI cable showing the anatomy of gland terminal fittings Courtesy of Tyco Thermal Controls

Metal-Clad Cable–Hazardous Locations (Type MC-HL)

Type MC-HL is permitted in Classes I and II, Division 1 hazardous (classified) locations. This is a multi-conductor, gas and vaportight continuous corrugated metal-sheathed cable provided with an overall polymeric jacket and an additional equipment grounding conductor sized in accordance with *NEC* 250.122. The termination fittings are specifically listed for Classes I and II, Division 1 locations. The *Code* currently permits any type of metallic sheath, but the product standard (UL 2225) limits the sheathing material to aluminum. Copper, copper-clad aluminum and aluminum conductors that employ thermoset or thermoplastic insulation are permitted as part of this type of cable assembly. The equipment grounding conductor is permitted to be insulated or bare. Cables are permitted to be rated up to 35 kV.

This type of cable is permitted in cable tray, in direct sunlight, and/or in direct burial or concrete encasement. The installation of MC-HL cable is limited by the *Code* to industrial establishments with restricted public access and facilities where the conditions of maintenance and supervision ensure that only qualified persons service the installation.

Where this wiring method is selected, the responsible decision-making party must be prepared to provide documentation to the authority having jurisdiction (AHJ) that those limiting conditions exist, and the AHJ must be prepared to evaluate the submitted documentation and determine if it meets the criteria specified for use of this method (see photo 5-03).

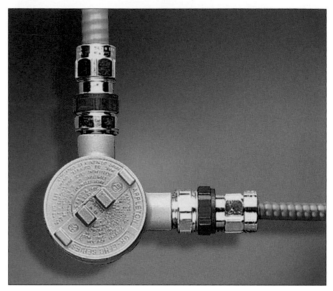

Photo 5-03. MC-HL cable is suitable for Classes I and II, Division 1 locations in industrial establishments with restricted public access. Courtesy of Thomas and Betts

Instrumentation Tray Cable (Type ITC-HL)

Type ITC-HL is suitable for use in Classes I and II, Division 1 hazardous (classified) locations. This is a multi-conductor, gas and vaportight continuous corrugated metal-sheathed cable provided with an overall polymeric jacket and may or may not include an additional equipment grounding conductor sized in accordance with 250.122 (see photo 5-04). The termination fittings are specifically listed for Classes I and II, Division 1 locations. Cables are rated for 300 volts, but limited by to use on circuits operating at 150 volts or less and 5 amperes or less [*NEC*, 727.1]. Instrumentation tray cable is evaluated for exposure to sunlight and may or may not be marked as sunlight resistant. This cable is permitted in direct burial applications or in concrete encasement. The installation of ITC-HL cable is limited by the *Code* to industrial establishments with restricted public access and facilities where the conditions of maintenance

Photo 5-04. Instrumentation Tray Cable (Type ITC-HL) Courtesy of Southwire Company

and supervision ensure that only qualified persons service the installation. Where this wiring method is selected, the responsible decision-making party must be prepared to demonstrate to the authority having jurisdiction (AHJ) through adequate documentation that those conditions do indeed exist.

Intrinsically Safe Systems

Intrinsically safe systems are covered by *NEC* 504. Where the circuits installed are intrinsically safe, as verified by the control drawings, the *Code* permits the use of any wiring method suitable for use in unclassified locations, including those permitted in chapters 7 and 8 [*NEC,* 504.20]. These circuits are not dependant on the wiring method to prevent ignition of a flammable atmosphere. When the circuits are intrinsically safe, the energy is maintained at a level where it cannot ignite the atmosphere if the circuit is opened, shorted, or faulted to ground at the same time a fault occurs at the source. Therefore, the wiring method is not limited. Although the wiring is not an ignition threat, due consideration should be given to the operation of the circuit. Should the circuit have a safety function that would be lost if the circuit were damaged, then the wiring method would become very important. The purpose is to ensure that the electrical system is not an ignition source. Even so, that may not be the only hazard that needs to be considered (see photo 5-05).

Therefore, it is extremely important to recognize the value and requirements of the control drawing for intrinsically safe systems. The control drawing is required for proper installation of these systems and is also necessary for making an inspection (see the annex for an example of a typical intrinsically safe system control drawing). Intrinsically safe systems include control drawings, and the zener diode barriers often reference a particular control drawing as well (see photos 5-06 and 5-07).

Identification

Other key requirements in Article 504 include rules for separation, identification, and conduit sealing. Intrinsically safe circuits are required to be identified at intervals not exceeding 7.5 m (25 ft) and must include the specific wording "Intrinsic Safety Wiring" (see figure 5-05). This identification requirement applies to raceways, cables, cable trays, and other wiring methods used for intrinsically safe system wiring.

Identification labels must be located to be readily visible and traceable for the

Photo 5-05. Intrinsically safe circuits installed using cable for level and leak sensors

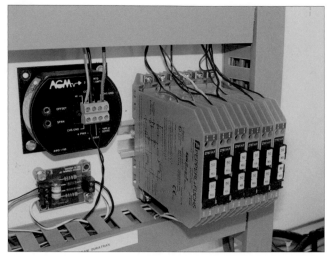

Photo 5-06. Intrinsically safe barriers installed in an IS control panel

Photo 5-07. Marks on an intrinsically safe barrier referencing a particular control drawing

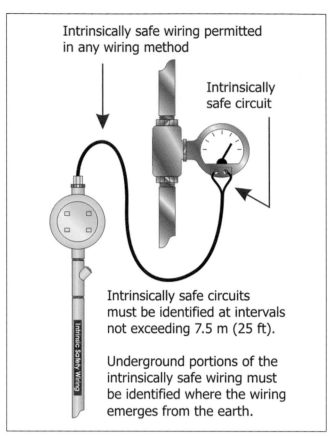

Figure 5-05. Identification is required for intrinsically safe circuits.

entire length of the wiring, except for any underground portions, which are re-identified as they emerge from the earth. Likewise, separate sections of this wiring created by walls, partitions, or other enclosures are required to be identified. Where a color code is used for intrinsically safe circuit conductors or wiring, such as raceways, boxes, and so forth, the color light blue is required [*NEC,* 504.80(C)].

Spacing Requirements

The *Code* permits any wiring method to be used for intrinsically safe circuits. However, there are specific spacing requirements between intrinsically safe circuits and those not instrinsically safe. The *Code* restricts intrinsically safe circuits from being installed in the same raceway, cable tray, or cable with conductors of any nonintrinsically safe circuit. Conductors of intrinsically safe circuits are permitted where they are separated from nonintrinsically safe circuit conductors by a space of not less than 50 mm (2 in.) or by grounded metal partitions or insulating barriers. The concern here is the possibility of compromising the intrinsic safety of the circuit through inductive or capacitive coupling conditions related to close proximities of other wiring. The identification rules covered above help installers and facilities maintain initial spacing when additional wiring or systems are installed.

Flexible Wiring in Class I, Division I Locations

When situations in an electrical installation warrant flexible connections in Class I, Division 1 locations, two options for the wiring methods are permitted: flexible fittings and flexible cord. The *Code* does not prescribe which option must be selected, but users must realize that this location has or could have ignitible concentrations of flammable vapors under normal operation. These days automation is evolving to a point where robots and mechanical devices are used to accomplish many tasks, even in hazardous (classified) locations. Movement of these mechanical devices requires more flexibility than was required in the past, which often necessitates the use of more flexible cords and greater lengths of flexible cord to complete electrical installations. In cases where increased use of robotics is employed, overall safety is improved because less human involvement is required to perform functions that were once extremely labor intensive. On the other hand, the use of flexible cord should always be minimized where other methods can be utilized to connect electrical circuits to equipment. The *Code* generally does not permit the use of flexible cord as a substitute for fixed wiring [*NEC*, 400.8(1)].

Explosionproof Flexible Fittings

Flexible fittings, sometimes called explosionproof flex, are available from several manufacturers in sizes ½ inch through 4 inch. Standard lengths begin at 4 inches in smaller sizes and range to 36 inches for the larger sizes. These fittings are available with either male or female threaded end fittings. Some sizes are listed only for Groups C and D, while others are available for Groups A, B, C and D. These fittings are very rugged and suitable for physical abuse while providing flexibility for difficult installation or vibration of equipment. The product standard used to evaluate these fittings is UL 886, *Outlet Boxes and Fittings for Use in Hazardous (Classified) Locations* (see photo 5-08).

Where flexible cord is installed as provided in 501.10(A) and 501.140, the cord must be listed for extra-hard usage and include an equipment grounding conductor, the braid or insulation of which is green or green with one or more yellow stripes. A review of *NEC* Table 400.4 will provide a description of the cords that are considered extra-hard usage. Other limitations for use of those cords are also included in that table. The cords must be continuous; they must be connected to their supply

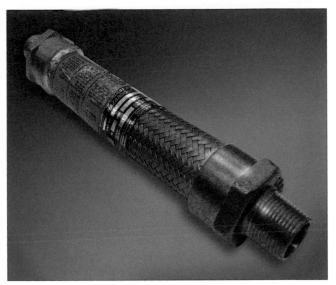

Photo 5-08. Explosionproof flexible conduit fitting for use in Class I, Groups A, B, C, and D and Class II, Groups E, F, and G, and Class III locations Courtesy of Cooper Crouse Hinds

terminals in an approved manner; they must be supported or secured to prevent tension on the terminal connections; and they must be sealed where they enter explosionproof enclosures or boxes to maintain the explosionproof integrity of the enclosure. Extreme care must be applied to select a fitting that matches the cord diameter to ensure that the explosionproof integrity of the enclosure is not compromised. As mentioned above, the provisions in 400.8 are applicable to cords installed in accordance with 501.140. It is important to consider all of the activities that take place on a normal basis that might subject flexible cords to physical damage and to provide proper precautions to protect the cord or cable where it is used.

Wiring Methods for Class I, Division 2 Locations
Class I, Division 2 wiring methods are installed in locations that are expected to include ignitible concentrations only under abnormal conditions. Under normal conditions, these locations might encounter releases of flammable liquids, gases or vapors that generally do not reach an ignitible concentration. These locations might also surround spaces that normally include ignitible concentrations. Since the ignitible concentrations are not expected to occur under normal conditions, the wiring methods allowed in these locations are not required to be as robust as those required in Division 1 locations. If arcs and/or

sparks from the wiring were to be released, chances are remote that an ignitible concentration would be present at the same time. Hence the risk of ignition has been determined to be acceptable. It should be recognized that normally arcing and sparking equipment located in Division 2 locations is to be protected by explosionproof enclosures. Where these explosionproof enclosures are provided, the wiring method is not permitted to compromise the integrity of the enclosure. Therefore, the wiring method from the enclosure to the seal would be limited to one of the methods permitted for Division 1 locations. Beyond the seal, the methods permitted for Division 2 would be acceptable.

Based on the historical evolution provided in sidebar 5-01, the current wiring methods permitted in Class I, Division 2 locations are provided in *NEC* 501.10(B), and include all of the wiring methods permitted in Division 1 locations as covered above and the following additional wiring methods.

Enclosed Gasketed Busways and Wireways

Installation requirements for an enclosed gasketed *busway* are provided in *NEC* Article 368. Article 376 provides the rules for enclosed gasketed *wireways*. These two types of wiring methods are evaluated to ordinary location product standards. The requirement for this equipment to be enclosed and gasketed provides an additional degree of protection in a fault condition. Gaskets minimize the possibilities that sparks might escape and be released into the atmosphere. That level of protection in a Class I, Division 2 area would include only ignitible concentrations under abnormal

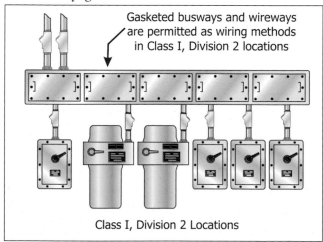

Gasketed busways and wireways are permitted as wiring methods in Class I, Division 2 locations

Class I, Division 2 Locations

Figure 5-06. Gasketed busways and wireways are permitted wiring methods in Class I, Division 2 locations.

conditions and has been determined to be an acceptable risk (see figure 5-06).

Power-Limited Tray Cable (PLTC)

Type PLTC cable is permitted to be installed in cable trays and raceways, to be supported by messenger wire, and also to be supported and protected by angles, struts, channels or other mechanical means. In industrial applications where qualified persons maintain the installations, PLTC cable is permitted to be exposed from cable tray to the utilization equipment. It must be secured at not more than 6 foot intervals and must comply with the crush and impact requirements of Type MC cable. The installation must be done in a manner that avoids stress on terminations.

Other Cables
Types ITC, MC, MV and TC Cable

Standard ITC, MC, MV, and TC cables installed in accordance with requirements in chapter 3 and Article 727 are permitted in Class I, Division 2 locations. These cables are all ordinary location wiring methods and are not required to have been subjected to any special product evaluation as required for MC-HL and ITC-HL used in Division 1 locations.

Where flexibility is required in Division 2 locations, flexible metal fittings, flexible metal conduit, liquidtight flexible metal conduit, liquidtight flexible nonmetallic conduit, and extra-hard usage cord are all permitted. Each of these wiring methods requires the use of listed fittings.

Nonincendive field wiring is also permitted for use in Class I, Division 2 locations where in accordance with the applicable control drawings. It is critical to follow the exact requirements of any control drawing whether it is for a nonincendive circuit or an intrinsically safe circuit. The integrity of this protection technique depends on strict conformance to the applicable control drawing.

For installations in Class I locations under the Zone system, all of the wiring methods permitted in Division 2 are permitted in Zone 2; all wiring methods permitted in Division 1 are permitted in Zone 1; and within areas designated as Zone 0, only intrinsically safe wiring installed in accordance with Article 504 is permitted.

Table 5-01. Summary of Wiring Methods for Class I Locations

Division 1 [NEC 501.10(A)]	Division 2 [NEC 501.10(B)
Threaded rigid metal conduit	All wiring methods indicated in Section 501.10(A)
Threaded intermediate metal conduit	Rigid metal conduit
Rigid nonmetallic conduit*	Intermediate metal conduit
Type MI Cable with listed termination fittings	Enclosed gasketed busways
Type MC-HL Cable**	Enclosed gasketed wireways
Fittings and bosses with threaded hubs that are dusttight	Type MC Cable with listed fittings
Dusttight flexible fittings	Type MI Cable with listed fittings
Liquidtight flexible metal conduit with listed fittings	Type PLTC per Article 725
Liquidtight flexible nonmetallic conduit with listed fittings	Type PLTC installed in cable trays
Type ITC-HL**	Type ITC as per 727.4
Flexible fittings listed for Class I, Division 1 locations	Type MC, MI, or TC with terminal fittings or in cable tray***
Flexible cord where listed for extra-hard usage and as provided in 501.140	Flexible metal fittings
Boxes and fittings that are approved for Class I, Division 1	Flexible metal conduit (listed fittings)
	Liquidtight flexible metal conduit (listed fittings)
	Liquidtight flexible nonmetallic conduit (listed fittings)
	Flexible cord listed for extra-hard usage
	Nonincendive field wiring
	Standard boxes or fittings****

* Where installed in accordance with the provisions of 501.10(A)(1) Exception

**Type MC-HL cable and Type ITC-HL, listed for use in Class I, Division 1 locations, with a gas/vaportight continuous corrugated metallic sheath, an overall jacket of suitable polymeric material, separate grounding conductors in accordance with 250.122, and provided with termination fittings listed for the application are permitted in industrial establishments with limited public access, where the conditions of maintenance and supervision ensure that only qualified persons service the installation.

*** Single Type MV cable must be either shielded or have a metallic armor

****Except as required by 501.105(B)(1), 501.115(B)(1), and 501.150(B)(1)

Table 5-01. Summary of wiring methods in Class I, Division 1 and 2 location

Sealing and Drainage Requirements in Class I Locations

Conduit and cable seals are required in classified locations and serve two primary purposes: (1) to contain explosions to explosionproof enclosures, and (2) to prevent the exploding gases and flames from migrating into the conduit system during such events. These seals are intended to prevent the passage of flames from one portion of the electrical installation to another. Sealing is also required to minimize the passage or communication of gases or vapors from a Class I location to one that is unclassified. Sealing fittings are available in vertical installation types and in types suitable for either vertical or horizontal installations (see photos 5-09 and 5-10).

Sealing methods and techniques for Class II locations are somewhat different, and primarily serve to prevent the passage of combustible dust into electrical equipment and dust-ignitionproof enclosures. Because gravity is continuously working to pull dusts in air suspension to the ground or floor level, sealing becomes more a matter of design and method of the conduit installation. Conduit seals and their requirements for Class II locations will be covered in more depth later in this chapter.

Photo 5-09. Conduit seal suitable for installation in vertical conduit runs

Photo 5-10. Conduit seal suitable for installation in vertical and horizontal conduit runs

Sealing is required where conduits and cables enter explosionproof and pressurized enclosures, and also where conduits and cables cross boundaries of classified locations [*NEC*, 501.15]. Seals installed at explosionproof and pressurized enclosures serve to complete the enclosure and maintain the integrity of the explosionproof protection technique. Boundary seals minimize the communication of gases and vapors from a more hazardous to a less hazardous location or unclassified location.

Conduit sealing fittings come in different types. There are vertical use sealing fittings, combination vertical and horizontal sealing fittings, sealing hubs (see figures 5-07 and 5-08), and sealing fittings that include drains (see photo 5-11). It is important to use correct damming fiber and compounds and proper installation techniques provided by the specific seal fitting manufacturer.

Some arcing devices have factory seals or contacts that are sealed. There is a difference in function between a conduit seal fitting and a process seal. Process seals are part of equipment installed into piping or vessels and are subject to a failure that would allow flammable liquid to enter the wiring system [*NEC*, 501.15(F)(3)]. Vertical sealing fittings can be used only when installed in the vertical position (see figure 5-09). Combination-type sealing fittings may be used in either the vertical or the horizontal position (see figure 5-10).

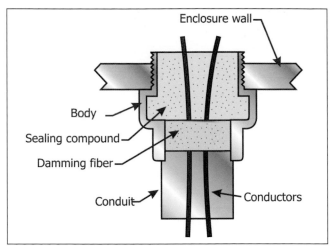

Figure 5-07. Sealing hub in threaded enclosure

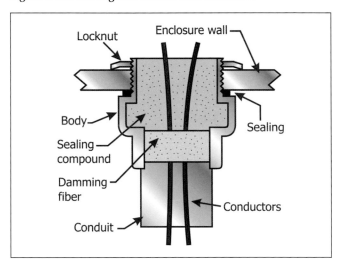

Figure 5-08. Sealing hub in standard enclosure with locknut

The primary difference between the two types has to do with how the sealing is accomplished in the fitting. In a vertical seal, the damming fiber is installed at the bottom of the fitting with the conductors separated for an effective seal between the compound and the conductors. In the horizontal sealing fitting, the damming fiber has to be packed in two ends of the fitting creating a bowl between the two conduit entries into which the compound is poured (see figure 5-11).

General Requirements for Conduit Seals

Before reviewing the specific locations that the *Code* requires conduit seals, one must understand the general requirements. The rules for conduit seals are provided in 501.15(C) and apply to conduit seals installed in Class I, Divisions 1 and 2 locations. These seals are generally required to be explosionproof,

Photo 5-11. Sealing fitting that includes a drain Courtesy of Hubbell/ Killark

Photo 5-12. Vertical sealing fitting Courtesy of Cooper Crouse Hinds

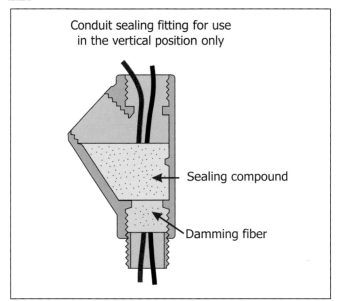

Figure 5-09. Vertical conduit sealing fitting

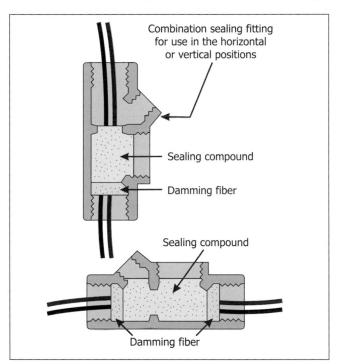

Figure 5-10. Combination vertical or horizontal sealing fitting

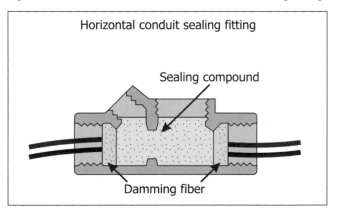

Figure 5-11. Anatomy of a horizontal conduit sealing fitting

except as permitted by 501.15(B)(2) or 504.70. The fittings are required to be listed for the location. Enclosures can include an integral means for sealing as well. Sealing fittings are required to use a damming material and compound specified by the seal manufacturer. The compound must not be affected by the surrounding atmosphere or liquids, and it is required to have a melting point of not less than 93°C (200°F). The reason for the minimum melting point temperature is to ensure that the seal will be maintained during normal operation. The listing requirement for these ensures that the sealing fitting in combination with the appropriate damming material and compound have been evaluated and listed for

Photo 5-13. Combination vertical and horizontal sealing fitting Courtesy of Cooper Crouse Hinds

providing a seal against the passage of gases or vapors and have the ability to contain an explosion within an explosionproof enclosure. Sealing fittings are required to be installed in accessible locations and are not permitted to contain any splices or taps. The thickness of the sealing compound cannot be any less than 16 mm (5/8 in.) and must not be less than the trade size of the fitting. Where conduit sealing fittings are installed, the conduit fill is impacted. The conduit fill is limited to not more than 25 percent of the cross-sectional area of the conduit of the same size, unless the seal fitting is specifically identified for a higher percentage of fill (see figure 5-10). The reason for the fill limitation is so that an effective sealing can be accomplished by separating the contained conductors during the damming process (see photos 5-14 and 5-15).

Cable Sealing Requirements

The primary purpose of cable sealing is to minimize the passage of gases or vapors through the cable core. Where cables are connected to explosionproof enclosures, sealing fittings meeting the requirements in 501.15(B)(1) are required for all cable entries to such enclosures.

In Class I, Division 1 locations, cable seals must be located and provided as required in 501.15(D)(1) through (D)(3).

Cable Terminations

Cables must be sealed at all terminations, or the

Photo 5-14. Conduit seal shown with the conductors separated and the damming fiber installed

cable and the sealing fitting are required to meet all of the rules in 501.15(C). Type MC-HL cables (with multiple conductors that include a gas/vaportight continuous corrugated metallic sheath and an overall jacket of suitable polymeric material) must be sealed with a listed fitting. The jacket, armor and any other covering must be removed so the sealing compound surrounds each individual insulated conductor to create a seal that minimizes the passage of gases and vapors.

If shielded cables and twisted pair cables are used, the shield is not required to be removed and separation of twisted pairs is not required, provided the termination is made in an approved means to minimize the entrance of gases or vapors and prevent propagation of flame into the cable core [*NEC*, 501.15(D)(1) and see photo 5-16].

Explosionproof Enclosures

Explosionproof seals are mandatory where cables enter enclosures required to be explosionproof in accordance with 501.15(B)(1). These sealing fittings are to maintain the explosionproof integrity of the enclosures. Where the cable sheath is capable of transmitting gases or vapors through the cable core, the sheath must be removed so that the sealing

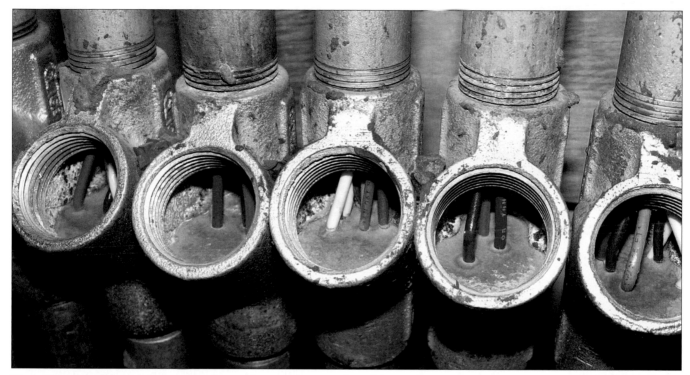

Photo 5-15. Conduit seal shown after the seal is poured (separation of the conductors is maintained and sealing compound forms a tight seal around the individual conductors).

process can be established around the individual conductors of multiconductor cables (see figure 5-12). Where multiconductor cables are installed in conduit connected to these types of enclosures, the seals must meet the requirements of 501.15(D).

Cables not capable of gas or vapor transmission through the cable core are required to be sealed only where they are connected to explosionproof or flameproof enclosures, unless otherwise required by 501.15(E)(2). Cables that are capable of gas or vapor transmission through the cable core are required to be sealed only where they are connected to explosionproof or flameproof enclosures, unless otherwise required by the requirements of 501.15(E)(3). Cables with an unbroken gas/vaportight continuous sheath are permitted to pass through Class I, Division 2 locations without being sealed.

Cables Without Gas/Vaportight Continuous Sheath

Cables that do not have a continuous gas/vaportight sheath are required to be sealed at the boundary of a Class I, Division 2 location to minimize the passage of gas or vapors from being communicated to the unclassified location through the cable core [NEC, 501.15(D)(4)].

Photo 5-16. Multiconductor cable is shown passing through a conduit sealing fitting (cable sheath is not removed) with damming material in place before the sealing compound is poured.

Integral Seals in Assemblies

Some equipment is manufactured to include two separate compartments: a specific compartment where terminations can be made is separated from the second compartment that contains arcing or sparking equipment or high temperatures (see photo 5-17). In these cases, if the specific compartment provides an integral seal between the two and the entire

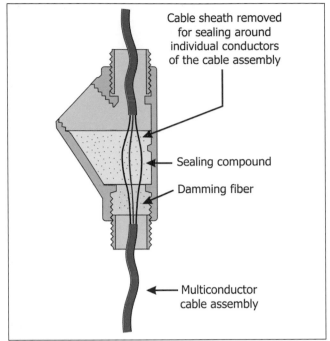

Figure 5-12. Sheath of cable is removed to seal around conductors individually.

assembly is identified for the location, additional seals are not necessary between the compartments. Conduits entering the compartment that contains the splices or taps must generally be sealed in Class I, Division 1 locations [*NEC*, 501.15(C)(5)].

Where Type MI cable is installed as the wiring method in Class I locations, the need for sealing fittings is eliminated. Type MI cable inherently prevents the passage of gases or vapors by the way it is constructed (see figure 5-14 and photo 5-18).

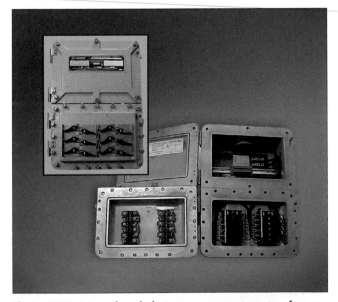

Photo 5-17. Integral seals between compartments of an assembly (panelboard) Courtesy of Appleton EGS Electrical Group

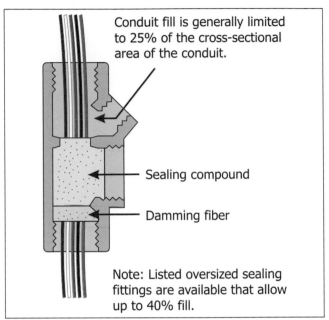

Figure 5-13. Conduit seals are limited to 25 percent fill unless specifically listed for higher percentages.

Type MI cable offers an effective wiring alternative that can be used in hazardous locations. Where it is used, the requirements to install sealing fittings are minimized. For example, if a circuit is installed in a Class I, Division 1 location to supply a motor, sealing fittings are not necessary at the boundary or the motor controller enclosure.

Propagation of flames is possible through the interstices between strands of standard stranded conductors larger than 2 AWG. Conductor constructions such as compact conductors are effective

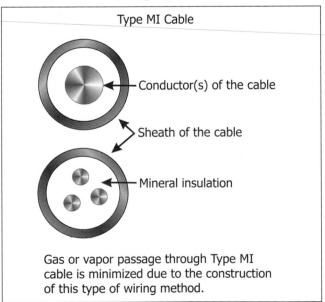

Figure 5-14. Type MI cable inherently prevents the passage of gases or vapors.

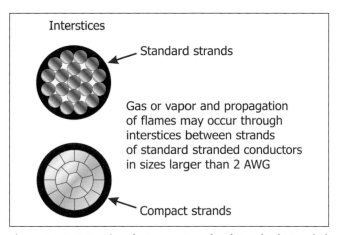

Figure 5-15. Interstices between strands of standard stranded conductors larger than 2 AWG can present sealing challenges.

in reducing the possibilities of leakage and flame propagation (see figure 5-15).

Electrical Process Seals

Both the *NEC* and the CE Code, Part I require that incendive components (those that produce arcs, sparks, or operate at high temperatures) be isolated from other parts of the explosionproof installation. This is accomplished by using explosionproof or flameproof seals, as previously reviewed. Seals used for isolating incendive equipment or components are usually constructed as explosionproof and are also used to minimize the passage of gases or vapors.

Photo 5-18. Type MI cable connected to an explosionproof enclosure

In many sealed systems, industrial control devices and process control devices are required to measure process liquids or gases. In order to accomplish this, some type of actual interface with the process piping system is necessary (see photo 5-19). Penetrations into the process piping always create increased risks of release of the contained process.

Instruments and devices used must be suitable for sealing against the potential release of process fluids into the electrical equipment (instrument or device) enclosure, conduit system, or the surrounding environment. Process seals are frequently used for measuring temperatures, pressures, levels, and fluid levels in equipment that can change the state of the process fluids, such as heaters, mixers, pumps, and so forth. Common examples of seals used in process sealing are "o" rings, ferrules, welded diaphragms, and thermowelds. Process seals will not necessarily be explosionproof or flameproof, but are intended to isolate industrial process fluids, gases, and so forth, from the electrical instrument enclosure and conduit system (see figure 5-16).

Electrical equipment that contains provisions for connection to a sealed process, such as temperature and pressure transmitting devices, must be provided with a process seal. The process seal is required to effectively block the passage of the process fluids or gases from the containment piping or system into the electrical enclosure and conduit system (see photo 5-20).

Single process seal devices are subject to more stringent pressure testing requirements to determine suitability. Equipment that includes two or more seals is tested at less pressure during the tests. A venting means is required between the primary and secondary seals so any leakage in the sealed process will become obvious. Secondary seals in such devices must be capable of preventing the passage of the process fluids or materials

Photo 5-19. Pressure sensor that includes a process seal connected to a high pressure natural gas lin

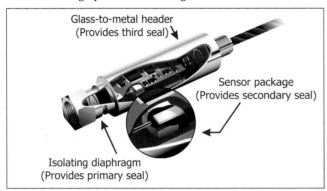

Glass-to-metal header
(Provides third seal)

Sensor package
(Provides secondary seal)

Isolating diaphragm
(Provides primary seal)

Figure 5-16. Process equipment that provides a diaphragm as the seal Courtesy of Emerson Controls Rosemount

Photo 5-20. Typical sensing device that utilizes process sealing
Courtesy of Emerson Controls Rosemount

at the venting pressure and temperature in case of a primary seal failure. Equipment may be marked "Factory Sealed – Conduit Seal Not Required" or equivalent. The *Code* indicates that listed equipment marked "Dual Seal" does not require an additional process seal when used within the manufacturer's ratings [*NEC*, 501.15(F)(3)].

Conductor Insulation

A review of 501.20 indicates that where conductor

insulation is exposed to vapors or liquids, it must be a type identified for use under such conditions. Gasoline and oil resistant insulated conductors are available and listed and identified for such use. No insulation has been evaluated for exposure to any other flammable material. The only additional option is the use of conductors protected by a lead sheath or other approved means. A review of the UL marking guide for cables and conductors indicates that currently no limited-energy cables have been evaluated for exposure to flammable liquids.

Exposed Uninsulated Parts

The voltage of uninsulated live parts installed in Class I, Class II, or Class III locations must be limited to 30 volts for dry locations and 15 volts for wet locations (no shock hazards permitted), and, in addition, must be part of an intrinsically safe system in Class I and/or Class II, Division 1 location. For Class I and/or Class II, Division 2 or a Class III location, the uninsulated part is permitted to be part of an intrinsically safe or nonincendive system to ensure that uninsulated live parts do not become an ignition or a shock hazard. Many workers will assume that these two issues are the same. Yet when these systems are closely evaluated, it is apparent that some Class 2, energy-limited circuits are ignition capable and some intrinsically safe and nonincendive circuits operate above the voltage limits established for shock hazards (see figure 5-17).

Multiwire Circuits

Multiwire circuits are those that consist of two or more ungrounded conductors that have a voltage

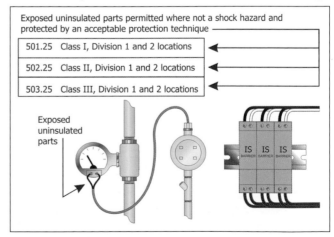

Exposed uninsulated parts permitted where not a shock hazard and protected by an acceptable protection technique

501.25   Class I, Division 1 and 2 locations
502.25   Class II, Division 1 and 2 locations
503.25   Class III, Division 1 and 2 locations

Exposed uninsulated parts

IS BARRIER   IS BARRIER   IS BARRIER

Figure 5-17. Exposed parts that are uninsulated are permitted.

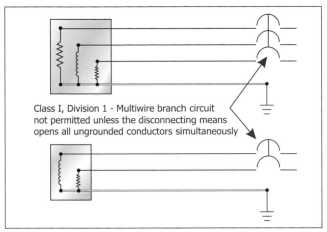

Figure 5-18. Multiwire branch circuits are not permitted in Class I, Division 1 locations unless the disconnecting means opens all ungrounded conductors of the multiwire branch circuit simultaneously. This can usually be accomplished by the installation of a suitable circuit breaker handle tie accessory device.

between them, and a grounded conductor that has equal voltage between it and each ungrounded conductor of the circuit and is connected to the neutral or grounded conductor of the system [Article 100, definition of *multiwire branch circuit*]. These circuits are not permitted to be installed in Class I and/or Class II, Division 1 locations unless the circuit disconnecting means opens all of the ungrounded conductors simultaneously (see figure 5-18). This restriction minimizes the opportunity for arcing and sparking of circuits that could become an ignition source and removes possibilities of neutral return current in multiwire branch circuits when the circuits are de-energized for service or repair operations. This same requirement applies to Class II, Division 1 locations.

Seal Requirements in Class I, Division 1 Locations

Seals at Enclosures

Where conduits enter an explosionproof enclosure, they are required to be sealed if the enclosure contains apparatus, such as switches, circuit breakers, fuses, relays, or devices, that may produce arcs or sparks or high temperatures considered to be an ignition source on the surface of the enclosure (see photo 5-21).

These high temperatures are considered to be those exceeding 80 percent of the autoignition temperature in degrees Celsius of the gas or vapor involved. For conduits of metric designator 53 (2 in.)

Photo 5-21. Conduit seals installed within 450 mm (18 in.) of switching devices (circuit breakers) and motor controllers

or larger entering enclosures that contain terminals, splices, or taps, seals must be provided [*NEC*, 501.15(A)(1) and see figures 5-19 and 5-20].

Conduit seals are not required for conduit entering enclosures where switches, circuit breakers, fuses, relays, or resistors meet one of four specific conditions:

• These devices (typically contact devices) are hermetically sealed.

• They are immersed in oil.

• They are in a factory-sealed explosionproof chamber within an enclosure that is identified for the location

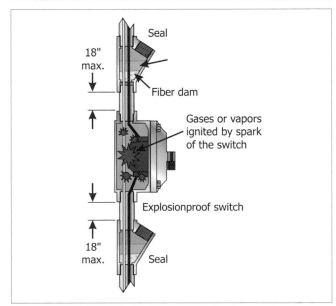

Figure 5-19. Conduit seals are required to be provided for enclosures containing arcing devices.

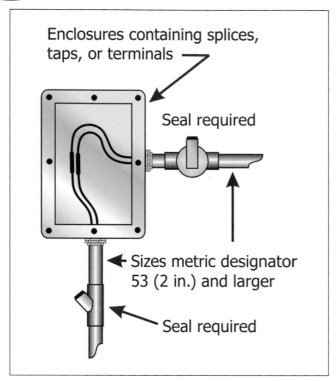

Figure 5-20. Seals are required in conduits that enter enclosures containing splices, taps, or terminals, and the conduit size is metric designator 53 (2 in.) [trade size 2] or larger.

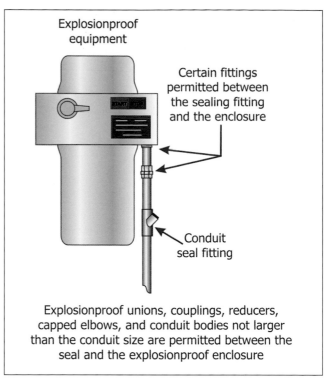

Figure 5-21. Certain fittings are permitted between the seal and an explosionproof enclosure.

and marked *factory sealed,* unless the enclosure entry is metric designator 53 (trade size 2) or larger

• They are nonincendive circuits [*NEC,* 501.15(A)(2) items (1) through (2)]

Enclosures that are factory-sealed are not permitted to satisfy a seal requirement for an adjacent explosionproof enclosure that is required to have a conduit seal. The sealing fitting must be located not more than 450 mm (18 in.) from the explosionproof enclosure. Explosionproof unions, couplings, reducers, elbows, capped elbows and conduit bodies not larger than the trade size of the conduit are the only fittings permitted between the seal and the explosionproof enclosure (see figure 5-21 and photos 5-22, 5-23 and 5-24).

Where pressurized enclosures are utilized, such as where the purged and pressurized protection technique is used, conduit seals are required to be as close as possible to the conduit entry into the enclosure, but not greater than 450 mm (18 in.) from the pressurized enclosure. Locating the seals close to pressurized enclosures helps reduce problems with purging dead air spaces within the pressurized enclosures (see figure 5-22 and photo 5-25).

A single conduit seal can satisfy the sealing requirements for two explosionproof enclosures connected by conduit nipples or lengths of conduit not exceeding 900 mm (36 in.) where the seal is located not more than 450 mm (18 in.) from either enclosure (see figure 5-23).

Seals at Boundaries

Where conduits cross a Class I, Division 1 boundary, a seal is required to be provided on either side of the boundary as long as it is located within 3.05 m (10 ft) of the boundary and no fittings other than explosionproof reducers are installed between

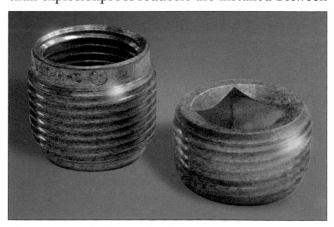

Photo 5-22. Explosionproof reducers   Courtesy of Cooper Crouse Hinds

Photo 5-23. Explosionproof unions Courtesy of Cooper Crouse Hinds

the conduit seal and the point where the conduit leaves the Division 1 location (see figure 5-24).

If a metal conduit that contains no fittings passes through a Class I, Division 1 location and there are no fittings within 300 mm (12 in.) beyond each boundary, seals are not required where the conduit terminates in an unclassified location [see *NEC*, 501.15(A)(4) Exception No. 1 and figure 5-25].

If conduits are located in the ground at the point of the boundary, the conduit is permitted to continue past the boundary point, but it must be sealed where the conduit emerges from the earth.

Photo 5-25. Seals located close to purged and pressurized enclosure

No fitting other than a listed explosionproof reducer at the sealing fitting is permitted in the conduit that emerges from the earth at that location [see *NEC*, 501.15(A)(4) Exception No. 2 and figure 5-26].

Seal Requirements in Class I, Division 2 Locations

Seals at Explosionproof Enclosures

For conduits connecting to explosionproof enclosures in Class I, Division 2 locations, conduit seals are to be provided in similar fashion to those required for explosionproof enclosures in Division 1 locations. The wiring method between the sealing fitting and the enclosure is required to be either rigid metal conduit or intermediate metal conduit [*NEC*, 501.15(B)(1) and 501.10(A)].

Seals at Boundaries

Where rigid metal conduit or intermediate metal conduit crosses a Class I, Division 2 boundary, a seal must usually be provided on either side of the boundary as long as it is located within 3.05 m (10 ft) of the boundary and no fittings other than explosionproof reducers are installed between the conduit seal and the point

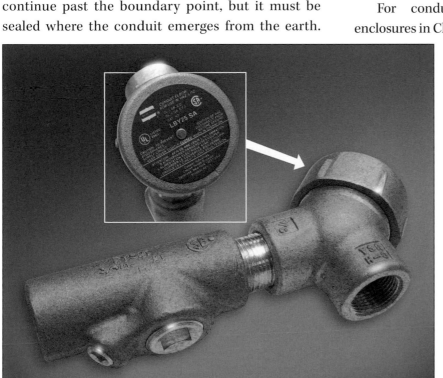

Photo 5-24. Explosionproof capped elbows Courtesy of Cooper Crouse Hinds

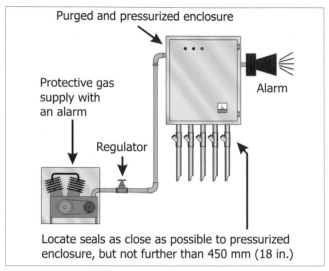

Figure 5-22. Seals for conduits entering pressurized enclosures shall be installed within 450 mm (18 in.) from such enclosures

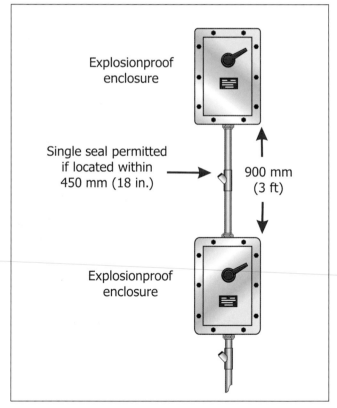

Figure 5-23. A single seal is permitted for two adjacent explosionproof enclosures under certain conditions.

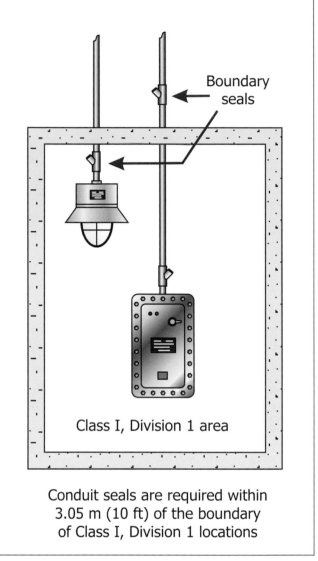

Figure 5-24. Seals are required within 3.05 m (10 ft) of either side of the boundary of Class I, Division 1 locations

where the conduit leaves the Division 2 location. As reviewed earlier, the primary purpose of the boundary seal is to minimize the passage of gas or vapors from a classified location to an unclassified location. Seals installed in conduits crossing a Class I, Division 2 boundary are not required to be explosionproof, but must be identified for the purpose of minimizing the passage of gases or vapors under normal operating conditions (see figure 5-27).

Similar to the allowance for Division 1 locations, for metal conduit that contains no fittings and passes through a Class I, Division 2 location and has no fittings within 300 mm (12 in.) beyond each boundary, seals are not required if the conduit terminates in an unclassified location [*NEC*, 501.15(B)(2) Exception No. 1].

If conduits pass into a Class I, Division 2 location from a pressurized enclosure or room that is unclassified as a result of pressurization, seals are not required at the boundaries.

Conduit systems terminating at an unclassified location where a wiring method transition is made

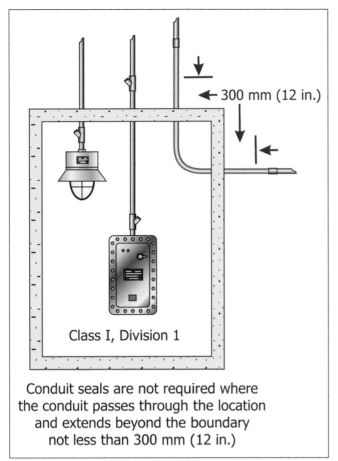

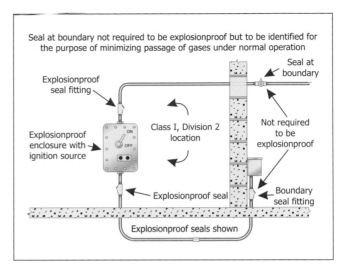

Figure 5-27. Seals are required at a Class I, Division 2 location boundary but are not required to be explosionproof [*NEC*, 501.15(B)(2)].

Figure 5-25. Conduit seals are not required under the conditions specified in Exception No. 1 to 501.15(A)(4).

to cable tray, cablebus, ventilated busway, Type MI cable, or open wiring, are not required to be sealed where they pass from the Class I, Division 2 location into the unclassified location. The unclassified lo-

cation shall be outdoors, or if the conduit system is all in one room, it shall be permitted to be indoors. The conduits shall not terminate at an enclosure containing an ignition source in normal operation.

Where segments of aboveground conduit systems pass from Class I, Division 2 locations to unclassified locations, the conduit is not required to be sealed if all of the following conditions are met:

• no part of the conduit system segment passes through a Class I, Division 1 location where the conduit contains unions, couplings, boxes, or fittings within 300 mm (12 in.) of the Class I, Division 1 location; and

• the conduit system segment is located entirely in outdoor locations; and

• the conduit system segment is not directly connected to canned pumps, process or service connections for flow, pressure, or analysis measurement, and so forth, that depend on a single compression seal, diaphragm, or tube to prevent flammable or combustible fluids from entering the conduit system; and

• the conduit system segment contains only threaded metal conduit, unions, couplings, conduit bodies, and fittings in the unclassified location; and

• the conduit system segment is sealed at its entry to each enclosure or fitting housing terminals, splices, or taps in Class I, Division 2 locations [*NEC*, 501.15(B)(2) Exception No. 4].

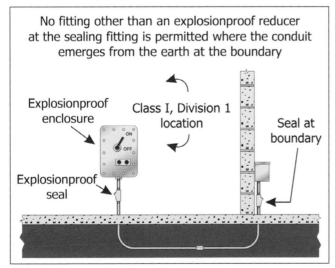

Figure 5-26. Seals are required at boundaries where the conduit emerges for termination in the electrical system. For underground conduits, the boundary is permitted to be at the location where the conduit emerges from the earth.

Photo 5-26. Type MC cable with a gas/vaportight continuous corrugated metallic sheath, with an overall nonmetallic covering, and used with suitable fittings Courtesy of Thomas and Betts

Class II Locations

Wiring Methods in Class II Locations

Class II, Division 1 Locations

Wiring methods, sealing, conductor insulation, uninsulated live parts, and multiwire circuit requirements are very similar to those for Division 1 locations with a few differences, especially in the requirements for conduit seals.

The specific wiring methods suitable for use in Class II, Division 1 locations are as follows:

• Threaded rigid metal conduit and threaded steel intermediate metal conduit

• Type MI cable with termination fittings listed for the location and installed in a manner to avoid tensile stress at the termination fittings

• Type MC cable with a gas/vaportight continuous corrugated metallic sheath, with an overall nonmetallic covering, and a properly sized equipment grounding conductor installed in industrial establishments with limited public access. The equipment grounding conductor size in such cable must meet the minimums specified in 250.122, and termination fittings listed for the application are required for this MC cable [see *NEC,* 502.10(A) and photo 5-26].

Fittings and boxes are required to be provided with threaded bosses for conduit or cable connections and must be dusttight; and where fittings and boxes contain taps, joints, or terminal connections or are used in Class II, Group E locations, they are to be identified for Class II locations.

Where flexible connections are necessary, the following flexible wiring methods are permitted:

• Dusttight flexible connectors

• Liquidtight flexible metal conduit used with listed fittings

• Liquidtight flexible nonmetallic conduit with listed fittings

• Type MC cable that includes interlocking metal tape-type construction, and is covered by a suitable jacket of polymeric material, and provided with fittings listed for use in Class II, Division 1 locations.

• Flexible cord listed for extra-hard usage that includes an equipment grounding conductor and is used with bushed fittings and meets all of the following additional installation requirements: (1) connected to terminals or supply conductors in a approved manner; (2) supported by clamps or other means in a manner that protects the cord from tension or stress on the terminal connections; (3) provided with suitable seals to prevent the entrance of dust where the cord enters boxes or fittings required to be dust-ignitionproof.

Class II, Division 2 Locations

Wiring methods recognized for use in Class II, Division 2 locations are as follows:

All of the wiring methods suitable for Class II, Division 1 locations as provided in Section 502.10(A) are also acceptable for Class II, Division 2 locations.

Rigid metal conduit, intermediate metal conduit, electrical metallic tubing and dusttight wireways are also permitted in these Division 2 locations.

Type MI cable and Type MC cable when used with listed fittings are also recognized for use in Division 2 locations; and power-limited tray cable and instrumentation tray cable where installed in cable trays are acceptable for use in Class II, Division 2 locations.

Types MC, MI, and TC cables installed in ladder, ventilated trough, or ventilated channel cable trays in a single layer, when specific spacing requirements are met, with the exception of Type MC cable listed for Class II, Division 1 locations [*NEC*, 502.10(B)(1)].

Flexible Connections

Where flexibility is necessary, the *Code* allows flexible cord to be installed in Class II, Division 2 locations as long as it meets all of the installation requirements for cords permitted in Class II, Division 1 locations in accordance with Section 502.10(A)(2). Care must be taken where the decision is made to utilize flexible cords in Class II locations. The "uses permitted" and "uses not permitted" rules for flexible cords in Article 400 must be considered as well (see 400.7 and 400.8 for general allowable uses for flexible cords and cables).

Nonincendive Field Wiring

Where nonincendive field wiring is installed in Class II, Division 2 locations, any of the wiring methods allowed for unclassified locations is permitted. To maintain its integrity, nonincendive field wiring systems must conform to all of the specific criteria of the applicable control drawing(s). Simple apparatus as defined in 504.2 is permitted to be connected to nonincendive field wiring circuit as long as the simple apparatus does not interconnect the nonincendive field wiring to any other circuit [*NEC*, 502.10(B)(3)].

Separate nonincendive field wiring circuits must be installed to meet one of the following criteria:

- In separate cables
- In multiconductor cables where the conductors of each circuit are contained within a grounded metal shield
- In multiconductor cables where the conductors of each circuit have a minimum insulation thickness of .25 mm (0.01 in.)
- Dusttight when any boxes or fittings are installed in Class II, Division 2 locations

Sealing Requirements for Class II Locations

Conduit sealing requirements for Class II locations deal with concerns about the migration of combustible dusts into dust-ignitionproof enclosures. The sealing means must prevent the entrance of dust into the

Table 5-02. Summary of Wiring Methods for Class II Locations

Division 1 [NEC 502.10(A)]

Threaded rigid metal conduit
Threaded intermediate metal conduit
Type MI Cable with listed termination fittings
Type MC Cable*
Fittings and bosses with threaded hubs that are dusttight
Dusttight flexible fittings
Liquidtight flexible metal conduit with listed fittings
Liquidtight flexible nonmetallic conduit with listed fittings
Type MC Cable*
Flexible cord where listed for extra-hard usage and as provided in 502.140

* Type MC cable, listed for use in Class II, Division 1 locations, with a gas/vaportight continuous corrugated metallic sheath, an overall jacket of suitable polymeric material, separate grounding conductors in accordance with 250.122, and provided with termination fittings listed for the application are permitted in industrial establishments with limited public access, where the conditions of maintenance and supervision ensure that only qualified persons service the installation.

Division 2 [NEC 502.10(B)]

All wiring methods indicated in Section 502.10(A)
Rigid metal conduit
Intermediate metal conduit
Electrical metallic tubing
Dusttight wireways
Type MC Cable with listed fittings
Type MI Cable with listed fittings
Type PLTC installed in cable trays
Type ITC installed in cable trays
Type MC, MI, or TC Cables installed in cable trays**

** MC, MI, and TC cable installed in ladder, ventilated trough, or ventilated channel cable trays in a single layer and generally with a space not less than the larger cable diameter between the two adjacent cables, shall be the wiring method employed.

Table 5-02. Summary of wiring methods in Class II, Division 1 and 2 locations

dust-ignitionproof enclosures. Where conduits are installed between two enclosures and one of the enclosures is required to be dust-ignitionproof, a suitable means for sealing the conduit is required (see figure 5-28). The method of accomplishing a seal is a bit different than those methods of sealing required for gases or vapors. Explosionproof sealing fittings are not necessary to accomplish the sealing required for Class II locations.

Electrical sealing putty or the manner of installation is permitted to accomplish a seal. For example, on a length of conduit or tubing installed horizontally for a distance of 3.05 m (10 ft) of length, sealing is not required; because, gravity is working to help the dust settle to the lowest point and dust does not easily migrate horizontally. A conduit run that enters the top of a dust-ignitionproof enclosure is to be sealed to prevent the dust from falling into the enclosure. Conduit or tubing installed from the bottom of a dust-ignitionproof enclosure for a vertical length downward not less than 1.5 m (5 ft) does not require a seal. A conduit installed horizontally and downward for a length equivalent to that provided in 502.15(2) or (3) does not require a seal. Seals are not required in a raceway installed between an enclosure required to be dust-ignitionproof and one located in an unclassified location. While seals for Class II locations are not required to be explosionproof types, they are required to be accessible [*NEC*, 502.15].

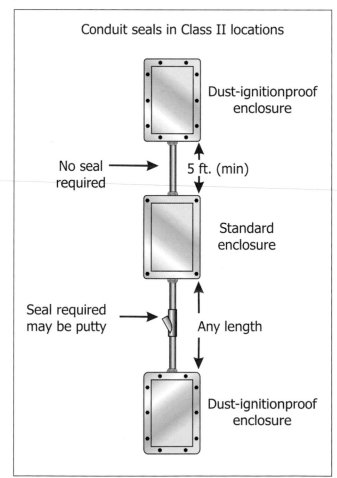

Conduit seals in Class II locations

Dust-ignitionproof enclosure

No seal required

5 ft. (min)

Standard enclosure

Seal required may be putty

Any length

Dust-ignitionproof enclosure

Figure 5-28. Seal is required in conduit between two enclosures in a Class II.

Multiwire Branch Circuits

Multiwire branch circuits are generally not permitted in Class II, Division 1 locations, except where the un-grounded conductors of the multiwire branch circuit can be disconnected simultaneously. This can usually be accomplished by the use of suitable circuit breaker handle tie accessories. [*NEC*, 502.40 and Exception]

Class III Locations
Class III Wiring Methods

In Class III locations (Divisions 1 and 2) the concerns are for fire and explosion hazards that may exist due to ignitible fibers and flyings. Specific concerns center on surface temperatures of electrical equipment reaching a level that could cause excessive dehydration or gradual carbonization of fibers and flyings, making them subject to spontaneous combustion. Wiring methods suitable for Class III, Division I locations are provided in 503.10(A), and those suitable for Class III, Division 2 locations are provided in 503.10(B).

Class III, Division 1 Locations

The wiring in Class III, Division 1 locations is required to be installed using any of the following methods:

- Rigid metal conduit
- Rigid nonmetallic conduit
- Intermediate metal conduit
- Electrical metallic tubing
- Dusttight wireways
- Type MC cable with listed termination fittings
- Type MI cable with listed termination fittings
- Dusttight when boxes and fittings are used

Flexible Connections

Where flexible connections are necessary, the following wiring methods are recognized by the *Code* for Class III, Division 1 locations:

- Dusttight flexible connectors
- Liquidtight flexible metal conduit with listed fittings
- Liquidtight flexible nonmetallic conduit with listed fittings
- Flexible cord installed to meet the requirements

of 503.140: cord to be listed for extra-hard usage, an equipment grounding conductor included in the cord, and the cord must be connected to the supply conductors in an approved manner. Where cord is used, it needs to be supported by suitable clamps or other means to prevent tension or stress on the terminal connections. Also, a suitable means of preventing the entrance of fibers or flyings at boxes or fittings is required.

Nonincendive Field Wiring

Where nonincendive field wiring is installed in Class III, Division 1 locations, any of the wiring methods allowed for unclassified locations is permitted. To maintain the nonincendive characteristic or integrity, nonincendive field wiring systems must conform to the specific criteria of the applicable control drawing(s). Simple apparatus as defined in 504.2 is permitted to be connected to nonincendive field wiring circuit, as long as the simple apparatus does not interconnect the nonincendive field wiring to any other circuit [*NEC*, 503.10(A)(3)].

Separate nonincendive field wiring circuits must be installed to meet one of the following criteria:
• In separate cables
• In multiconductor cables where the conductors of each circuit are contained within a grounded metal shield
• In multiconductor cables where the conductors of each circuit have a minimum insulation thickness of .25 mm (0.01 in.)

Class III, Division 2 Locations

Wiring installed in a location classified as Class III, Division 2 is generally required to meet all of the rules for wiring installed in Class III, Division 1 locations. One exception permits open wiring on insulators in areas used solely for storage and containing no machinery, but only where installed in accordance with the rules in Article 398. Protection from physical damage, as required by Section 398.15(C), must be provided where the open wiring on insulators is not run in roof spaces and located out of reach.

There are no specific sealing requirements for conduits installed in Class III locations.

Table 5-03. Summary of Wiring Methods for Class III Locations

Division 1 [NEC 503.10(A)]

Rigid metal conduit
Intermediate metal conduit
Rigid nonmetallic conduit
Electrical metallic tubing
Dusttight wireways
Type MI Cable with listed termination fittings
Type MC Cable with listed termination fittings
Dusttight boxes and fittings
Dusttight flexible connectors
Liquidtight flexible metal conduit with listed fittings
Liquidtight flexible nonmetallic conduit with listed fittings
Flexible cord where listed for extra-hard usage and as provided in 503.140
Dusttight boxes and fittings
Nonincendive field wiring in accordance with 503.10(A)(3)

Division 2 [NEC 503.10(B)*

Rigid metal conduit
Intermediate metal conduit
Rigid nonmetallic conduit
Electrical metallic tubing
Dusttight wireways
Type MI Cable with listed termination fittings
Type MC Cable with listed termination fittings
Dusttight boxes and fittings
Dusttight flexible connectors
Liquidtight flexible metal conduit with listed fittings
Liquidtight flexible nonmetallic conduit with listed fittings
Flexible cord where listed for extra-hard usage and as provided in 503.140
Dusttight boxes and fittings
Nonincendive field wiring in accordance with 503.10(A)(3)

* In sections, compartments, or areas used solely for storage and containing no machinery, open wiring on insulators shall be permitted where installed in accordance with Article 398, but only on condition that protection as required by 398.15(C) be provided where conductors are not run in roof spaces and are well out of reach of sources of physical damage.

Table 5-03. Summary of wiring methods in Class III, Division 1 and 2 locations

Zone System

Wiring Outside the Classified Area

Article 505 does not specifically address or restrict wiring requirements outside of classified locations. Therefore, those involved with electrical installations should be aware that many of the occupancy standards and recommended practices do limit wiring methods or modify general wiring requirements in unclassified locations near classified spaces. In some situations, an electrical system (wiring and/or equipment) outside the classified space could provide ignition of a flammable atmosphere by releasing ignition capable particles that could communicate to the classified spaces.

Wiring Methods for Class I, Zone 0 Locations

Just as for the Division system, the *Code* specifies certain wiring methods for use in hazardous (classified) locations using the Zone system of area classification. Wiring methods required in Zone 1 and Zone 2 locations, while similar to those required for Division 1 and 2 locations, utilize primarily cable methods. However, wiring methods required for Zone 0 locations are more restrictive as far as the protection technique required. Wiring installed in Zone 0 locations is required to be in any wiring method that utilizes intrinsically safe (ia) protection techniques in accordance with Article 504. Note the restriction

Table 5-04. Summary of Wiring Methods for Class I, Zones 0, 1, and 2

Zone 0 Only intrinsically safe wiring methods in accordance with Article 504	**Zone 2 [NEC 505.15(C)]**
Zone 1 [NEC 505.15(B)]	All wiring methods indicated in Section 505.15(B)
Intrinsically safe circuits and systems per 505.15(A)	Rigid metal conduit
Threaded rigid metal conduit	Intermediate metal conduit
Threaded intermediate metal conduit	Enclosed gasketed busways
Rigid nonmetallic conduit*	Enclosed gasketed wireways
Type MI Cable with listed termination fittings	Type MC Cable with listed fittings
Type MC-HL Cable**	Type MI Cable with listed fittings
Fittings and bosses with threaded hubs that are dusttight	Type PLTC per Article 725
Dusttight flexible fittings	Type PLTC installed in cable trays
Liquidtight flexible metal conduit with listed fittings	Type ITC as per 727.4
Liquidtight flexible nonmetallic conduit with listed fittings	Type MC, MI, or TC with terminal fittings or in cable tray***
Type ITC-HL**	Flexible metal fittings
Flexible fittings listed for Class I, Zone 1 or Division 1 locations	Flexible metal conduit (listed fittings)
Flexible cord where listed for extra-hard usage and as provided in 505.17	Liquidtight flexible metal conduit (listed fittings)
Boxes and fittings that are approved for Class I, Zone 1 or Division 1	Liquidtight flexible nonmetallic conduit (listed fittings)
	Flexible cord listed for extra-hard usage and per 505.17
	Nonincendive field wiring
	Standard boxes or fittings****

* Where installed in accordance with the provisions of 505.10(B)(1)(f)

**Type MC-HL cable and Type ITC-HL, listed for use in Class I, Zone 1 or Division 1 locations, with a gas/vaportight continuous corrugated metallic sheath, an overall jacket of suitable polymeric material, separate grounding conductors in accordance with 250.122, and provided with termination fittings listed for the application are permitted in industrial establishments with limited public access, where the conditions of maintenance and supervision ensure that only qualified persons service the installation.

*** Single Type MV cable must be either shielded or have a metallic armor

****Except as required by 501.105(B)(1), 501.115(B)(1), and 501.150(B)(1)

Table 5-04. Wiring methods in the Zone system (Class I, Zones 0, 1, and 2)

to two-circuit (ia) intrinsically safe systems or circuit [*NEC*, 505.15(A)].

Intrinsically safe protection techniques are covered in chapter 3 of this book.

Wiring Methods for Class I, Zone 1 Locations

In Class I, Zone 1 locations, any wiring method suitable for Zone 0 locations, as specified in 505.15(A), is permitted in Zone 1 locations. The intrinsically safe protection technique is the key to acceptability of any wiring method being used in the Zone 1 locations, because IS circuits are not capable of being an ignition source. General wiring methods are permitted. There are a variety of cables suitable for use as wiring methods in Class I, Zone 1 locations.

• Type MC-HL cable is permitted in industrial establishments with limited public access.

• Type ITC-HL cable is also permitted in industrial establishments with limited public access.

• Type MI cable is permitted when used with terminal fittings listed for Zone 1 and Division 1 locations.

• Rigid nonmetallic conduit is permitted where concrete-encased and where it meets the restrictions provided in 505.15(B)(1)(f).

Where flexible connections are necessary, flexible cord is permitted in Class I, Zone 1 locations when used with fittings listed for those locations and meeting the following requirements:

• The flexible cord includes an equipment grounding conductor in addition to the other conductors in the cord.

• The flexible cord is connected to terminals or supply conductors in an approved manner.

• The flexible cord is supported by clamps or other means in a manner that protects it from tension or stress on the terminal connections.

• Listed sealing fittings are provided where the cord enters boxes or fittings that are required to be explosionproof or flameproof.

Wiring Methods for Class I, Zone 2 Locations

All of the wiring methods for Class I Zone 1 locations as provided in 505.15(B) are permitted in Class I, Zone 2 locations.

Various cables are recognized as wiring methods acceptable for use in Class I, Zone 2 locations when used with suitable terminal fittings or installed in cable trays in a manner to avoid tensile stresses at the terminal fittings. The following cables are permitted:

• Type MI cable with termination fittings
• Type MC cable with termination fittings
• Type TC cable with termination fittings
• Type MV cable with terminal fittings

Note that single conductor Type MV cables are required to be shielded or metallic-armored.

Type ITC and PLTC Cables

Instrumentation tray cable (Type ITC) as provided in 727.4 is permitted as a wiring method in Zone 2 locations.

Type PLTC cable meeting the requirements in Article 725 is permitted in Class I, Zone 2 locations if it is installed in a manner to avoid tensile stress at the termination fittings.

Enclosed gasketed busways and enclosed gasketed wireways are also permitted in Class I, Zone 2 locations, in addition to threaded rigid metal conduit and threaded steel intermediate metal conduit.

Nonincendive Field Wiring

Where nonincendive field wiring is installed in Class I, Zone 2 locations, any of the wiring methods allowed for unclassified locations is permitted. To maintain the nonincendive characteristic or integrity, nonincendive field wiring systems must meet all of the specific criteria of the applicable control drawing(s). Simple apparatus as defined in 504.2 is permitted to be connected to nonincendive field wiring circuits, as long as the simple apparatus does not interconnect the nonincendive field wiring to any other circuit [*NEC*, 505.15(C)(1)(g)].

Separate nonincendive field wiring circuits must be installed to meet one of the following criteria:

• In separate cables
• In multiconductor cables where the conductors of each circuit are contained within a grounded metal shield
• In multiconductor cables where the conductors of each circuit have a minimum insulation thickness of .25 mm (0.01 in.)

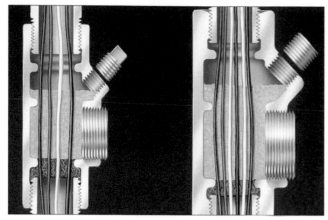

Photo 5-27. Sealing fittings are generally limited to no more than 25 percent fill unless listed for higher percentages of fill.
Courtesy of Appleton EGS Electrical Group

Sealing Requirements Under the Zone System

Conduit and cable sealing requirements are provided in Article 505 for installation under the Zone system. Many of the rules that relate to the seal itself are consistent with those provided for the use under the Division system. Enclosures or equipment are generally required to provide an integral means for sealing; otherwise, sealing fittings listed for the location must be used. Listed sealing fittings require specific damming fiber (packing material) and compounds to be used, and the compound is not permitted to have a melting point in excess of 93°C (200°F). Minimum thickness of the compound is required to be not less than the trade size of the conduit-sealing fitting and, at a minimum, must not be less than 16 mm (5/8 in.) in thickness.

Cable sealing fittings are not required to have a thickness equal to the trade size of the cable fitting, as these fittings have a few different physical characteristics.

Splices or taps are not permitted within a sealing fitting, and the fitting is required to be installed in accessible locations. Just as for seal fittings installed under the Division system, the conductor fill at the seal is generally limited to not more than 25 percent of the cross-sectional area of the conduit unless the seal fitting is listed for a higher percentage of fill (see photo 5-27). Manufacturers of conduit sealing fittings have listed oversized seals that allow for a 40 percent fill limitation for the conduit generally [*NEC,* 505.16(D)].]

Seal Locations in the Zone System

Seals for conduits and cables installed in areas

classified under the Zone system are required to meet the applicable rules provided in 505.16(A) through 505.16(E). Where Type MI cable is used as the wiring method, sealing compound that will exclude moisture or other fluids must be used in the terminal fittings.

Class I, Zone 0 Locations

Conduit seals are required at the boundary of Zone 0 locations and must be within 3.05 m (10 ft) of either side of the boundary. No fitting other than a listed reducer is permitted between the sealing fitting and the point where the conduit leaves the Zone 0 location. With the understanding that the only protection technique permitted for use in a Zone 0 location is the intrinsically safe (ia) type, seals are required for the boundaries only. Any unbroken length of rigid conduit that passes through a Zone 0 location and extends not less than 300 mm (12 in.) beyond the boundary is not required to have a sealing fitting, as long as the conduit terminates in an unclassified location (see figure 5-29). Cable seals are required on cables terminating in a Zone 0 location, and must be provided at the first point of termination after the cable enters the location. Seals for Zone 0 locations are not required to be explosionproof or flameproof.

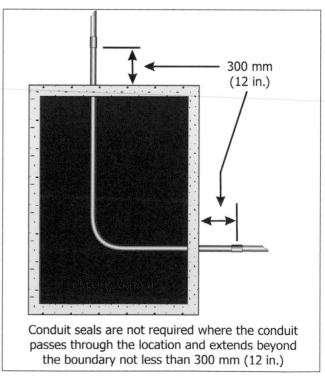

300 mm (12 in.)

Class I, Zone 0

Conduit seals are not required where the conduit passes through the location and extends beyond the boundary not less than 300 mm (12 in.)

Figure 5-29. Seals are not required where conduit extends at least 300 mm (12 in.) beyond the boundary.

Class I, Zone 1 Locations

Equipment Enclosures

Conduit sealing fittings are generally required within 50 mm (2 in.) of flameproof enclosures (Type "d" protection technique) or increased safety enclosures (Type "e" protection technique). If a flameproof enclosure is marked to indicate that a seal is not required, no additional field-installed conduit seal is necessary. This marking typically reads as follows: "Factory-Sealed — No Additional Seal Required." Where Type "e" protection is used, conduits including only NPT to NPT raceway joints or fittings listed for Type "e" protection are permitted between the enclosure and the seal, and the seal does not have to be within 50 mm (2 in.) of the entry. Conduits with NPT to NPT raceway joints installed between Type "e" protection enclosures are not required to be sealed [*NEC,* 505.16(B)(1) Exceptions].

Conduit sealing requirements for explosionproof equipment and pressurized enclosures installed under the Zone system are provided in 505.16(B)(2) and (3) and are similar to those required for explosionproof equipment installed under the Division system, which is covered in detail earlier in this chapter.

Cable Sealing Requirements

The primary purpose of cable sealing is to minimize the passage of gases or vapors through the cable core and where cables are connected to explosionproof or flameproof enclosures. Sealing fittings meeting the requirements in 505.16(D) are required at cable entries to such enclosures.

Explosionproof and Flameproof Enclosures

Explosionproof seals are required where cables enter enclosures required to be explosionproof or flameproof in accord with 505.16(D). These sealing fittings are required to maintain the explosionproof or flameproof integrity of the enclosures. Where the cable sheath is capable of transmitting gases or vapors through the cable core, the sheath must be removed so that the sealing process can be established around the individual conductors of multiconductor cables. Where multiconductor cables are installed in conduit connected to these types of enclosures, the seals must meet the requirements of 505.16(B)(4).

Cables not capable of gas or vapor transmission through the cable core are required to be sealed only where they are connected to explosionproof or flameproof enclosures, unless otherwise required by 505.16(C)(2)(a). Cables that are capable of gas or vapor transmission through the cable core are required to be sealed only where they are connected to explosionproof or flameproof enclosures, unless otherwise required by the requirements of 505.16(C)(2)(a). Cables with an unbroken gas/vaportight continuous sheath are permitted to pass through Class I, Zone 2 locations without being sealed.

Cables Without Gas/Vaportight Continuous Sheath

Cables that do not have a continuous gas/vapor-tight sheath are required to be sealed at the boundary of a Class I, Zone 2 location to minimize the passage of gas or vapors from being communicated to the unclassified location through the cable core [*NEC,* 505.16(C)(2)(d)].

Seals at Boundaries

Class I, Zone 1 Boundary

Boundary seals for conduit systems are to be provided in the same fashion and locations as those required at the boundaries classified under the Division system. The seal is permitted on either side of and within 3.05 m (10 ft) of the boundary, and must be designed to minimize the passage of gases or vapors from being communicated from the Zone 1 location to the conduit beyond the seal. Only listed reducers are permitted between the conduit seal and the point where the conduit leaves the Zone 1 location. If metal conduit that contains no fittings passes through a Class I, Zone 1 location and has no fittings within 300 mm (12 in.) beyond each boundary, seals are not required if the conduit terminates in an unclassified location [*NEC,* 505.16(B)(4) Exception and see figure 5-30].

Class I, Zone 2 Boundary

Conduit seal requirements for Class I, Zone 2 locations are provided in Section 505.16(C)(1) and are similar to the seal requirements for Class I, Division 2 locations. Where the conduit connects to

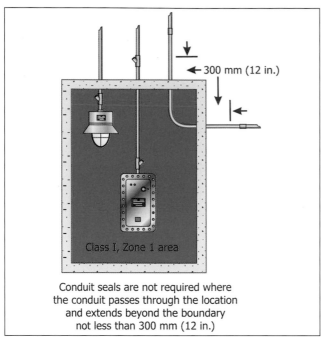

Figure 5-30. Seals are not required as indicated in 505.16(B)(4) Exception.

flameproof enclosures (type "d") or increased safety enclosures ("e" types), seals are required; and the sealing fitting must generally be located within 50 mm (2 in.) of these enclosures [see exceptions to 505.16(B)(1) also]. For explosionproof enclosures, the requirements for sealing fitting are the same as are applicable to explosionproof enclosures installed under the Division system. Where the conduit passes from a Class I, Zone 2 location into an unclassified location, a sealing fitting is required; and it is permitted to be located within

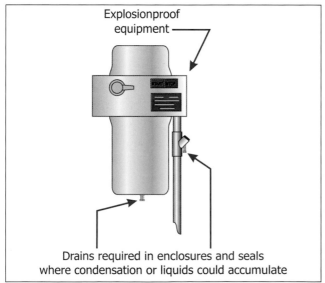

Figure 5-31. Drains are required in enclosures and seals where condensation or liquids could accumulate.

3.05 m (10 ft) of either side of the boundary. These seals must also be designed and installed to minimize the passage of gases or vapors within the Zone 2 location from being communicated to the conduit beyond the seal.

Drainage Requirements

Where condensation of vapors or liquids could be trapped within enclosures or at any point in the raceway system, an approved means is to be provided to prevent this accumulation or provide periodic draining of these accumulations of liquids or vapors (see figure 5-31).

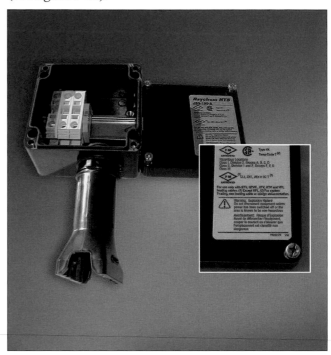

Photo 5-28. Increased safety "e" terminals in increased safety equipment

Conductors and Conductor Insulation

Insulation on conductors exposed to condensed vapors or liquids or in contact with such materials must be identified for the use, or the insulation must be protected by a lead sheath or other approved means. Where field-wired conductors are connected to equipment identified as Type "e", they must be connected to a Type "e" terminal. The integrity of the terminations at this type of equipment is critical to maintaining the integrity of this protection technique (see figures 5-32 and 5-33). Copper conductors are required where the Type "e" protection technique is used [*NEC*, 505.18 and see photo 5-28].

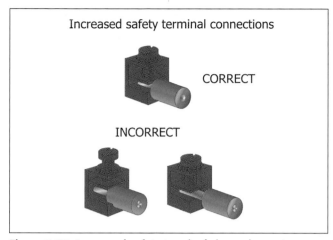

Figure 5-32. Increased safety terminals in equipment

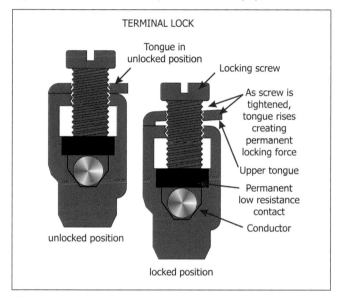

Figure 5-33. Anatomy of an increased safety terminal is shown with conductor connected. Concepts for 5-32 and 5-33 courtesy of Appleton

Multiwire Branch Circuits in Zone 1 Locations

Multiwire branch circuits are generally not permitted in Class I, Zone 1 locations, except where ungrounded conductors of the multiwire branch circuit can be disconnected simultaneously. This can usually be accomplished by the use of suitable circuit breaker handle tie accessories [*NEC*, 505.21 and Exception and see figure 5-34].

Summary

Where areas are classified as hazardous locations, electrical system design should endeavor to locate as much of the electrical and electronic equipment and associated wiring as possible and practical outside the classified location. Electrical wiring outside the hazardous locations usually can be

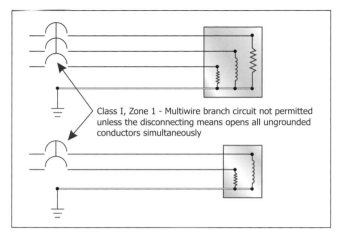

Figure 5-34. Multiwire branch circuits generally are not permitted in Class I, Zone 1 locations unless a means to disconnect all ungrounded conductors is provided.

installed in accordance with the general rules of the *NEC*. When electrical wiring and equipment are installed in Class I, II, or III locations, wiring methods must be any of those recognized as suitable for the particular location. Sections 501.10, 502.10, and 503.10 include the various wiring methods suitable for use in these hazardous locations. Where the electrical wiring is connected to equipment, conduit and cable seals are often required. Understanding why conduit and cable seals are required and where they are to be located is important to safe electrical wiring installations in these locations. This chapter has provided a general overview of the various wiring methods, conduit and cable sealing and drainage rules, and rules for multiwire branch circuits in hazardous (classified) locations.

Chapter six provides information about several special occupancies that include hazardous locations and the rules specific to each of those occupancies. These rules are covered by Articles 511 through 517. Article 510 indicates that the general requirements in the *Code* and the rules for any of the special occupancies (hazardous locations) covered in 511 through 517 can modify or amend the general provisions for hazardous (classified) locations included in 500 through 504. When unusual conditions exist in a specific occupancy, the authority having jurisdiction is required to exercise judgment with respect to the application of specific *Code* rules.

Review Questions

1. The metal clad cable that is permitted for use in Class I, Division 1, locations is _____.

    a.   continuous sheath MC
    b.   interlocked-type MC
    c.   corrugated sheath MC
    d.   MC-HL

2. In Class I, Division 2, locations _____ type metal clad cable is permitted.

    a.   continuous sheath
    b.   interlocked
    c.   MC-HL
    d.   all of the types above

3. In Class II, Division 1, locations where it is necessary to employee flexible connections, liquidtight flexible nonmetallic conduit is permitted.

    a.   True
    b.   False

4. Where raceways provide communication between a dust-ignitionproof enclosure and one that is not, an explosionproof seal is required.

    a.   True
    b.   False

5. Where branch circuit wiring is installed from an unclassified location to connect a piece of equipment located in a Class III, Division 1, location, neither double-locknut nor locknut-bushing type contacts are permitted as bonding means from that equipment to _____.

    a.   other equipment in the Division 1 location
    b.   the Division 2 boundary
    c.   the boundary of the unclassified location
    d.   point of grounding for the service or separately derived system

6. Wireways in Class III, Division 1, locations shall _____.

    a.   not be permitted
    b.   be dusttight
    c.   be dust ignitionproof
    d.   be explosionproof

7. Wireways in Class II, Division 1, locations shall _____.

    a.   not be permitted
    b.   be dusttight
    c.   be dust ignitionproof
    d.   be explosionproof

8. Where multiwire branch circuits are installed in Class II, Division 1, locations, the circuit disconnect device(s) shall open all ungrounded conductors of the multiwire circuit simultaneously.

    a.   True
    b.   False

9. Electrical metallic tubing is not permitted in _____ locations

    a.   Class III, Division 1
    b.   Class II, Division 2
    c.   Class I, Division 2
    d.   Class III, Division 2

10. Unless protected by a lead sheath, conductors in Class I locations that are exposed to condensed vapors or liquids shall be identified for use under such conditions.

    a.   True
    b.   False

11. Explosionproof conduit seals are not evaluated or suitable for the process sealing that is required in 501.15(F)(3).

    a.   True
    b.   False

12. All conduit seals installed in Class I locations are required to be explosionproof.

    a.   True
    b.   False

13. Which cables that are permitted in Class I locations is required to have boundary seals?

    a.   Cables without gas/vaportight sheath
    b.   MC-HL
    c.   MI
    d.   ITC-HL

14. The cross-sectional area of conductors generally permitted in a seal fitting is limited to ____ percent of the cross-sectional area of the conduit.

    a.   40
    b.   53
    c.   25
    d.   31

15. Sealing requirements in Class II locations are not provided for containing explosions, but to minimize the chance of communicating dust into the dust ignitionproof enclosures.

    a.   True
    b.   False

Chapter 6

Requirements for Special Occupancies

This chapter contains information on requirements related to hazardous locations for specific occupancies or portions of occupancies covered by Articles 511 through 517. In accordance with 90.3 Code Arrangement, these requirements amend, or supplement, and in many cases modify, the general requirements of chapters 1 through 4 of the *Code*.

Article 510 provides an overview detailing the arrangement of Articles 511 through 517.

As previously reviewed, Articles 500 through 504 provide the general rules for Class I, II, and III locations. Various *Code* articles also contain specific requirements for hazardous locations in special occupancies. Sometimes rules in any of these special occupancy articles modify general provisions in Articles 500 through 504 [*NEC* 510.2]. These articles provide specific designations of the hazardous (classified) locations and areas that are unclassified (see table 6-01). This chapter examines the hazardous (classified) locations for each of these occupancies and the rules that apply to electrical installations in these areas. As discussed in chapter one, area classification is not always provided in the *NEC* and a careful process must be implemented to establish each hazardous (classified) location. Sometimes this process is simple in nature, but often it is very complex.

Section 510.2 gives the authority having jurisdiction (AHJ) the responsibility of determining how the specific rules apply to any unusual conditions that exist. The AHJ should exercise great care when determining which rules to apply to unique circumstances and unusual electrical installations in hazardous locations.

Photo 6-01. Typical commercial repair garage

Commercial Garages, Repair and Storage

Article 511 applies to service and repair locations for self-propelled vehicles that use volatile flammable liquids or flammable gases for power. Examples of such fuels are gasoline, hydrogen, natural gas, and liquefied petroleum gases. Some of these materials are lighter-than-air while others are heavier-than-air, and the properties of the particular material need to be considered when determining the extent of the classified areas. Hydrocarbons, such as gasoline, are heavier-than-air; but other fuels, such as natural gas and hydrogen, are lighter-than-air. Service stations and repair shops for automobiles, buses, trucks, and tractors are included in the classified area, but facilities limited to repairing electric vehicles would not be included [*NEC,* 511.1].

The scope does not mention storage facilities but they are included in the title and other sections of the article.

For additional information see NFPA 30-2003, *Flammable and Combustible Liquids Code*, and NFPA 30A-2003, *Code for Motor Fuel Dispensing Facilities and Repair Garages*, and NFPA 88A-2002, *Standard for Parking Structures*.

Hazardous Location Occupancies in the NEC

Article 511	Commercial Garages, Repair and Storage
Article 513	Aircraft Hangars
Article 514	Motor Fuel Dispensing Facilities
Article 515	Bulk Storage Plants
Article 516	Spray Application, Dipping, and Coating Processes
Article 517	Health Care Facilities

Table 6-01. Hazardous Location Occupancies in the *NEC*

Major repair garages and minor repair garages are defined in NFPA 30A. *Major repair garages* include those where fuel tanks or fuel lines are involved in the work performed, such as during engine overhauls or other major repair operations.

Section 511.3 provides details on unclassified locations in (A) and classified locations in (B). Unclassified locations are those that are determined not to need classification [*NEC,* 500.2].

Photo 6-02. Parking garages are typically unclassified

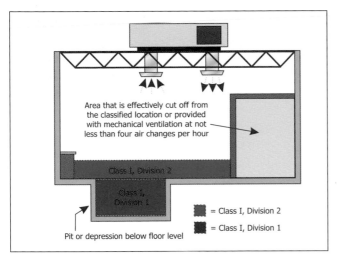

Figure 6-01. Areas effectively cut off from classified areas, or areas that are mechanically ventilated with four or more air changes per hour

Unclassified Locations

Garages used for parking or storage need not be classified if the details included in *NEC* 511.3(A)(2) through 511.3(A)(7) are followed (see photo 6-02). Two significant concerns are whether the ventilation rate is sufficient and the means of exhaust is located where any hazardous material is likely to be present [*NEC*, 511.3(A)(1)].

Storing, handling, or dispensing alcohol-based windshield washer fluid is not sufficient reason to require an area be classified [*NEC*, 511.3(A)(2)].

If adjacent areas to classified locations in commercial repair garages are mechanically ventilated at a rate of at least four or more air changes per hour, or are designed with positive air pressure, or are effectively cut off by walls or partitions, and flammable vapors are not likely to be released, classification is not required [see figure 6-01 and *NEC*, 511.3(A)(3)].

Pits, belowgrade and subfloor work areas in lubrication or service rooms are not required to be classified if exhaust ventilation is provided when the building is occupied or when vehicles are parked in or over them. Class I liquids, such as gasoline, cannot be transferred in these rooms or classification becomes necessary. The ventilation rate must be at least 0.3 m³/min/m² (1 cfm/ft²) based on the floor area, and the exhaust air *pickup point* must be not more than 12 inches above the floor level of the pit, belowgrade area, or subfloor area [*NEC*, 511.3(A)(4) and see figure 6-02].

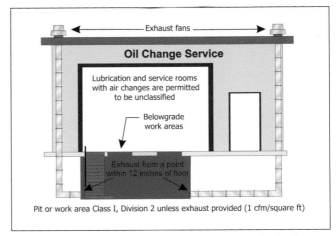

Figure 6-02. Pits or subfloor areas provided with air changes can be unclassified.

The area up to 18 inches above floor level in lubrication or service rooms is also not classified if at least four air changes per hour or one cubic foot per minute of exchange air for each square foot of floor area is provided by mechanical ventilation. This applies even where Class I liquids are transferred in the rooms [*NEC*, 511.3(A)(5)].

If flammable liquids or gasses are not transferred, those locations are unclassified. But unventilated pits, belowgrade and subfloor areas, and the area 18 inches above them are classified for heavier-than-air materials. In major repair garages, the area within 18 inches of the ceiling is also classified if unventilated and if vehicles that use gases, such as natural gas or hydrogen, are serviced [*NEC*, 511.3(A)(6) and see figure 6-03].

In ventilated major repair garages, such as those involving work on fuel lines or fuel tanks and where fuel

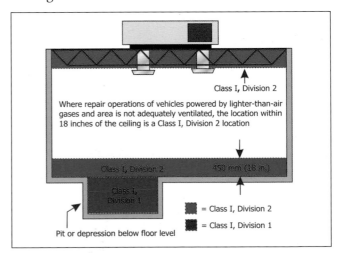

Figure 6-03. Classified areas near the ceiling where not adequately ventilated

is lighter-than-air, such as natural gas or hydrogen, the area within 18 inches of the ceiling is unclassified. To maintain this classification, however, the ventilation rate must be at least 1 cubic foot per minute per square foot of ceiling area and be taken within 18 inches of the ceiling's highest point [*NEC*, 511.3(A)(7)].

Classified Locations

If flammable fuel is dispensed into vehicle fuel tanks, those areas must comply with Article 514 as motor fuel dispensing facilities [*NEC*, 511.3(B)(1)].

In lubrication or service rooms, even if flammable fuels are not transferred, unventilated areas that can collect liquids or vapors, such as pits and the space 18 inches above and within 3 feet horizontally of those areas, must be classified [*NEC*, 511.3(B)(2)].

In lubrication or service rooms where flammable fuels are transferred, certain areas must be classified.

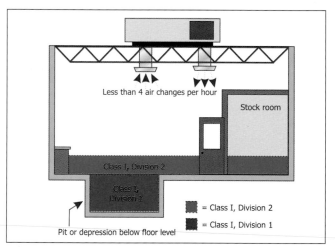

Figure 6-04. Pits or depressions below floor levels are Class I, Division 1 locations.

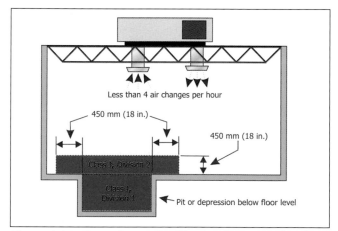

Figure 6-05. General area classification for unventilated service rooms extends to 450 mm (18 in.) above the finished floor and extends out 900 mm (3 ft) from the pit.

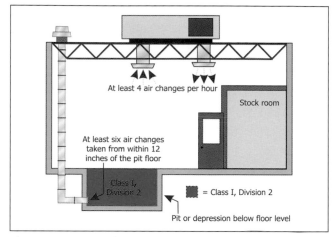

Figure 6-06. Pits with ventilation within 12 inches of the floor of the pit are permitted to be Class I, Division 2 locations

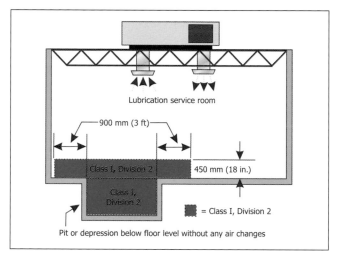

Figure 6-07. Pit and area 450 mm (18 in.) above pit and floor is classified as Class I, Division 2, extending out 900 mm (3 ft) in all directions from the pit opening.

Class I, Division 1

Unventilated depressions, such as pits up to the floor level, are generally classified as Class I, Division 1 locations (see figure 6-04).

In commercial repair garages where vehicles that use lighter-than-air gases—such as natural gas or hydrogen—are repaired, the space within 450 mm (18 in.) of a ceiling is a Class I, Division 2 location [*NEC*, 511.3(B)(4)]. However, if ventilation of at least 1 cfm/sq ft of ceiling area is provided from a point within 450 mm (18 in.) of the highest point in the ceiling, the area is considered unclassified [*NEC*, 511.3(A)(7)].

Class I, Division 2

The area up to 18 inches above each floor level is generally classified as a Class I, Division 2 location unless adequate ventilation is provided (see figure 6-05).

Pits ventilated at a rate of six air changes per hour with the means of exhaust within 12 inches of the pit floor are classified as Class I, Division 2 locations (see figure 6-06).

The space above unventilated pits up to 18 inches above the floor and extending out three feet is a Class I, Division 2 location (see figure 6-07).

For flammable dispensers for liquids other than fuels, the space within three feet of the fill or dispensing point is a Class I, Division 2 location [*NEC*, 511.3(B)(3)].

Major repair garages where vehicles use lighter-than-air fuels must be classified Class I Division 2 if they do not have sufficient ventilation [*NEC*, 511.3(B)(4)].

Wiring and Equipment in Class I Locations

Wiring and equipment in areas classified as covered in 511.3 must be installed using the portions of Article 501 that apply. If fuel dispensers are located in

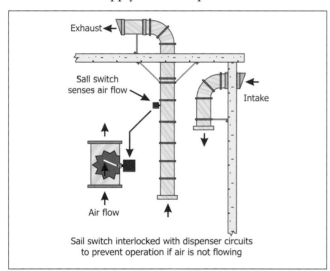

Figure 6-08. Sail switch or pressure differential switch used for mechanical ventilation interlocking to fuel dispensing equipment circuits.

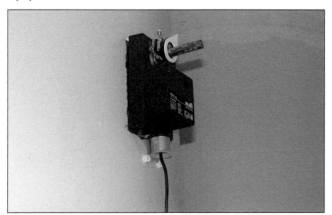

Photo 6-03. Sail (air flow) switch installed in air exhaust duct

a building, Article 514 applies. Any mechanical ventilation for the dispensing area must be interlocked so that no dispensing can occur without ventilation. Verifying actual air movement ensures that a broken belt does not stop air movement. This is usually accomplished by installing a sail switch or pressure differential switch within the duct (see figure 6-08 and photo 6-03).

Portable lighting must be identified for use in a Class I Division 1 location, unless the lamp and cord are installed in such a way that they cannot be used in the classified location. A handle, suitable lampholder, hook, and substantial guard must be included. The exterior surface must be either nonconductive or insulated, and switches or receptacles are not permitted.

Wiring and Equipment Above Class I Locations

Spaces above classified locations have special requirements that limit the types of wiring methods and equipment permitted because sparks could fall and ignite any flammable atmospheres present.

Cellular metal floor raceways and cellular concrete floor raceways may be used to supply ceiling outlets or equipment below the floor, but these raceways cannot have any connection to a classified location above the floor. Pendants must use flexible cord listed for hard usage [*NEC*, 511.7(A)].

Fixed equipment must be located above the level of the classified area or be identified for that location. Any equipment that could release sparks, arcs or hot particles must be totally enclosed or otherwise be able to contain the hot particles. Fixed lighting must be at least 12 feet above floor level or be equipped to contain any hot particles if subject to physical damage [*NEC*, 511.7(B) and see figure 6-09 and photo 6-04].

Conduit Sealing

Seals for enclosures and all boundaries must be provided in conduits and cable systems in accordance with 501.15 and 501.15(B)(2) [*NEC*, 511.9].

Special Equipment

Batteries, battery charging equipment and their controls must not be located in classified locations [*NEC*, 511.10(A)].

Photo 6-04. Commercial repair garage showing luminaires installed to meet the minimum height requirements in 511.7(B)

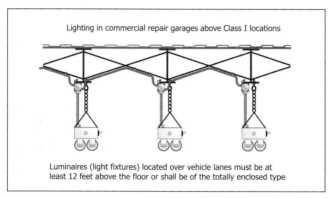

Lighting in commercial repair garages above Class I locations

Luminaires (light fixtures) located over vehicle lanes must be at least 12 feet above the floor or shall be of the totally enclosed type

Figure 6-09. Fixed lighting above vehicle lanes must be at least 12 feet above the floor, or be of an enclosed type, or be equipped to contain hot particles.

Electrical vehicle charging equipment has some additional requirements in Article 625 that must be followed. All flexible cords must be identified for extra-hard usage, and connectors must not be in the classified locations. Cords for vehicle plug connections must not be allowed to sag closer than 6 inches above the floor, if the cord is suspended. An additional connector is not necessary if automatic means are provided to pull the cord and plug from where they are exposed to physical damage [*NEC*, 511.10(B)].

Ground-Fault Circuit Interrupter (GFCI) Protection for Personnel

GFCI protection is required for all 15- and 20-ampere 125-volt receptacles for certain equipment. This

protection can be provided by either breaker-type or receptacle-type GFCI devices. Class A GFCI devices are listed to UL Standard 943 and are defined in Article 100. Frequent flexing of cords and the type of use associated with vehicle repair warrant additional protection for these receptacles. Where vehicles are insulated from the ground by rubber tires, the possibilities of vehicles becoming energized and presenting shock and electrocution hazards are amplified. GFCI protection for receptacles in these work areas provides security from these hazards [see figure 6-10 and *NEC*, 511.12].

Grounding and Bonding Requirements

Essentially all normally non-current-carrying metal parts of electrical equipment must be grounded as provided in Article 250. This applies to all voltage levels because of the concern for igniting flammable atmospheres due to any arcing or sparks generated [*NEC*, 511.16(A)].

The specific grounding and bonding provisions of 501.30 must also be followed. These more restrictive bonding rules apply to all intervening metal raceways all the way back to the supply service or source point of grounding within the building or structure. [See chapter 2 for specific grounding and bonding requirements in hazardous (classified) locations]. Grounding type devices must be used for portable equipment and pendants that include a grounded conductor, and the grounded conductor

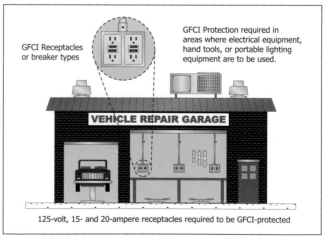

GFCI Receptacles or breaker types

GFCI Protection required in areas where electrical equipment, hand tools, or portable lighting equipment are to be used.

VEHICLE REPAIR GARAGE

125-volt, 15- and 20-ampere receptacles required to be GFCI-protected

Figure 6-10. GFCI protection is required for all 125-volt, 15- and 20-ampere receptacles in commercial repair garages.

Hazardous Locations

Photo 6-05. Typical aircraft hangar for servicing commercial aircraft

of the flexible cord must always be connected to the screw shell of the lampholder. Equipment grounding continuity must be maintained between the non-current-carrying metal parts of portable equipment and the fixed wiring system [*NEC*, 511.16(B)].

Aircraft Hangars

Article 513 applies to buildings or structures where aircraft might be serviced, repaired or stored (see photos 6-05 and 6-06). The aircraft must contain, or have contained, flammable or combustible liquids at temperatures sufficient to form an ignitible mixture. This article does not cover locations used for unfueled aircraft. NFPA 409, *Standard on Aircraft Hangars*, defines an *unfueled aircraft* as one that has had the flammable or combustible liquid removed so no part of the fuel system contains more than 1/2 percent of its volumetric capacity. The Division and Zone systems are both permitted for classification of aircraft hangars [*NEC*, 513.1]. For additional information see NFPA 409, *Standard on Aircraft Hangars* and NFPA 30, *Flammable and Combustible Liquids Code*.

Photo 6-06. Smaller "T" hangar for small aircraft

REQUIREMENTS FOR SPECIAL OCCUPANCIES

Definitions are included for specific equipment with electric components. *Portable equipment* can be moved by a single person without mechanical aids. *Mobile equipment* needs mechanical aids or wheels to be moved by persons or powered devices [*NEC*, 513.2].

Classification of Locations

Class I, Division 1 or Zone 1
Unventilated depressions, such as pits, up to the hangar floor level are classified as a Class I, Division 1 or Zone 1 location.

Class I, Division 2 or Zone 2
All of the hangar not suitably cut off is Class I, Division 2 or Zone 2 up to 18 inches above the floor. This includes adjacent and communicating areas (see figure 6-11).

Areas from the floor to five feet above the engine enclosures and upper wing surfaces, and those areas five feet horizontally from the aircraft power plants or aircraft fuel tanks are Class I, Division 2, or Zone 2 locations (see figure 6-11).

Unclassified Areas
Adjacent areas are not classified if adequately ventilated and effectively separated from the hangar by walls or partitions. These areas include stock rooms and electrical control rooms in which flammable liquids or vapors are not likely to be released. Adequate ventilation prevents significant concentrations from exceeding 25 percent of the lower flammable limit of the particular material present, as covered in NFPA 497, *Recommended Practice for the Classification of Flammable Liquids, Gases, or Vapors and of Hazardous (Classified) Locations*

for Electrical Installations in Chemical Process Areas.

Wiring and Equipment in Class I Locations
Locations that have or may have flammable gases or vapors present in quantities sufficient to produce explosive or ignitible mixtures are defined as Class I locations in 500.5 and 505.5.

Wiring and equipment installed or operated in those Class I locations described in 513.3 must comply with Article 501 or 505, depending on which classification system is used. Attachment plugs and receptacles must either be designed so connections cannot be made while the devices are energized, or be identified for use in the hazardous locations [*NEC*, 513.4(A)].

Articles 501 and 505 must also be applied to electrical equipment mounted on or attached to framework and structures used for inspecting or repairing aircraft. This includes stanchions, rostrums, and docks [*NEC*, 513.4(B)].

Wiring and Equipment Not Installed in Class I Locations
Fixed wiring installed in a hangar but not in a hazardous location is limited to metal raceways, mineral-insulated cable, tray cable, or metal-clad cable. An exception allows any wiring method included in chapter 3 of the *NEC* for areas suitably cutoff and adequately ventilated [*NEC*, 513.7(A)].

Flexible cord used for pendants must include a separate equipment grounding conductor and be identified for hard usage or extra-hard usage [*NEC*, 513.7(B)].

Spaces above those areas classified as hazardous have additional requirements for arcing equipment.

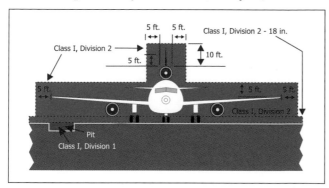

Figure 6-11. Typical aircraft hangar area classification based on classified areas designated in Section 513.3. Concept derived from *NEC Handbook* Exhibit 513.1

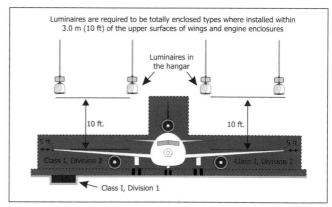

Figure 6-12. Luminaires are required to be totally enclosed types where installed within 10 ft of the upper surfaces of aircraft wings in hangars.

Hazardous Locations

This type of electrical equipment within ten feet of the upper surface of wings and engine enclosures shall be totally enclosed or constructed to keep sparks or hot metal particles from escaping (see figure 6-12).

Lamps and lampholders for fixed lighting, cutouts, switches, receptacles, charging panels, generators, motors, or other equipment having make-and-break or sliding contacts are included in the types covered by this section. An exception allows general-purpose enclosures, such as NEMA Type 1, in areas suitably cutoff and adequately ventilated [*NEC*, 513.7(C)]. See the annex for additional detailed information about the various types for electrical enclosures, NEMA enclosure types, and their uses.

Fixed lighting cannot contain lampholders that have metal shells with fiber liners [*NEC*, 513.7(D)].

If stanchions, rostrums and docks will not be within or near hazardous locations, then associated equipment does not have to be specifically rated. Stanchions, rostrums, or docks cannot be located or be likely to be located five feet horizontally from the aircraft power plants or aircraft fuel tanks, including the area from the floor to five feet above the engine enclosures and upper wing surfaces. Equipment still has to be limited to that specified in 513.7. All wiring within 18 inches of the floor must be suitable for the location as covered in Article 501 or Article 505. Only locking type attachment plugs and receptacles are allowed to be used, so that they will not be readily disconnected [*NEC*, 513.7(E)].

Mobile stanchions must have a permanent sign warning persons to keep the stanchion five feet from

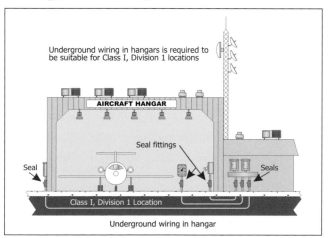

Figure 6-13. Underground wiring installed at aircraft hangars must meet the requirements of Article 501.

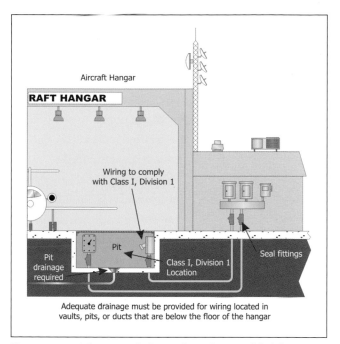

Figure 6-14. Adequate drainage is to be provided in accordance with 513.8(A).

aircraft engines and fuel tank areas. Mobile equipment needs mechanical aids or wheels to facilitate being moved by persons or powered devices as defined in 513.2 [*NEC*, 513.7(F)].

Underground Wiring

Wiring and equipment in the floor (slab), under it, or underground must be suitable for Class I Division 1 in accordance with Article 501. This also applies to uninterrupted raceways, even where they extend above or below the floor [*NEC*, 513.8 and see figure 6-13].

If wiring is located in pits, vaults, or ducts at the floor level, adequate drainage is to be provided (see figure 6-14).

Sealing Requirements

Seals for enclosures and all boundaries must be provided in conduits and cable systems in accordance with 501.15 or 505.16 [*NEC*, 513.9].

Special Equipment

Aircraft electrical systems cannot be energized when aircraft is stored in hangars. Also, during maintenance the electrical systems must not be energized, if possible. Some testing or troubleshooting activities are examples of when systems might need to be energized [*NEC*, 513.10(A)(1)].

Whenever aircraft are within hangars or even partially within hangars, the aircraft batteries may not be charged [*NEC*, 513.10(A)(2)].

It is preferred that battery chargers and their control equipment be located in separate buildings or in adjacent areas not classified because of adequate ventilation and effective separation as specified in 513.3(D). Battery chargers and their control equipment, tables, racks, trays, and wiring cannot be located in the classified locations described in 513.3. Tables, racks, trays, and wiring additionally must be in accordance with Article 480 for storage batteries. Mobile battery chargers must have a permanent sign warning persons to keep the stanchion five feet from aircraft engines and fuel tank areas. *Mobile equipment* is defined, in 513.2, as needing mechanical aids or wheels to facilitate its being moved by persons or powered devices [*NEC*, 513.10(B)].

Mobile energizers must have a permanent sign warning persons to keep the stanchion 5 feet from aircraft engines and fuel tank areas [*NEC*, 513.10(C)(2)].

Flexible cords associated with aircraft energizers must: (1) be suitable for the type of service, (2) be of the extra-hard usage type, and (3) include an equipment grounding conductor. Included in these restrictions are flexible cords used for energizers and those that connect to ground support equipment [*NEC*, 513.10(C)(3)].

Electrically powered mobile equipment, such as vacuum cleaners, air compressors, and air movers, used for servicing aircraft must either be installed (designed and mounted) so all fixed wiring and equipment is more than 18 inches above the floor or be suitable for that location. Mobile equipment must have a permanent sign warning persons to keep the stanchion five feet from aircraft engines and fuel

tank areas [*NEC*, 513.10(D)(1)].

Flexible cords associated with mobile equipment must: (1) be suitable for the type of service, (2) be of the extra-hard usage type, and (3) include an equipment grounding conductor. All attachment plugs and receptacles must be identified as being suitable for the location they are used in. They must also include connections for the equipment grounding conductor [*NEC*, 513.10(D)(2)].

Any equipment not judged suitable for a Division 2 location is not to be operated where or when maintenance likely cause a release of flammable liquids of vapors is taking place [*NEC*, 513.10(D)(3)].

Portable equipment is defined in 513.2 as suitable of being moved by a person without mechanical aids. All portable lighting equipment used in hangars must be identified for the particular location it is used in. Flexible cords for portable lamps must: (1) be suitable for the type of service, (2) be of the extra-hard usage type, and (3) include an equipment grounding conductor [*NEC*, 513.10(E)(1)].

All portable utilization equipment used in a hangar must be suitable for Class I, Division 2 or Zone 2 locations, depending on the classification system used.

Flexible cords for portable utilization equipment must also: (1) be suitable for the type of service, (2) be of the extra-hard usage type, and (3) include an equipment grounding conductor [*NEC*, 513.10(E)(2)].

Ground-Fault Circuit Interrupter (GFCI) Protection for Personnel

GFCI protection is required for 15- and 20-ampere, 50/60-Hz, single-phase, 125-volt receptacles where electrical diagnostic equipment, electrical hand tools, or portable lighting equipment are used. The frequent flexing of cords and type of use associated with the repair of aircraft warrants additional protection for these receptacles. Only 50- and 60-Hz receptacles are covered in this section because other frequencies, such as 400 Hz, are used associated with aircraft [*NEC*, 513.12 and see figure 6-15].

Grounding and Bonding Requirements

Essentially all normally non-current-carrying metal parts of electrical equipment must be grounded as

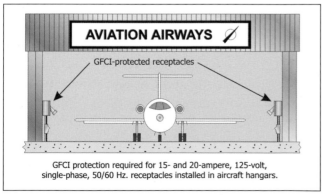

Figure 6-15. GFCI protection is required for 125-volt, single-phase, 15- and 20-ampere receptacles operating at 50/60 hertz.

Hazardous Locations

Photo 6-10. Typical propane (LPG) dispensing equipment

Photo 6-07. Grounding (bonding) bushings and jumpers installed to meet the more restrictive bonding requirements specified in 501.30 and 250.100

provided in Article 250. This applies to all voltage levels because of the concern for igniting flammable atmospheres due to any arcing or sparks generated. The specific grounding provisions of 501.30 or 505.25, depending on which classification system is used, must also be followed. This applies all the way back to the supply source within the building or structure [*NEC*, 513.16(A)]. Photo 6-07 shows bonding methods that meet the requirements of 501.30.

Grounding type devices must be used for portable equipment and pendants that include a grounded conductor in hazardous locations. The grounded conductor must be connected to the screw shell of the lampholder. Equipment grounding continuity must be maintained for the non-current-carrying metal parts of portable equipment to the fixed wiring system [*NEC*, 513.16(B)].

Motor Fuel Dispensing Facilities

Article 514 applies to facilities where fuel dispensing occurs. Previously, the title of this article was limited to gasoline, but because of the variety of fuels used it was changed to broaden the scope (see photos 6-08, 6-09, and 6-10). Gasoline stations, propane dispensing stations, watercraft (marine) fueling stations, and group (fleet) fueling stations are included [*NEC*, 514.1]. For additional information see NFPA 30A-2003, *Code for Motor Fuel Dispensing Facilities and Repair Garages*.

The definition of a *motor fuel dispensing facility* includes the concept of fuel storage in conjunction with fuel dispensing. Fixed equipment is used to dispense fuel into the tanks of vehicles or marine craft or into approved containers. This definition is extracted from NFPA 30A, which provides consistency between that code and the *NEC* [*NEC*, 514.2].

A fine print note refers to Articles 510 and 511 for additional information on other areas such as lubritoriums, service rooms, repair rooms, salesrooms, compressor rooms and similar locations.

Classification of Locations

If flammable liquids with a flash point below 100°F are not used or dispensed (handled), the authority having jurisdiction (AHJ) may determine that the area can be unclassified. Combustible liquids, such as diesel fuel, are not flammable liquids because they do not give off sufficient vapor to form an ignitible mixture with the air (at normal temperatures) hence the AHJ may not require classification. The AHJ in this case is typically not the electrical inspector; it may be a fire marshall, other governmental official, or other designated entity. Many times a group determines the classifications instead of just one individual [*NEC*, 514.3(A)].

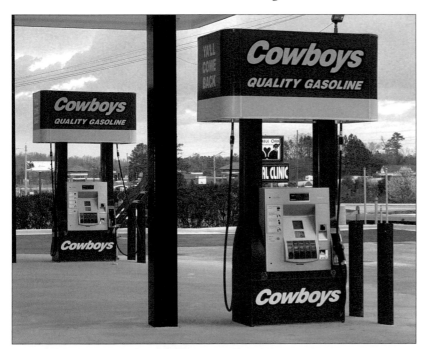

Photo 6-08. Typical motor fuel dispensing (gasoline and diesel) facility

Requirements for Special Occupancies

Where flammable liquids are stored, handled or dispensed, *NEC* Table 514.3(B)(1) is to be used in determining the extent of the classification. This table also includes details for areas and equipment in commercial garages used for repair and storage as covered by Article 511. The extent of classification ends at an unpierced wall, roof or other solid partition. *NEC* Table 515.3 is to be used when classifying locations for aboveground tanks. The information in this section and table is extracted from NFPA 30A, *Code for Motor Fuel Dispensing Facilities and Repair Garages* [*NEC*, 514.3(B)].

Table 514.3(B)(1) contains typical equipment used at motor fuel dispensing facilities, and the classification and extent of the classified location for Group D materials. Included are underground tanks; dispensing devices; remote pumps; lubrication or service rooms; special enclosures inside buildings; sales, storage, and rest rooms; and vapor processing systems. For marine applications, *grade level* is described as the surface of a pier down to the water level. An FPN in the table provides information that the space inside a dispenser is covered in ANSI/UL 87, *Power-Operated Dispensing Devices for Petroleum Products*. Figure 6-16 graphically

Photo 6-09. Compressed natural gas (CNG) fuel dispensing facility

illustrates the classified area associated with gasoline dispensers.

Table 6-02 provides a general overview of the various hazardous (classified) locations associated with gasoline motor fuel dispensing facilities. Review *NEC* Table 514.3(B)(1) for specific details.

Figures 6-17 through 6-20 and photos 6-11 through 6-13 illustrate the various classified locations provided in Table 514.3(B)(1) associated with motor fuel dispensing facilities. Figures 6-17 and 6-18 show the classified location at standard and high-hose types of gasoline fuel dispensers (see photos 6-11 and 6-12). Figures 6-19 and 6-20 show the classified areas associated with underground tank fill points (points of transfer) and underground fuel tank vents (see photos 6-12 and 6-13).

Where compressed natural gas, liquefied natural gas, and liquefied petroleum gas are stored, handled or dispensed, *NEC* Table 514.3(B)(2) is to be used in determining the extent of the classification. A choice can be made where a canopy or enclosure is above compressed natural gas or liquefied natural gas dispensers. Either the canopy or enclosure has to be designed to prevent ignitible vapors from accumulating or becoming entrapped or all electrical equipment must be suitable for a Class I Division 2 location. Natural gas, which consists primarily of methane, is considerably lighter-than-air and will rise and collect under any enclosing structures. Liquefied petroleum gas dispensers must be located at least five feet from dispensing devices for flammable liquids. Propane is a hydrocarbon and is, therefore, heavier-than-air. The information in this section and table is extracted from NFPA 30A.

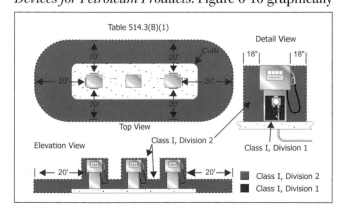

Figure 6-16. Typical hazardous locations associated with gasoline motor fuel dispensing facilities

Table 6-02. Class I Motor Fuel Dispensing Facilities

Class I, Division 1

Location	Extent of Classification
Pits and boxes	Any part within the classified location
Remote outdoor pumps	Within 10 feet horizontally of the pump
Open vent	All space within 3 feet
Dispenser enclosures	All space within enclosure
Equipment enclosures	Where liquid or vapor is normally present within

Class I, Division 2

Location	Extent of Classification
Underground tank, loose fill connection	Up to 18 inches above grade, 10 feet horizontally
Underground tank, tight fill connection	5 feet horizontally
Open vent	Space between 3 and 5 feet in all directions
Dispenser enclosures	Within 18 inches horizontally down to grade level
Dispensing device — indoor with mechanical ventilation	Up to 18 inches above grade and 20 feet horizontally of any edge
Dispensing device — indoor with gravity ventilation	Horizontal dimension extends to 25 feet
Outdoor remote pumps	3 feet in all directions from the pump edge and 10 feet horizontally up to 18 inches above grade
Indoor remote pumps	5 feet in all directions from the pump edge and 25 feet horizontally up to 3 feet above grade.
Lubrication or service room where flammable liquids could be released	Entire unventilated area in all pits, belowgrade and subfloor areas, and 3 feet horizontally from those "subsurface areas" up to 18 inches vertically.
Vapor processing equipment located within protective housings	Within 18 inches in all directions to grade level out to 10 feet
Vacuum-assist blowers above grade out to 10	Within 18 inches in all directions to grade level and 18 inches feet horizontally

Unclassified Areas Location	Extent of Classification
Lubrication or service rooms without dispensing Pits that have at least 1 cubic feet per minute per square foot of floor area of exhaust ventilation.	The ventilation must be operational when the building is occupied or when vehicles are parked in the building. The exhaust intake must be located within 12 inches of the floor of the pit, belowgrade work area or subfloor work area
Sales, storage, and rest rooms	Unless there is any opening to an area classified as Division 1, then the entire room must be classified Division 1

Table 6-02. Class I Locations, Motor Fuel Dispensing Facilities for gasoline

Photo 6-11. Typical motor fuel dispensers for gasoline (standard type)

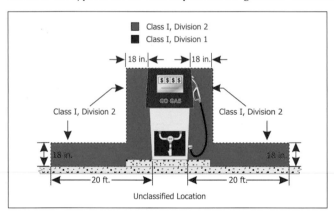

Figure 6-17. Classified locations at typical gasoline dispenser (standard type)

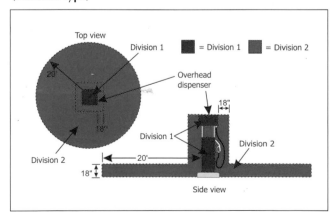

Figure 6-18. Classified locations at typical gasoline dispenser (high-hose style)

Photo 6-12. Typical motor fuel dispenser for gasoline (high-hose style)

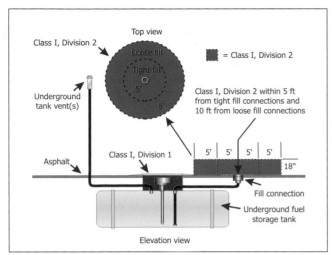

Figure 6-19. Classified locations at underground fuel tank fill locations (points of fuel transfer)

Photo 6-13. Point of transfer showing a tight fill connection between mobile vessel and underground fuel storage tanks

Photo 6-14. Typical underground fuel storage tank vents located in close proximity to a pole-mounted luminaire (lighting fixture)

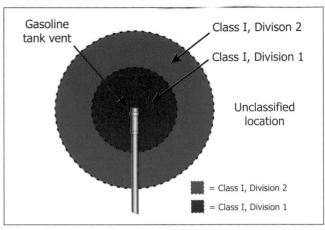

Figure 6-20. Classified locations at underground tank vents

Fine print notes provide informational references to NFPA 58, *Liquefied Petroleum Gas Code*, NFPA 59, *Utility Liquefied Petroleum Gas Code*, and 555.21 for motor fuel dispensers in marinas and boatyards. At marinas and boatyards, power and lighting installed on wharfs, piers, and docks must be on the opposite side from the liquid piping system.

Table 6-03 provides a general overview. Review *NEC* Table 514.3(B)(2) for specific details.

Figure 6-21 and photos 6-15 through 6-20 illustrate the various classified locations provided in Table 514.3(B)(2) associated with motor fuel dispensing facilities for compressed natural gas, liquefied natural gas, and liquefied petroleum gas. Figure 6-21 shows the area classification associated with a compressed natural gas dispenser (see photo 6-18). Photos 6-15 and 6-16 show mobile and permanently installed liquefied natural gas (LNG) dispensers; and photo 6-17 shows a typical liquefied petroleum gas (LPG) dispenser. Photos 6-18 through 6-20 are of typical compressed natural gas (CNG) equipment showing the compressor and storage tanks and associated control equipment.

Wiring and Equipment Installed in Class I Locations
Equipment and wiring in locations classified as provided in 514.3 must be installed using Article 501, except for underground wiring that is installed in accordance with 514.8.

Section 501.20 requires conductor insulation to be suitable for the material it will be exposed to, such as gasoline. Where circuits are installed for motor fuel dispensing equipment, the conductors

Table 6-03. Electrical Equipment Classified Areas for Dispensing Devices

Class I, Division 1 Location	Extent of Classification
Compressed natural gas	Entire space within dispenser enclosures
Liquefied natural gas	5 feet in all directions from the dispenser enclosure
Liquefied petroleum gas	18 inches from the dispenser enclosure up to 4 feet above the dispenser base. All of the pit or open space below the dispenser out to 20 feet, if the pit or trench is not mechanically ventilated

Class I, Division 2 Location	Extent of Classification
Compressed natural gas	5 feet in all directions from the dispenser enclosure
Liquefied natural gas	Space between 5 feet and 10 feet from the dispenser enclosure
Liquefied petroleum gas	18 inches above ground and 20 feet horizontally from the dispenser enclosure. Pits and trenches are included in this classification if they are provided with adequate ventilation. Adequate ventilation prevents the significant concentrations from exceeding 25 percent of the lower flammable limit of the particular material present as covered in NFPA 497, *Recommended Practice for the Classification of flammable Liquids, Gases, or Vapors and of Hazardous (Classified) Locations for Electrical Installations in Chemical Process Areas.*

Table 6-03. Class I Locations, Electrical Equipment Classified Areas for Dispensing Devices for compressed natural gas (CNG), liquefied natural gas (LNG) and liquefied petroleum gas (LPG)

are generally gasoline-resistant and oil-resistant and are so identified [*NEC*, 514.4] (see photo 6-21).

Wiring and Equipment Above Class I Locations
This section requires that installations above classified locations comply with the requirements in 511.7, which covers commercial garages. These are as follows:

• Spaces above classified locations have special requirements that limit the types of wiring methods and equipment permitted, because sparks could fall and ignite any flammable atmospheres present.

• Cellular metal floor raceways and cellular concrete floor raceways may be used to supply ceiling outlets or equipment below the floor, but they cannot have any connection to a classified location above the floor. Pendants must use flexible cord listed for hard usage [*NEC*, 511.7(A)].

• Fixed equipment must be located above the level of the classified area or be identified for that location. Any equipment that could release sparks,

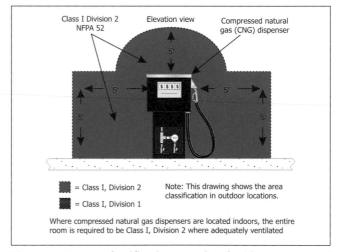

Figure 6-21. Area classification associated with a compressed natural gas (CNG) dispenser

arcs or hot particles must be totally enclosed or otherwise designed to contain the hot particles. If subject to physical damage, fixed lighting must be at least 12 feet above floor level or constructed to contain hot particles [*NEC*, 511.7(B) and see photos 6-22 and 6-23].

Photo 6-15. Liquefied natural gas (LNG) dispenser (mobile type)

Photo 6-16. Liquefied natural gas (LNG) dispenser (permanently installed) showing LNG storage facility being constructed in the background

Photo 6-17. Typical liquefied petroleum gas (LPG) dispenser and bulk storage tank

Photo 6-18. Compressed natural gas (CNG) dispenser showing compressor and storage tanks in the background

Photo 6-19. Natural gas compressing equipment (electrical motor-driven) and storage tanks

Photo 6-20. Compressed natural gas (CNG) dispenser showing compressor (combustion engine type) in the background

Photo 6-21. Conductors used for wiring at motor fuel dispensing facilities are required to be suitable for exposure to gasoline. Conductors installed at motor fuel dispensing equipment are to be gasoline- and oil-resistant.

Photo 6-22. Typical canopy and luminaires (light fixtures) over gasoline dispensing equipment must meet the requirements in 511.7(B). Note that the installation meets the requirements for height and total enclosure type.

Underground Wiring for Motor
Fuel Dispensing Facilities

In general, only threaded rigid metal conduit or threaded steel intermediate conduit are allowed below the surface of motor fuel dispensing classified areas. A seal is required within 10 feet of where the conduit emerges above grade. Only explosionproof reducers are permitted at the conduit seal; no other fittings, including couplings, are permitted between the seal and grade. Explosionproof reducers are sometimes used with larger trade size sealing fittings. Standard sealing fittings have only a 25 percent fill

Photo 6-23. Totally enclosed luminaires (light fixtures) in canopy over motor fuel dispensers

capacity, which limits the number of conductors in a conduit to less than the 40 percent generally permitted for over two conductors. In the past, the area below a classified location was classified with no lower boundary. That concept has changed, because the basis for classifying an area is dependent on sufficient quantities of an ignitible concentration of a material in air. The space belowgrade is concrete, earth, or some other material—not air—so it should not be possible for there to be an ignitible mixture.

Exception one allows mineral-insulated cable. This is a metal-sheathed cable, typically resembling copper tubing, with a highly compressed refractory mineral insulation.

Exception two allows rigid nonmetallic conduit if buried below 24 inches of cover. Cover includes earth, concrete, and so forth, from finished grade to the top surface of the conduit as stated in a note to *NEC* Table 300.5. Threaded rigid metal conduit or threaded steel intermediate conduit must be used for the last 24 inches before it emerges abovegrade. An equipment grounding conductor is required to ensure continu-

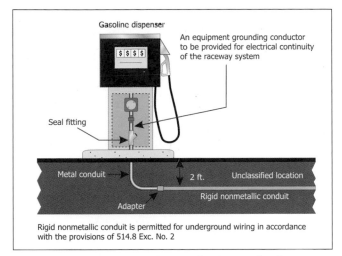

Figure 6-22. Rigid nonmetallic conduit is permitted as an underground wiring method for motor fuel dispensing facilities in accordance with 514.8.

ity of the raceway system and to provide an effective ground-fault path for the connected electrical equipment [*NEC*, 514.8 and see figure 6-22].

Conduit Sealing

Seals must be listed and be located in every conduit connected to a dispenser or any other directly connected enclosure. They must be the first fitting abovegrade as the conduit emerges to connect to the dispensing equipment. Seals are also required at all vertical and horizontal boundaries of classified locations [*NEC*, 514.9 and see figures 6-23 and 6-24 and photos 24 and 25].

Circuit Disconnects

A means to disconnect all conductors of all circuits of dispensing equipment and remote pumping systems

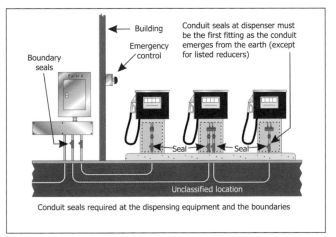

Figure 6-23. Conduit seals are required at dispensers and at boundaries.

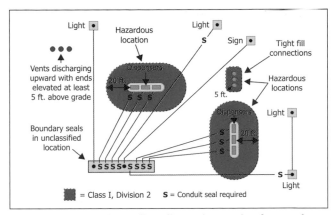

Figure 6-24. Typical gasoline dispensing station layout showing locations where conduit seals are required Concept is derived from Appleton EGS Electrical Group and NFPA 70 *Handbook* Exhibit 514.5

Photo 6-24. Sealing fittings are shown in conduits emerging from the earth at a gasoline dispenser.

Photo 6-25. Sealing fittings are shown on conduits at the boundary (emerging from the earth) in a building for termination to electrical system.

must be installed at a readily accessible place. *Readily accessible* (accessible, readily) is defined in Article 100 and means capable of being reached quickly without having to climb over or remove obstacles or use portable ladders. The maximum height above the floor is usually limited to 6 feet 7 inches as covered in 404.8(A). This disconnecting means must actually disconnect all circuit conductors at the same time. If a grounded conductor (may be a neutral) is present, it must also be disconnected by the same device. Handle ties on single-pole circuit breakers are not to be used for this purpose. The disconnect requirements in this section are permitted to open dispenser(s) and, if used, remote pump(s) circuits individually or collectively. The disconnecting means must clearly indicate its purpose [*NEC*, 514.11(A) and see figure 6-25 and photos 6-26 and 6-27].

Emergency Controls

In addition to the circuit disconnect required in 514.11(A), emergency controls that will disconnect all power for all dispensing equipment at the station is required by 514.11(B) or (C). This emergency control

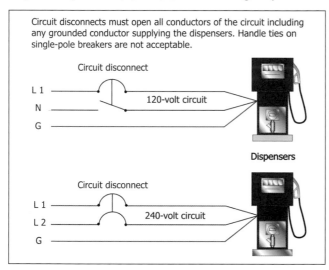

Figure 6-25. Circuit disconnects are required to open all conductors of the circuit, including any grounded conductor.

Photo 6-26. Panelboard with neutral-break circuit breakers to comply with 514.11(A)

Photo 6-27. Circuit breakers that open the grounded conductor to comply with 514.11(A)

is also required to remove all sources of supply and all conductors, including the grounded conductor. The location of the emergency control depends on whether the motor fuel dispensing facility is attended or unattended. The control device in these sections is required to provide a means to disconnect all of the power to all of the dispensing equipment collectively in the event of an emergency. That location is also required to be approved by an authority having jurisdiction and that authority is probably someone other than the electrical inspector

Attended Self-Service Motor Fuel Dispensing Facilities

The emergency disconnecting means control must be within 100 feet of the dispensers and be located where acceptable to the authority having jurisdiction (see figure 6-26 and photos 6-28 and 6-29). The disconnecting means is required to be readily accessible to the attendant by 6.7.1 of NFPA 30A, *Code for Motor Fuel Dispensing Facilities and Repair Garages* [*NEC*, 514.11(B)].

Unattended Self-Service Motor Fuel Dispensing Facilities

For self-service motor fuel dispensing facilities that have no attendant, the disconnecting means control must also be within 100 feet of the dispensers but not closer than 20 feet (see figure 6-27 and photo 6-30). The disconnecting means is required to be readily accessible to the patrons by 6.7.2 of NFPA 30A, *Code for Motor Fuel Dispensing Facilities and Repair Garages*. If there are groups of dispensers, additional emergency controls must be located on each group or on the outdoor equipment that it controls. The manner of manually resetting the emergency control must be approved by the authority having jurisdiction [*NEC*, 514.11(C)].

There are a few common methods of providing

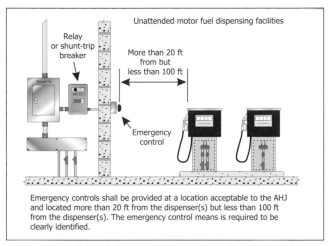

Figure 6-27. Emergency controls are required less than 100 feet of dispensers but not closer than 20 feet, where unattended.

emergency controls for motor fuel dispensing facilities. For those that include only a single fuel dispenser and the pump is included in the dispenser, the emergency control might be provided by a properly located single switching device that may also meet the circuit disconnect requirement in 511.14(A). Other larger facilities are more complex and involve the use of a shunt-trip breaker or contactor for a whole panel that supplies multiple dispenser and remote pump branch circuits. It should be emphasized that the emergency controls are for emergency disconnecting purposes, such as a fire or major leaks in the fuel system and require that all equipment that could supply fuel in that event and all circuits that could provide an ignition source be disconnected simultaneously.

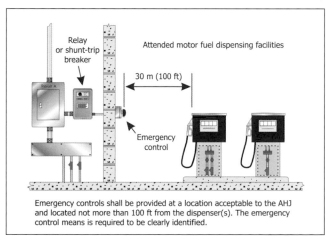

Figure 6-26. Emergency controls are required within 100 feet of dispensers, where attended.

Provisions for Maintenance and Service of Dispensing Equipment

A means to remove all external voltages, including those used for feedback, during maintenance and servicing purposes must be available for each dispenser. The means must be capable of being locked in the open (off) position and may be located other than within or adjacent to the dispensing device [*NEC*, 514.13 and see figure 6-28 and photo 6-31].

This requirement is written in objective rather than prescriptive terms. That objective is to ensure that ALL voltage is removed and prohibited from occurring while a

Photo 6-28. Typical emergency control device *(on left post)* installed at an attended motor fuel dispensing facility

Photo 6-29. Emergency control switch properly identified

maintenance or service person is working in the dispenser. The complexity of meeting this requirement will vary based on the amount of equipment and the features included with the equipment.

In a simple installation, this requirement can be met by providing a means to lock out a single breaker that controls the branch circuit to a dispenser which includes the pump as part of that dispenser. The requirement will be much more complex where multiple dispensers are supplied by common remote pumps and the dispensers have data, intercom, lighting, and other features. In larger facilities where the owner or operator would like to provide maintenance on single or small groups of dispenser while continuing to operate others, this could be even more complex.

Grounding and Bonding
Essentially all normally non-current-carrying metal parts of electrical equipment must be grounded as provided in Article 250. This applies to all voltage levels because of the concern for igniting flammable atmospheres due to any arcing or sparks generated. The specific grounding provisions of 501.30 must also be followed. This applies all the way back to the supply source within the building or structure [*NEC*, 514.16].

Leak Detection and Tank Level Monitoring Systems
Many motor fuel dispensing facilities are equipped with vapor recovery systems, leak detection systems, and tank fluid level monitoring systems (see photos 6-33 and 6-34). Concerns about the environment generally mandate these systems where motor fuel is stored or dispensed (transferred) or both. The fuel dispensing equipment used today is usually equipped

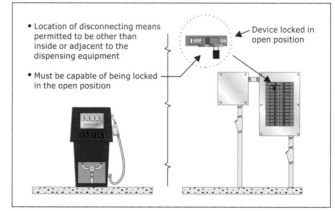

- Location of disconnecting means permitted to be other than inside or adjacent to the dispensing equipment
- Must be capable of being locked in the open position

Device locked in open position

Figure 6-28. Circuit disconnects are required to be capable of being locked in the open position.

Photo 6-30. Typical unattended motor fuel dispensing facility

and installed with vapor and leak recovery enclosures installed under the product dispensers (see photo 6-32). The electrical power wiring, electrical control wiring, intercom, product sheer valves, etc., are located in these enclosures to which the dispensing equipment is connected.

Leak detection and tank level monitoring systems are usually installed using intrinsically safe (IS) circuits and systems (see photos 6-33 and 6-34).

One of the most important requirements for intrinsically safe circuits and systems is to adhere to the specifications provided on the applicable control drawing(s). Article 504 provides the minimum *Code* requirements that apply where intrinsically safe circuits and systems are installed. Section 504.10(A)

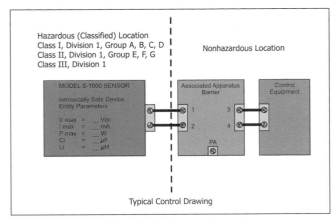

Figure 6-29. Example of a basic control drawing

Photo 6-31. Circuit breaker is shown with accessory device that allows the breaker to be locked in the open position. Note that the accessory remains with the switch or circuit breaker whether the lock is installed or not.

requires these systems and associated apparatus to be installed in accordance with the control drawing (see figure 6-29). More detailed examples of control drawings are provided in the annex in figures A-04 through A-08.

Many intrinsically safe systems are complex in nature, and control drawings can get fairly extensive. Some of the items specified on control drawings include, but are not limited to, separation requirements, types of conductors or cables to use, maximum and minimum length of conductors or cables, and special grounding requirements. It is important for the installer and designer to be familiar with the control drawings. They are essential to installing an

Photo 6-32. Vapor and leak recovery pit under a motor fuel dispenser showing electrical supply conduits and product lines

intrinsically safe system; they are also essential for making an inspection.

Other important requirements for IS systems provided in the *Code* include a requirement for listing [*NEC* 504.4], separation between other wiring [*NEC* 504.30], identification of the IS wiring [*NEC* 504.80], and grounding and bonding rules [*NEC* 504.50 and 504.60].

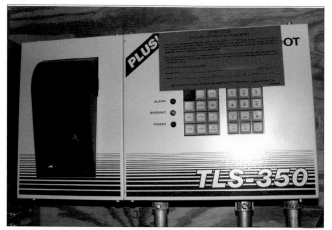

Photo 6-33. Typical intrinsically safe system Manufacturer, Veeder-Root

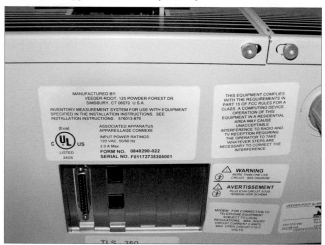

Photo 6-34. Listing marks and other identification marks on an intrinsically safe control panel

Photo 6-35. Bulk storage tanks and required containment dikes

Photo 6-36. Typical bulk storage facility storage tanks

Because intrinsically safe circuits are incapable of causing ignition of mixtures of combustible or flammable materials in air, general wiring methods are permitted for use [*NEC* 504. 20]. Be sure to meet any applicable wiring method rules indicated on the control drawing.

Intrinsically safe circuits and systems are being used more and more commonly for wiring in hazardous (classified) locations. Chapter 3 provides more detailed information about this protection technique and its use.

Bulk Storage Facilities

Article 515 applies where flammable liquids are stored or blended in bulk. Flammable liquids have flash points below 100°F. The liquids are received by tank vessels, pipelines, tank cars, or tank vehicles and distributed by tank vessels, pipelines, tank cars, tank vehicles, portable tanks, or containers [*NEC, 515.1* and see photos 6-35, 6-36, and 6-37). For additional information see NFPA 30, *Flammable and Combustible Liquids Code.*

The definition of a *bulk plant or terminal* is essentially the same as the scope of Article 515 [*NEC, 515.2*].

Class I Locations

NEC Table 515.3 is to be used in determining the extent of classifications. Classification ends at floors, walls, roofs or other solid partitions that have no communicating openings.

A fine print indicates the listed classifications assume the installation is in accordance with chapter 5 of NFPA 30, *Flammable and Combustible Liquids Code.*

A second fine print note points to the requirement in 555.21 for motor fuel dispensing stations at marinas

Table 6-04. Electrical Area Classifications

Class I, Division 1 or Zone 0

Location	Extent of Classification
Indoor and outdoor equipment	Entire area where flammable gases or vapors are present continuously or for long periods of time
Tank with a floating roof with a fixed outer roof	Inside and the area between the floating and fixed roof sections and within the shell.
Vent	Area inside of vent piping or openings Area inside drums, containers, and tanks

Class I, Division 1 or Zone 1

Location	Extent of Classification
Indoor equipment	Area within 5 feet in all directions, where vapors are present continuously or for long periods of time
Outdoor equipment	Area within three feet
Tank storage installations inside buildings	All equipment below grade level
Tank — aboveground	Area inside tank dikes, where the dike height is more than the distance between the tank and the dike for more than 1/2 of the tank circumference
Vent opening for an aboveground tank	Within 5 feet in all directions
Tank with a floating roof without a fixed outer roof	Area above the floating roof and within the shell of a tank
Tank with a floating roof without a fixed outer roof	Area above the floating roof and within the shell of a tank
Underground tank fill openings	Any pit, space below grade, if any part is within a classified location
Underground tanks and drums and container filling operations	Within 3 feet in all directions of vent openings
Pit without mechanical ventilation	If any portion is within a classified location
Tank vehicle and tank car open domes	Within 3 feet in all directions
Venting for bottom loading connections and closed dome loading	Within 3 feet in all directions
Tank vehicle storage and repair garages	All pits or spaces below floor level

Class I, Division 2 or Zone 2

Location	Extent of Classification
Indoor equipment where vapors are present continuously or for long periods of time	Area between 5 feet and 8 feet in all directions; Up to 3 feet above the floor or grade between 5 feet and 25 feet horizontally of the equipment
Outdoor equipment where vapors are present continuously or for long periods of time	Area between 3 feet and 8 feet in all directions; Up to 3 feet above the floor or grade between 3 feet and 10 feet horizontally of the equipment (see photo 6-xx).
Tank storage inside buildings	Equipment at or above grade
Aboveground tanks	Within 10 feet of shells, ends, or roofs of tanks and the area inside the dike. The area between 5 feet and 10 feet in all directions of vent openings
Underground tanks	18 inches above grade; within 10 feet of a loose fill connection and within 5 feet of a tight fill connection

Table 6-04. Hazardous Location Classification for Bulk Storage Plants

Table 6-04. Electrical Area Classifications (continued)

Class I, Division 2 or Zone 2

Location	Extent of Classification
Vent — discharging upward	Area between 3 feet and 5 feet in all directions
Drum and container filling—outdoors or indoors	Area 18 inches above grade within 10 feet of the vent or fill opening
Indoor pumps, bleeders and withdrawal fittings	Area within 5 feet in all directions and 25 feet horizontally up to 3 feet above grade
Outdoor pumps, bleeders and withdrawal fittings	Area within 3 feet in all directions and 10 feet horizontally up to 18 inches above grade
Pits and sumps with adequate mechanical ventilation	Entire area if any part is within a classified location
Pits and sumps containing valves, fittings or piping	Entire pit or sump if not within a classified location
Outdoor drainage ditches, separators, and impounding basins	Area up to 15 feet horizontally from the edge and 18 inches above that space and 18 inches above grade
Tank vehicle and tank car open domes	Area between 3 and 15 feet in all directions
Bottom loading connections and atmospheric venting	Between 3 feet and 15 feet in all directions. Also 10 feet horizontally from the loading connection up to 18 inches above grade
Loading through bottom connections with atmospheric venting	Between 3 feet and 15 feet in all directions of venting for bottom loading connections and closed dome loading and within 3 feet in all directions of the dome and fill and vapor line connections
Bottom loading with vapor control and any bottom unloading	Within 3 feet in all directions and 10 feet horizontally up to 18 inches above grade
Inside rooms or storage lockers used for flammable liquids	Entire Room

Table 6-04 (continued). Hazardous Location Classification for Bulk Storage Plants

and boatyards. At marinas and boatyards, power and lighting installed on wharfs, piers, and docks must be on the opposite side from the liquid piping system [*NEC,* 515.3].

Bulk storage plants and terminals can be classified under the Division system or the Zone system of classification. Table 6-04 provides a general overview of the extent of classified areas. Review *NEC* Table 515.3 for specific details. [See figures 6-30, 6-31, and 6-32 for typical area classifications associated with bulk storage tanks classified in accordance with *NEC* Table 515.3].

Ordinary Locations

Offices and rest rooms; garages for other than tank vehicles; outdoor drum storage; and indoor warehousing with no flammable liquid transfer and without any openings to classified locations are all classified as ordinary locations.

Wiring and Equipment Located in Class I Locations

All wiring and equipment in classified locations must be installed in accordance with Article 501 or Article 505, depending on the classification system used [*NEC,* 515.4].

Wiring and Equipment Above Class I Locations

Only metal raceways, Schedule 80 PVC conduit (or its equivalent), mineral-insulated, power and control tray cable, or metal-clad cable are to be used for fixed wiring above classified locations [*NEC,* 515.7(A)].

Any fixed equipment that could release sparks, arcs or hot particles must be totally enclosed or otherwise constructed to contain the hot particles. This includes lamps, lampholders for fixed lighting, cutouts, switches, receptacles, motors or any other equipment that has make-and-break or sliding contacts [*NEC,* 515.7(B)].

Photo 6-37. Bulk storage facility loading terminal

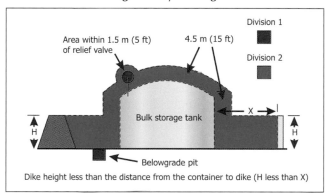

Figure 6-30. Bulk storage tanks and dike Concept derived from NFPA 70 *Handbook* Exhibit 515.6

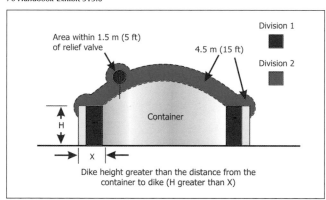

Figure 6-31. Bulk storage tanks and dike Concept derived from NFPA 70 *Handbook* Exhibit 515.6

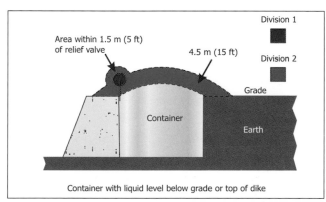

Figure 6-32. Bulk storage tanks and dike Concept derived from NFPA 70 *Handbook* Exhibit 515.6

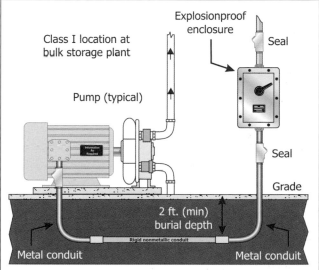

Rigid nonmetallic conduit permitted under not less than 2 feet of cover and rigid metal conduit of intermediate metal conduit is used for the last two feet before it emerges from grade

Figure 6-33. Underground wiring is permitted to be installed in rigid nonmetallic conduit.

Portable Lamps or Other Utilization Equipment

Where utilization equipment, including portable lamps and their flexible cords, is used above a classified location, it must be rated based on the classification of that location. Article 501 or Article 505 is applicable depending on which classification system is used [*NEC,* 515.7(C)].

Underground Wiring

Threaded rigid metal conduit or threaded steel intermediate conduit must be used; unless two feet of cover is provided, then rigid nonmetallic conduit or listed cables may be used. The rigid nonmetallic conduit must be changed to rigid metal or steel intermediate for the last two feet before it emerges above grade. If

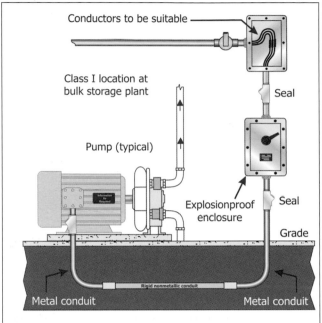

Figure 6-34. Conductors are required to be suitable for the materials to which they are exposed (markings can include "gasoline-resistant" and "oil-resistant").

cable is used, it must be enclosed in rigid metal or steel intermediate conduit from a minimum depth of two feet to where the cable emerges above grade [*NEC,* 515.8(A) and see figure 6-33].

Insulation

At bulk storage plants and terminals, conductor insulation must be suitable for the material, such as gasoline, it will be exposed to, in compliance with 501.20. Conductor markings can include "gasoline-resistant" and "oil-resistant" [*NEC,* 515.8(B) and see figure 6-34].

Nonmetallic Wiring

An equipment grounding conductor is required for rigid nonmetallic conduit and for cables with nonmetallic sheaths. This is to ensure electrical continuity of the raceway system and to provide an effective ground-fault path for the connected electrical equipment [*NEC,* 515.8(C)].

Conduit Sealing

Seals must be provided for all boundaries of the classified areas. Raceways and cables buried under classified locations are considered to be in the classified locations. This is different from the concept in 514.8 for motor fuel dispensing facilities [*NEC,* 515.9].

Special Equipment—Gasoline Dispensers

If volatile flammable liquids or liquefied flammable gases are dispensed, the portions of Article 514 that apply must be used [*NEC,* 515.10].

Grounding and Bonding

Essentially all normally non-current-carrying metal

Photo 6-38. Static protection equipment installed and operating at a bulk storage loading terminal. (Note the green light is on, indicating it is safe to transfer product.) Usually these systems are interlocked with the pumping equipment.

Photo 6-39. Static protection equipment connected to a mobile vessel (tanker truck) during the product transferring process.

parts of electrical equipment must be grounded as provided in Article 250. Section 250.100 requires electrical continuity of normally non-current-carrying metal parts of equipment, raceways, and other enclosures in hazardous locations defined in Article 500. This continuity (bonding) must be assured by any of the methods specified in 250.92(B)(2) through (B)(4) that are approved for the wiring method used. This more substantial bonding is required whether or not any equipment grounding conductors (wire types) are installed. This applies to all voltage levels because of the concern for igniting flammable atmospheres due to any arcing or sparks generated. The specific grounding provisions of 501.30 must also be followed. This more robust method of bonding is required all the way back to the supply source within the building or structure [*NEC*, 515.16].

A fine print note points out that NFPA 30 provides information on static protection grounding in 4.5.3.4 and 4.5.3.5. Static grounding and bonding

Photo 6-40. Typical indoor spray paint booth covered by the requirements in Article 516

Photo 6-41. Typical enclosed spray paint booth showing dedicated exhaust system

protection systems are often installed at bulk storage facilities. Protection against static electricity is essential to minimize the hazards of explosions in hazardous locations (see photos 6-38 and 6-39).

Spray Application, Dipping, and Coating Processes

Article 516 applies where flammable liquids, combustible liquids and combustible powders are regularly or frequently applied (see photo 6-40). Vapors in air and residue deposits need to be considered when classifying areas and selecting equipment. Classifications include both the Division system and the Zone system.

For additional information see NFPA 33 *Standard for Spray Application Using Flammable and Combustible Materials*, and NFPA 34 *Standard for Dipping and Coating Processes Using Flammable or Combustible Liquids*. Ventilation information is available in NFPA 91, *Standard for Exhaust Systems for Air Conveying of Vapors, Gases, Mists, and Noncombustible Particulate Solids*.

Definitions

Three definitions are provided in 516.2:

Spray area is usually an unconfined space and is outside of buildings; or if inside, it is only a portion of the room or total space. For automated processes, it is the maximum direct spray area. For manual processes, it is the maximum direct spray area when the sprayer is 180 degrees perpendicular to the surface being sprayed.

Spray booth is an enclosure or partial enclosure inside a larger room used for spraying, coating, or dipping processes. Spray booths may be fully enclosed or have one or more openings, including those for associated conveyors. A dedicated ventilation exhaust may draw supply air from the room or be provided with a separate supply (see photo 6-41).

Spray room is an enclosed room intended for spraying, coating, or dipping processes; it is also provided with a dedicated ventilated supply and exhaust. The room is designed and sized based on the objects to be painted. For large items, the room may actually be the entire building or a majority of it.

Classification of Locations

Determining the extent of classification is based on the quantity of vapors, combustible mists, residues, dusts, or deposits present. The Division system and the Zone system for classifying hazardous locations are both permitted for locations or operations covered by Article 516. Spaces are classified as follows:

Class I, Division 1 or Class I, Zone 0 Locations

Interiors of any open and closed container for flammable liquids, dip tank, or coating tank are considered Class I, Division 1 or Class I, Zone 0 [*NEC*, 516.3(A)].

Class I or Class II, Division 1; or Class I, Zone 1 Locations

The following areas are considered Class I or Class II, Division 1 or Class I, Zone 1 locations [*NEC*, 516.3(B)]:

• Interiors of spray booth and spray room, unless the space is adjacent to enclosed dipping or coating processes

   • Interiors of exhaust ducts

   • Direct spray path area

• An area that is within a 5-foot radius of open coating and dipping vapor sources and extends from the source down to the floor. Vapor source includes exposed liquid, drainboard, and any coated or dipped object that emits measurable vapors exceeding 25 percent of the lower flammable limit within one foot of the source.

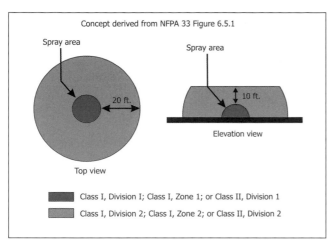

Concept derived from NFPA 33 Figure 6.5.1

Spray area

Spray area

20 ft.

10 ft.

Elevation view

Top view

■ Class I, Division I; Class I, Zone 1; or Class II, Division 1

■ Class I, Division 2; Class I, Zone 2; or Class II, Division 2

Figure 6-35. Classified locations for open spraying operations
Concept derived from NFPA 70 Figure 516.(B)(1)

• Subsurface spaces, such as sumps, pits or channels, that are within 25 feet horizontally of a vapor source. Where those subsurface spaces extend beyond 25 feet of the vapor source, a vapor stop must be provided or the entire length is to be classified as Class I, Division 1.

• Within 3 feet in all directions of open containers, supply containers, spray gun cleaners, and solvent distillation units that contain flammable liquids.

Class I or Class II, Division 2 Locations; or Class I Zone 2

For open spraying, the space beyond the area classified as Division 1 or Zone 1 out to 20 feet horizontally and 10 feet vertically is considered Class I or Class II, Division 2 locations or Class I, Zone 2. Adjacent areas separated by partitions are not required to be classified. *NEC* Figure 516.3(B)(1) provides an illustration of the classified location boundaries (see figure 6-35).

For spraying in rooms or booths with closed-tops but open-faces or open-fronts, the area within specific dimensions of openings is considered Class I or Class II, Division 2 locations or Class I, Zone 2. This space includes three feet vertically above the open-front or open-face and three feet from conveyor openings. *NEC* Figure 516.3(B)(2) provides an illustration of the classified location boundaries. Horizontal dimensions are determined based on whether the exhaust ventilation system is interlocked with the spraying equipment. Interlocked systems extend to five feet horizontally and non-interlocked systems extend to ten feet. Interlocking must prevent spraying if the exhaust system either stops functioning or is not

Photo 6-42. Sail switch or pressure differential is used to detect airflow and is interlocked with the spray and ventilation system.

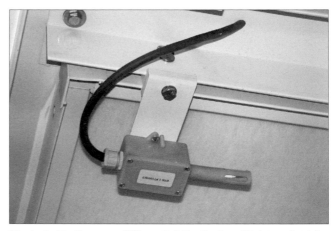

Photo 6-43. Pressure differential (in the booth) is used to detect airflow and is interlocked with the spray and ventilation system.

functioning properly. The sensing device must verify actual air movement to ensure that a malfunction, such as broken belt, does not stop air movement. A sail switch or pressure differential sensor is often used for this purpose (see photos 6-42 and 6-43).

For spraying in an open-top booth, the space three feet above the booth and within three feet of other openings is considered Class I or Class II, Division 2 or Class I, Zone 2 location.

For spraying in enclosed booths or rooms, the space out to three feet in all directions from any openings as shown in Figure 516.3(B)(4) is considered Class I or Class II, Division 2 or Class I, Zone 2 location.

Spaces three feet beyond the five-foot Division 1 or Zone 1 space surrounding dip tanks and drainboards as defined in 516.3(B)(4) and as shown in Figure 516.3(B)(5) are considered Class I or Class II, Division 2 or Class I, Zone 2 locations.

Spaces extending 20 feet horizontally beyond the five-foot Division 1 or Zone 1 space [516.3(B)(4)] of dip tanks and drain boards and up to 3 feet above the floor are considered Class I or Class II, Division 2 or Class I, Zone 2 locations.

An exception permits that area to be unclassified under all of the following conditions: (1) vapor source area is 5 square feet or less; (2) tank or container does not contain more than 5 gallons; (3) vapor concentration is not more than 25 percent of the lower flammable limit.

For open containers, the space extending two feet in all directions beyond the three-foot Division 1 or Zone 1 space [516.3(B)(6)] is considered Class I or Class II, Division 2 or Class I, Zone 2 location.

Also the space five feet beyond the three-foot Division 1 or Zone 1 space up to 18 inches above the floor or grade has the same classification.

Enclosed Coating and Dipping Operations

Adjacent spaces to enclosed dipping and coating processes are considered unclassified. But the space out to three feet in all directions from any enclosure openings is classified as Division 2 or Zone 2 [*NEC*, 516.3(D)].

Adjacent Locations

Locations adjacent to areas classified due to the presence of flammable liquids or vapors or combustible dusts may be considered unclassified if separated by tight partitions, with no communicating openings, and the flammable vapors or combustible powders are not be likely to be released in those adjacent areas [*NEC*, 516.3(E)].

Unclassified Locations

Drying, curing, or fusion apparatus that is adequately ventilated mechanically to prevent accumulations of flammable vapor concentrations and is interlocked to de-energize all electrical equipment may be unclassified. If certain safeguards are provided, such as

Photo 6-44. Drying and curing booth are permitted to be unclassified if adequately mechanically ventilated.

mechanical ventilation and interlocks that de-energize electrical equipment suitable for general use, the authority having jurisdiction is allowed to accept an area as being unclassified. A fine print note points to NFPA 86, *Standard for Ovens and Furnaces*, for additional information [*NEC*, 516.3(F) and see photo 6-44).

Wiring and Equipment in Class I Locations

Wiring and Equipment—Vapors

All equipment and electric wiring in a classified location containing vapors but no residues must comply with the requirements of Article 501 or 505, depending on the classification system used [*NEC*, 516.4(A)].

Wiring and Equipment—Vapors and Residues

Only rigid metal conduit, intermediate metal conduit, mineral-insulated cable and metal boxes or fittings without splices, taps or terminal connections are permitted in locations where deposits can accumulate. Other electrical equipment must be specifically listed for that location. Accumulation of paint or other coating residues and deposits on equipment can cause overheating and the equipment could ignite the material. Heat causes organic material to dehydrate, making it easier to ignite [*NEC*, 516.4(B)].

Illumination

Areas containing material capable of being ignited may be illuminated through glass or other panels that allow light to pass through them under the following specific conditions (see photos 6-45 and 6-46). Lighting units must be fixed and identified for the location they are installed in. Panels must effectively isolate the classified location from the lighting units. Panels must be made of material not likely to be broken or must be protected so breakage is not likely to occur. The installation must not allow normal residue accumulations to be raised to a temperature by the illumination source so they could ignite [*NEC*, 516.4(C)].

Portable Equipment

Portable electrical equipment, including portable electric lamps, is not to be used in a spray area while spraying is being done. Exception one allows portable electric lamps if identified for Division 1 or Zone 1 lo-

Photo 6-45. Luminaires (light fixtures) installed in the walls of an enclosed spray booth

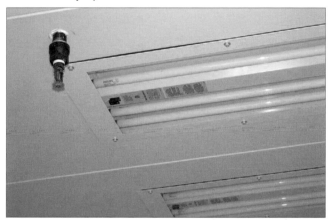

Photo 6-46. Luminaires (light fixtures) installed in the ceiling of an enclosed spray booth

cations for processes not readily illuminated by fixed lighting. Exception two allows portable electric drying apparatus in automobile spray booths used for refinishing under all of the following conditions: (1) the apparatus and its electrical connections are removed during spraying operations; (2) any electrical equipment within 18 inches of the floor must be identified for Division 2 or Zone 2 locations; (3) all drying apparatus metallic parts are electrically bonded and grounded; (5) spraying equipment must be interlocked so that it cannot be operated when the drying apparatus is in the booth. It must also provide a 3-minute purge of the booth and shut off the drying equipment if the ventilation stops functioning [*NEC*, 516.4(D)].

Electrostatic Equipment

Electrostatic spraying and detearing equipment are covered by 516.10. This type of equipment minimizes over spray and material consumption by establishing different charges between the spraying equipment and the object being coated. The material is attracted to the object but not to other nearby surfaces [*NEC,* 516.4(E)].

Wiring and Equipment Not Within Class I and II Locations

All fixed wiring above these classified locations is limited to specific wiring methods. Only metal raceways, rigid nonmetallic conduit, electrical nonmetallic tubing, mineral-insulated cable, power and control tray cable or metal-clad cable are allowed. Cellular metal floor raceways may be used to supply ceiling outlets or equipment below the floor of a classified location but cannot have any connection to a classified location above the floor unless seals are provided [*NEC,* 516.7(A)].

Equipment

Any fixed equipment, installed above classified locations or where freshly finished parts are handled, that could release sparks, arcs or hot particles must be totally enclosed or otherwise constructed to contain the hot particles. This includes lamps, lampholders for fixed lighting, cutouts, switches, receptacles, motors or any other equipment that has make-and-break or sliding contacts [*NEC,* 516.7(B)].

Fixed Electrostatic Equipment

Equipment that uses electrostatically charged elements to atomize, charge, or precipitate hazardous material for coating objects must be listed and comply with specific requirements. Robotic devices and other equipment that uses mechanical supports or manipulators for similar purposes are also covered. Equipment or robots that are manually held or manipulated during programming while spraying with the high-voltage equipment energized are covered by the hand spraying equipment requirements in 516.10(B) [*NEC,* 516.10(A)].

Electrical equipment, including transformers, high-voltage supplies, and control apparatus, must be located either outside the classified location (516.3) or be identified for it. High-voltage grids, electrodes, electrostatic atomizing heads and their connections are allowed in the hazardous location.

Electrodes and electrostatic atomizing heads must be insulated from ground but still be adequately supported and permanently located. Attaching them to their bases, supports, reciprocators, or robots is considered acceptable even though movement may occur.

High-voltage leads must be insulated and protected from mechanical damage or exposure to chemicals that could affect them. Exposed high-voltage elements must be permanently supported by insulators and be guarded from unexpected contact or grounding.

Objects to be coated must be supported from conveyors or hangers in a manner that keeps them from swinging. Electrical contact must provide a resistance to ground not exceeding 1 megohm.

Automatic means must be provided to quickly de-energize the electrostatic apparatus under these conditions: (1) ventilation stops functioning, (2) the conveyor stops unexpectedly, (3) excessive high-voltage current leakage, or (4) primary input power is interrupted.

Electrically conductive objects—such as paint containers, wash cans, guards, hose connectors, brackets, or other devices—in the spray area must be adequately grounded. Obviously objects that need to be energized at high voltage because of the process do not have to be grounded.

To maintain a safe separation of the process, safeguards such as booths, fencing, railings, interlocks, or other means should be placed around the equipment or incorporated into it.

Signs must be provided to identify the process area as being dangerous due to possible fire and accidents. These signs must also identify grounding requirements and restrict access of unqualified persons.

Insulators Must Not Become Wet or Dirty

Spraying equipment, other than nonincendive equipment, has additional requirements. *Nonincendive equipment* is, as defined in 500.2, equipment that will not cause ignition under normal conditions. Conveyors and hangers must keep the objects being painted at least twice the sparking distance from charged conductors. Warning signs must provide the safe distance dimension. If the distance between the objects being painted and the electrodes or atomizing heads is reduced to less than twice the sparking distance, the high-voltage elements must be automatically de-energized.

Electrostatic Hand-Spraying Equipment

Hand-spraying equipment that uses electrostatically charged elements to atomize, charge, or precipitate hazardous material for coating objects must also be listed and comply with specific requirements.

High-voltage circuits must not produce a spark capable of igniting the vapor-air mixture likely to be present or result in a significant shock hazard upon coming in contact with a grounded object under normal conditions. An actuator must be provided to energize the exposed elements and control the supply of coating material.

Electrical equipment, including transformers, power packs, and control apparatus, must be located either outside the classified location (516.3) or be identified for it. An exception allows the handgun and its power supply connections to be in the hazardous location.

Provisions must be made to prevent a static charge buildup on the operator's body. A metallic connection to ground must be made to the spraying gun handle and intimate contact with the operator must be ensured. Signs must warn others in the spray area of the need to be grounded.

Electrically conductive objects, such as paint containers, wash cans, or other devices, in the spray area must be adequately grounded. A permanently installed warning must be provided to give notice about the need for grounding.

Objects to be painted must be kept in contact with the conveyor or grounded support. Contact areas must be sharp points or knife-edges where possible. These contacts must be regularly cleaned to maintain a resistance to ground not exceeding 1 megohm. Object support points must not be exposed to random spray if possible; and conveyor attachment points must not be located where they collect spray material.

Powder Coating

Processes that apply combustible dry powders can have hazards, depending on the properties of the material, including composition, particle size, shape and distribution.

As powder coating typically includes combustible dusts, all equipment and ignition sources must be installed in accordance with Article 502. Portable electric lamps are not to be used in the classified location during the finishing operation. If used during cleaning or repairing activities, they must be identified for Class II Division 1 locations, and exposed metal parts must be effectively grounded. An exception allows portable electric lamps if listed for Class II Division 1 locations for processes not readily illuminated by fixed lighting.

Fixed electrostatic spraying equipment used for powder coating must comply with both the requirements for fixed equipment in 516.10(A) and the requirements in 516.10(C)(1) for powder coating.

Hand-spraying equipment used for powder coating must comply with both the requirements for hand-spraying equipment in 516.10(B) and the requirements in 516.10(C)(1) for powder coating.

Electrostatic fluidized beds and their associated equipment must be identified for the use. High-voltage circuits must not produce a discharge of sufficient intensity to ignite the powder-air mixture or cause a significant shock hazard.

Electrical equipment, including transformers, power packs, and control apparatus, must be located either outside the powder-coating area or be identified for it. An exception allows the charging electrodes and their power supply connections in the powder coating area.

Electrically conductive objects in the powder-coating area must be adequately grounded. A permanently installed warning must be provided to give notice about the need for grounding.

Objects being coated must be kept in contact with the conveyor or grounded support. Contact areas must be sharp points or knife-edges where possible, and these contacts must be regularly cleaned to maintain a resistance to ground not exceeding 1 megohm.

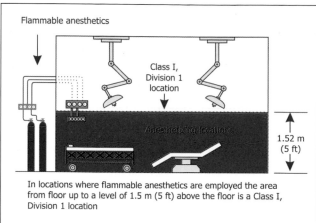

Figure 6-36. Class I, Division 1 location where flammable anesthetics are employed

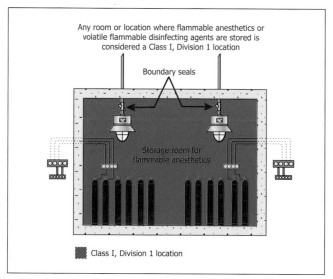

Figure 6-37. Class I, Division 1 location where flammable anesthetics are stored (includes a room or location)

The equipment and compressed air supplies must be interlocked with the ventilation system to prevent the equipment's use if the ventilating system is not operating.

Grounding and Bonding

Essentially all normally non-current-carrying metal parts of electrical equipment must be grounded as provided in Article 250. Section 250.100 requires electrical continuity of normally non-current-carrying metal parts of equipment, raceways, and other enclosures in hazardous locations defined in Article 500. This continuity (bonding) must be assured by any of the methods specified in 250.92(B)(2) through (B)(4) that are approved for the wiring method used. This more substantial bonding is required whether

Photo 6-47. A gas bottle storage room in a medical center that uses only nonflammable gases as anesthetizing agents (unclassified location)

or not any equipment grounding conductors (wire types) are installed. This applies to all voltage levels because of the concern for igniting flammable atmospheres due to any arcing or sparks generated. The specific grounding provisions of 501.30, 502.30, or 505.25 must also be followed. This applies all the way back to the supply source within the building or structure [*NEC,* 516.16].

Health Care Facilities

Up until *NEC-1968,* Article 517 was titled "Flammable Anesthetics." In *NEC*-1971 the title changed to

Photo 6-48. A gas bottle storage room in a medical center that uses only nonflammable gases as anesthetizing agents (unclassified location)

Photo 6-49. Isolated power system equipment

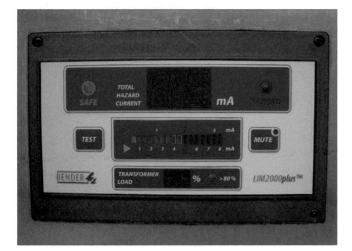

Photo 6-50. Isolated power system equipment showing a closeup of the line isolation monitor (LIM).

"Health Care Facilities" and electrical requirements for circuits systems and equipment in health care facilities were in the scope of the article. Many of the requirements for electrical circuits, systems, and equipment were derived from the information contained in NFPA 99. The electrical requirements in the *Code* for health care facilities to this day include rules that are also part of NFPA 99.

In the early years of medical practice, it was common to utilize flammable gases as anesthetizing agents for patients. Many explosions related to the use of these flammable anesthetics resulted in area classification for health care facilities. Hazardous (classified) locations for these areas are provided in Section 517.60(A) and (B) [see figure 6-36].

Where flammable anesthetics are employed, the area from the floor upward to a height of 1.52 m (5 ft)

is a Class I, Division 1 location. The storage room for flammable anesthetics or volatile disinfecting agents is to be considered a Class I, Division 1 location. This includes the whole room (see figure 6-37). It is interesting that there is no Class I, Division 2 location associated with anesthetizing agents in health care facilities.

Any area used for inhalation of nonflammable anesthetizing agents or any room used for storing nonflammable gases is considered an other-than-hazardous (classified) or unclassified location (see photos 6-47 and 6-48).

Wiring and equipment installed in a flammable anesthetizing location is to be supplied from an isolated power system that is listed and installed to meet the requirements of 517.160 see photos 6-49 and 6-50).

Photo 6-51. Reference grounding terminal bar in a listed isolated power panel

Isolated Power Systems

Isolated power systems were commonly used in flammable anesthetizing locations of health care facilities to minimize the possibilities of arcing on ground-fault conditions. The hazards of fires and explosions in operating rooms and critical care areas were a serious concern until the introduction and acceptance of the first nonflammable anesthetic agent, halothane. Although the danger from using flammable anesthetics has been significantly reduced, continued vigilance is still necessary whenever an increased oxygen concentration is employed in the presence of an ignition source.

Isolated power systems also help to reduce the possibilities of patients being subjected to electrical shock or electrocution and to monitor insulation leakage levels in branch circuits and equipment-connected circuits supplied by these systems. Although these systems are ungrounded, equipment grounding conductors for devices and equipment supplied by isolated power systems are connected to the reference grounding terminal bus located in isolated power panels (see photo 6-51).

Controlling static electricity and differences of potential is generally accomplished by using patient equipment grounding point as an optional technique [*NEC*, 517.19(C)]. In earlier years, it was common to see conductive floors installed in operating rooms. Reminders of the explosive history with health care facilities endure in the form of conductive flooring in operating rooms and the occasional drag chain on the rolling operating tables and stretchers used to reduce potential differences between conductive parts.

In 517.19(E), the *Code* specifies the use of isolated power systems in critical care areas only as an optional protection technique. However, in wet locations of critical care areas where interruption by a ground-fault circuit interrupter cannot be tolerated, branch circuits supplying those wet locations must be supplied by an isolated power system that is listed and installed to meet all of the rules in 517.160.

Wiring Methods in the Hazardous Locations

Electrical wiring installed in Class I, Division 1 locations generally must meet the requirements of 501.10(A).

Equipment and Flexible Cords

Where a box, fitting, or enclosure is partially, but not entirely, within a hazardous (classified) location, the classification shall be extended to include the entire box, fitting, or enclosure. Receptacles or attachment plugs located in hazardous (classified) locations are required to be listed for use in Class I, Group C and must include provisions for the connection of a grounding conductor. Flexible cords used in hazardous (classified) locations for connection to portable utilization equipment, including lamps operating at more than 8 volts between conductors, must be suitable for extra-hard usage and include an additional conductor for grounding.

Wiring Methods and Equipment
Above the Hazardous Location

Electrical wiring installed above a hazardous (classified) location as delineated in 517.60 must be in rigid metal conduit, electrical metallic tubing, intermediate metal conduit, MI cable, or MC cable that employs a continuous, gas/vaportight metal sheath.

Any equipment that may produce arcs, sparks, or particles of hot metal, such as lamps and lampholders for fixed lighting, cutouts, switches, generators, motors, or other equipment having make-and-break or sliding contacts, must be totally enclosed or be constructed to prevent escape of sparks or hot metal particles.

Any surgical or other luminaires (lighting fixtures) must meet the requirements in 501.130(B).

Receptacles and Attachment Plugs

Receptacles and attachment plugs located above hazardous (classified) anesthetizing locations must be listed for hospital use. They must be suitable for services of prescribed voltage, frequency, rating, and number of conductors and have provisions for connection of the equipment grounding conductor if of the 2-pole, 3-wire grounding type for single-phase, 120-volt, nominal, ac service.

Sealing Requirements

Suitable seals are to be provided at horizontal and vertical boundaries of the anesthetizing locations defined as hazardous (classified) locations. Seals are required to meet the applicable rules in 501.15, including seal locations. Chapter five provides a detailed review of conduit and cable sealing rules.

Grounding and Bonding

In any anesthetizing area, all metal raceways and metal-sheathed cables and all non–current-carrying conductive portions of fixed electric equipment are required to be grounded, with the exception of equipment operating at not more than 10 volts between conductors. The specific grounding and bonding requirements in 501.30 must be used in Class I locations. As reviewed in chapter two, this more restrictive method of bonding must extend all the way back to the point of grounding for the applicable derived system or service.

Summary

Not many health care facilities use flammable anesthetics these days, but the *Code* still provides for instances where classification is necessary. This chapter provided a review of the specific occupancy requirements in Articles 511 through 517 of the *NEC*.

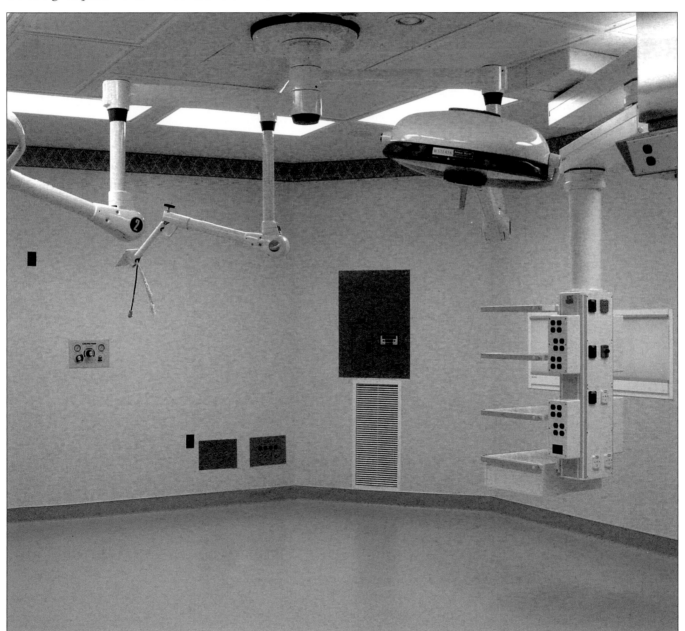

Photo 6-52. Operating room that does not use flammable anesthetizing agents

Review Questions

1. Section 511.3(A) of the *NEC* includes a number of commercial garage applications that are permitted to be unclassified locations. These facilities are not required to meet any of the requirements in Article 511.

   a. True
   b. False

2. Classified spaces in repair garages will be near the floor or in pits or below grade areas unless the repair operation involves vehicles _____.

   a. with oversized fuel tanks
   b. of large fleet operations
   c. fueled by lighter-than-air fuels
   d. multiple fuel tanks

3. GFCI protection is required for all _____ receptacles installed in areas where electrical diagnostic equipment, electrical hand tools, or portable lighting equipment is used in commercial garages.

   a. single-phase
   b. 125-volt, single-phase, 15- and 20-ampere
   c. 15- and 20-ampere
   d. 125-volt, 50/60 Hz, single-phase, 15- and 20-ampere

4. Spaces near the floor and areas around the aircraft are potentially hazardous classified locations within an aircraft hangar. Wiring and equipment located outside of those hazardous (classified) locations is only required to comply with the general requirements in Chapters 1 through 4 of the *NEC*.

   a. True
   b. False

5. GFCI protection is required for all _____ receptacles installed in areas where electrical diagnostic equipment, electrical hand tools, or portable lighting equipment is used in an aircraft hangar.

   a. single-phase
   b. 125-volt, single-phase, 15- and 20-ampere
   c. 15- and 20-ampere
   d. 125-volt, 50/60 Hz, single-phase, 15- and 20-ampere

6. All wiring installed in or under an aircraft hangar floor shall comply with the requirements for a _____ _____ location.

   a. Class I, Division 1
   b. Class I, Division 2
   c. Class I, Zone 0
   d. Class I, Zone 1

7. Area classification and electrical installation requirements from Article 505, Class I, Zone 0, 1, and 2, locations are not allowed in aircraft hangars.

   a. True
   b. False

8. Hazardous (classified) areas around dispensing devices at motor fuel dispensing facilities will vary based on the fuel being dispensed.

   a. True
   b. False

9. Circuit disconnects for circuits leading to or through dispensing or remote pumping equipment are required to _____ all conductors of the circuits, including the grounded conductor, where provided.

   a. lock-out
   b. simultaneously disconnect
   c. to be located at the equipment for
   d. be rated 20 ampere, 250 volt for

10. Dispensing devices are required to be provided with means to remove _____ voltage sources during maintenance and service events.

a. power

b. control

c. communication

d. external

11. Area classification and electrical installation requirements from Article 505, Class I, Zone 0, 1, and 2 locations are not allowed in motor fuel dispensing facilities.

    a. True

    b. False

12. Where the authority having jurisdiction can determine that a motor fuel dispensing facility will only handle and dispense combustible liquids with a flash point above 100° F, such location shall not be required to be classified.

    a. True

    b. False

13. Rigid nonmetallic conduit installed underground at bulk storage plants must comply with the requirements in 501.10(A)(1) exception.

    a. True

    b. False

14. Facilities involved in spray applications, or a dipping and coating process may include spaces classified either Class I, or Class II, or Class I and II.

    a. True

    b. False

15. Depending on the facility and the application, requirements in Article 516 might apply only to a booth within a room or building, or might apply to an area within a room or building, or might apply to an entire room or building.

    a. True

    b. False

16. Emergency controls are required to be installed not more than 30 m (100 ft) from the dispensers at an attended motor fuel dispensing facility.

    a. True

    b. False

17. Emergency controls are required to be located not less than _____ and not more than _____ from the dispensers at an unattended motor fuel dispensing facility.

    a. 900 mm (3 ft), 2.0 m (6 ½ ft)

    b. 1.8 m (6 ft), 3.0 m (10 ft)

    c. 6 m (20 ft), 30 m (100 ft)

    d. 7.5 m (25 ft), 15 m (50 ft)

18. The area within a motor fuel dispenser for gasoline is classified as a _____ location.

    a. Class III, Division 1

    b. Class II, Division 2

    c. Class I, Division 2

    d. Class I, Division 1

19. The area within _____ in all directions from a compressed natural gas dispenser is a Class I, Division 2 location

    a. 450 mm (18 in.)

    b. 900 mm (3 ft)

    c. 1.5 m (5 ft)

    d. All of the above

20. The area within 900 mm (3 ft) in all directions from an underground gasoline tank vent is classified as a _____ location.

    a. Class II, Division 1

    b. Class I, Division 1

    c. Class I, Division 2

    d. Class I, Zone 2

Ready

Reference

Charts

and

Tables

Chemical	CAS No.	Class I Division Group	Type[a]	Flash Point (°C)	AIT (°C)	%LFL	%UFL	Vapor Density (Air = 1)	Vapor Pressure[b] (mm Hg)	Class I Zone Group[c]	MIE (mJ)	MIC Ratio	MESG (mm)
Acetaldehyde	75-07-0	C[d]	I	−38	175	4.0	60.0	1.5	874.9	IIA	0.37	0.98	0.92
Acetic Acid	64-19-7	D[d]	II	43	464	4.0	19.9	2.1	15.6	IIA		2.67	1.76
Acetic Acid-tert-Butyl Ester	540-88-5	D	II			1.7	9.8	4.0	40.6				
Acetic Anhydride	108-24-7	D	II	54	316	2.7	10.3	3.5	4.9				
Acetone	67-64-1	D[d]	I		465	2.5	12.8	2.0	230.7	IIA	1.15	1.00	1.02
Acetone Cyanohydrin	75-86-5	D	IIIA	74	688	2.2	12.0	2.9	0.3				
Acetonitrile	75-05-8	D	I	6	524	3.0	16.0	1.4	91.1	IIA			1.50
Acetylene	74-86-2	A[d]	GAS		305	2.5	99.9	0.9	36600	IIC	0.017	0.28	0.25
Acrolein (Inhibited)	107-02-8	B(C)[d]	I		235	2.8	31.0	1.9	274.1	IIB	0.13		
Acrylic Acid	79-10-7	D	II	54	438	2.4	8.0	2.5	4.3				
Acrylonitrile	107-13-1	D[d]	I	−26	481	3.0	17.0	1.8	108.5	IIB	0.16	0.78	0.87
Adiponitrile	111-69-3	D	IIIA	93	550			1.0	0.002				
Allyl Alcohol	107-18-6	C[d]	I	22	378	2.5	18.0	2.0	25.4				0.84
Allyl Chloride	107-05-1	D	I	−32	485	2.9	11.1	2.6	366			1.33	1.17
Allyl Glycidyl Ether	106-92-3	B(C)[e]	II		57			3.9					
Alpha-Methyl Styrene	98-83-9	D	II		574	0.8	11.0	4.1	2.7				
n-Amyl Acetate	628-63-7	D	I	25	360	1.1	7.5	4.5	4.2				1.02
sec-Amyl Acetate	626-38-0	D	I	23		1.1	7.5	4.5		IIA			
Ammonia	7664-41-7	D[d,f]	I		498	15.0	28.0	0.6	7498.0	IIA	680	6.85	3.17
Aniline	62-53-3	D	IIIA	70	615	1.3	11.0	3.2	0.7	IIA			
Benzene	71-43-2	D[d]	I	−11	498	1.2	7.8	2.8	94.8	IIA	0.20	1.00	0.99
Benzyl Chloride	98-87-3	D	IIIA		585	1.1		4.4	0.5				
Bromopropyne	106-96-7	D	I	10	324	3.0							
n-Butane	3583-47-9	D[d,g]	GAS		288	1.9	8.5	2.0			0.25	0.94	1.07
1,3-Butadiene	106-99-0	B(D)[d,e]	GAS	−76	420	2	12	1.9		IIB	0.13	0.76	0.79
1-Butanol	71-36-3	D[d]	I	36	343	1.4	11.2	2.6	7.0	IIA			0.91
2-Butanol	78-92-2	D[d]	I	36	405	1.7	9.8	2.6		IIA			
Butylamine	109-73-9	D	GAS	−12	312	1.7	9.8	2.5	92.9			1.13	
Butylene	25167-67-3	D	I		385	1.6	10.0	1.9	2214.6				
n-Butyraldehyde	123-72-8	C[d]	I	−12	218	1.9	12.5	2.5	112.2				0.92
n-Butyl Acetate	123-86-4	D[d]	I	22	421	1.7	7.6	4.0	11.5	IIA		1.08	1.04
sec-Butyl Acetate	105-46-4	D	II	−8		1.7	9.8	4.0	22.2				
tert-Butyl Acetate	540-88-5	D	II			1.7	9.8	4.0	40.6				
n-Butyl Acrylate (Inhibited)	141-32-2	D	II	49	293	1.7	9.9	4.4	5.5				
n-Butyl Glycidyl Ether	2426-08-6	B(C)[e]	II										

Table A-1. Selected Chemicals [Reproduction of Table 4.4.2 from NFPA 497; reprinted with permission of NFPA]

Selected Chemicals

Chemical	CAS No.	Class I Division Group	Type[a]	Flash Point (°C)	AIT (°C)	%LFL	%UFL	Vapor Density (Air = 1)	Vapor Pressure[b] (mm Hg)	Class I Zone Group[c]	MIE (mJ)	MIC Ratio	MESG (mm)
n-Butyl Formal	110-62-3	C	IIIA						34.3				
Butyl Mercaptan	109-79-5	C	I	2				3.1	46.4				
Butyl-2-Propenoate	141-32-2	D	II	49		1.7	9.9	4.4	5.5				
para tert-Butyl Toluene	98-51-1	D	IIIA										
n-Butyric Acid	107-92-6	D[d]	IIIA	72	443	2.0	10.0	3.0	0.8				
Carbon Disulfide	75-15-0	d,h	I	−30	90	1.3	50.0	2.6	358.8	IIC	0.009	0.39	0.20
Carbon Monoxide	630-08-0	C[d]	GAS		609	12.5	74.0	0.97		IIA			0.84
Chloroacetaldehyde	107-20-0	C	IIIA	88					63.1				
Chlorobenzene	108-90-7	D	I	29	593	1.3	9.6	3.9	11.9				
1-Chloro-1-Nitropropane	2425-66-3	C	IIIA										
Chloroprene	126-99-8	D	GAS	−20		4.0	20.0	3.0					
Cresol	1319-77-3	D	IIIA	81	559	1.1		3.7					
Crotonaldehyde	4170-30-3	C[d]	I	13	232	2.1	15.5	2.4	33.1	IIB			0.81
Cumene	98-82-8	D	I	36	424	0.9	6.5	4.1	4.6	IIA			
Cyclohexane	110-82-7	D	I	−17	245	1.3	8.0	2.9	98.8	IIA	0.22	1.0	0.94
Cyclohexanol	108-93-0	D	IIIA	68	300			3.5	0.7	IIA			
Cyclohexanone	108-94-1	D	II	44	245	1.1	9.4	3.4	4.3	IIA			0.98
Cyclohexene	110-83-8	D	I	−6	244	1.2		2.8	89.4			0.97	
Cyclopropane	75-19-4	D[d]	I		503	2.4	10.4	1.5	5430	IIB	0.17	0.84	0.91
p-Cymene	99-87-6	D	II	47	436	0.7	5.6	4.6	1.5	IIA			
Decene	872-05-9	D	II		235			4.8	1.7				
n-Decaldehyde	112-31-2	C	IIIA						0.09				
n-Decanol	112-30-1	D	IIIA	82	288			5.3	0.008				
Decyl Alcohol	112-30-1	D	IIIA	82	288			5.3	0.008				
Diacetone Alcohol	123-42-2	D	IIIA	64	603	1.8	6.9	4.0	1.4				
Di-Isobutylene	25167-70-8	D[d]	I	2	391	0.8	4.8	3.8			0.96		
Di-Isobutyl Ketone	108-83-8	D	II	60	396	0.8	7.1	4.9	1.7				
o-Dichlorobenzene	955-50-1	D	IIIA	66	647	2.2	9.2	5.1		IIA			
1,4-Dichloro-2,3 Epoxybutane	3583-47-9	D[d]	I			1.9	8.5	2.0			0.25	0.98	1.07
1,1-Dichloroethane	1300-21-6	D	I		438	6.2	16.0	3.4	227				1.82
1,2-Dichloroethylene	156-59-2	D	I	97	460	5.6	12.8	3.4	204	IIA			
1,1-Dichloro-1-Nitroethane	594-72-9	C	IIIA	76				5.0					
1,3-Dichloropropene	10061-02-6	D	I	35		5.3	14.5	3.8					
Dicyclopentadiene	77-73-6	C	I	32	503				2.8				0.91
Diethylamine	109-87-9	C[d]	I	−28	312	1.8	10.1	2.5		IIA			1.15
Diethylaminoethanol	100-37-8	C	IIIA	60	320			4.0	1.6	IIA			
Diethyl Benzene	25340-17-4	D	II	57	395			4.6					
Diethyl Ether (Ethyl Ether)	60-29-7	C[d]	I	−45	160	1.7	48	2.6	538	IIB	0.19	0.88	0.83
Diethylene Glycol Monobutyl Ether	112-34-5	C	IIIA	78	228	0.9	24.6	5.6	0.02				
Diethylene Glycol Monomethyl Ether	111-77-3	C	IIIA	93	241				0.2				
n-n-Dimethyl Aniline	121-69-7	C	IIIA	63	371	1.0		4.2	0.7				
Dimethyl Formamide	68-12-2	D	II	58	455	2.2	15.2	2.5	4.1				1.08
Dimethyl Sulfate	77-78-1	D	IIIA	83	188			4.4	0.7				
Dimethylamine	124-40-3	C	GAS		400	2.8	14.4	1.6		IIA			
2,2-Dimethylbutane	75-83-2	D[g]	I	−48	405				319.3				
2,3-Dimethylbutane	78-29-8	D[g]	I		396								
3,3-Dimethylheptane	1071-26-7	D[g]	I		325				10.8				
2,3-Dimethylhexane	31394-54-4	D[g]	I		438								
2,3-Dimethylpentane	107-83-5	D[g]	I		335				211.7				
Di-N-Propylamine	142-84-7	C	I	17	299				27.1				
1,4-Dioxane	123-91-1	C[d]	I	12	180	2.0	22.0	3.0	38.2	IIB	0.19		0.70
Dipentene	138-86-3	D	II	45	237	0.7	6.1	4.7					1.18

Table A-1. Selected Chemicals [Reproduction of Table 4.4.2 from NFPA 497; reprinted with permission of NFPA]

Chemical	CAS No.	Class I Division Group	Type[a]	Flash Point (°C)	AIT (°C)	%LFL	%UFL	Vapor Density (Air = 1)	Vapor Pressure[b] (mm Hg)	Class I Zone Group[c]	MIE (mJ)	MIC Ratio	MESG (mm)
Dipropylene Glycol Methyl Ether	34590-94-8	C	IIIA	85		1.1	3.0	5.1	0.5				
Diisopropylamine	108-18-9	C	GAS	−6	316	1.1	7.1	3.5					
Dodecene	6842-15-5	D	IIIA	100	255								
Epichlorohydrin	3132-64-7	C[d]	I	33	411	3.8	21.0	3.2	13.0				
Ethane	74-84-0	D[d]	GAS	−29	472	3.0	12.5	1.0		IIA	0.24	0.82	0.91
Ethanol	64-17-5	D[d]	I	13	363	3.3	19.0	1.6	59.5	IIA		0.88	0.89
Ethylamine	75-04-7	D[d]	I	−18	385	3.5	14.0	1.6	1048		2.4		
Ethylene	74-85-1	C[d]	GAS	0	450	2.7	36.0	1.0		IIB	0.070	0.53	0.65
Ethylenediamine	107-15-3	D[d]	I	33	385	2.5	12.0	2.1	12.5				
Ethylenimine	151-56-4	C[d]	I	−11	320	3.3	54.8	1.5	211		0.48		
Ethylene Chlorohydrin	107-07-3	D	IIIA	59	425	4.9	15.9	2.8	7.2				
Ethylene Dichloride	107-06-2	D[d]	I	13	413	6.2	16.0	3.4	79.7				
Ethylene Glycol Monoethyl Ether Acetate	111-15-9	C	II	47	379	1.7		4.7	2.3			0.53	0.97
Ethylene Glycol Monobutyl Ether Acetate	112-07-2	C	IIIA		340	0.9	8.5		0.9				
Ethylene Glycol Monobutyl Ether	111-76-2	C	IIIA		238	1.1	12.7	4.1	1.0				
Ethylene Glycol Monoethyl Ether	110-80-5	C	II		235	1.7	15.6	3.0	5.4				0.84
Ethylene Glycol Monomethyl Ether	109-86-4	D	II		285	1.8	14.0	2.6	9.2				0.85
Ethylene Oxide	75-21-8	B(C)[d,e]	I	−20	429	3.0	99.9	1.5	1314	IIB	0.065	0.47	0.59
2-Ethylhexaldehyde	123-05-7	C	II	52	191	0.8	7.2	4.4	1.9				
2-Ethylhexanol	104-76-7	D	IIIA	81		0.9	9.7	4.5	0.2				
2-Ethylhexyl Acrylate	103-09-3	D	IIIA	88	252				0.3				
Ethyl Acetate	141-78-6	D[d]	I	−4	427	2.0	11.5	3.0	93.2		0.46		0.99
Ethyl Acrylate (Inhibited)	140-88-5	D[d]	I	9	372	1.4	14.0	3.5	37.5	IIA			0.86
Ethyl Alcohol	64-17-5	D[d]	I	13	363	3.3	19.0	1.6	59.5				0.89
Ethyl Sec-Amyl Ketone	541-85-5	D	II	59									
Ethyl Benzene	100-41-4	D	I	21	432	0.8	6.7	3.7	9.6				
Ethyl Butanol	97-95-0	D	II	57		1.2	7.7	3.5	1.5				
Ethyl Butyl Ketone	106-35-4	D	II	46				4.0	3.6				
Ethyl Chloride	75-00-3	D	GAS	−50	519	3.8	15.4	2.2					
Ethyl Formate	109-94-4	D	GAS	−20	455	2.8	16.0	2.6		IIA			0.94
Ethyl Mercaptan	75-08-1	C[d]	I	−18	300	2.8	18.0	2.1	527.4			0.90	0.90
n-Ethyl Morpholine	100-74-3	C	I	32				4.0					
2-Ethyl-3-Propyl Acrolein	645-62-5	C	IIIA	68				4.4					
Ethyl Silicate	78-10-4	D	II					7.2					
Formaldehyde (Gas)	50-00-0	B	GAS	60	429	7.0	73.0	1.0					0.57
Formic Acid	64-18-6	D	II	50	434	18.0	57.0	1.6	42.7				1.86
Fuel Oil 1	8008-20-6	D	II	72	210	0.7	5.0						
Furfural	98-01-1	C	IIIA	60	316	2.1	19.3	3.3	2.3				0.94
Furfuryl Alcohol	98-00-0	C	IIIA	75	490	1.8	16.3	3.4	0.6				
Gasoline	8006-61-9	D[d]	I	−46	280	1.4	7.6	3.0					
n-Heptane	142-82-5	D[d]	I	−4	204	1.0	6.7	3.5	45.5	IIA	0.24	0.88	0.91
n-Heptene	81624-04-6	D[g]	I	−1	204			3.4					0.97
n-Hexane	110-54-3	D[d,g]	I	−23	225	1.1	7.5	3.0	152	IIA	0.24	0.88	0.93
Hexanol	111-27-3	D	IIIA	63				3.5	0.8	IIA			0.98
2-Hexanone	591-78-6	D	I	35	424	1.2	8.0	3.5	10.6				
Hexene	592-41-6	D	I	−26	245	1.2	6.9		186				
sec-Hexyl Acetate	108-84-9	D	II	45				5.0					
Hydrazine	302-01-2	C	II	38	23		98.0	1.1	14.4				

Table A-1. Selected Chemicals [Reproduction of Table 4.4.2 from NFPA 497; reprinted with permission of NFPA]

Chemical	CAS No.	Class I Division Group	Type[a]	Flash Point (°C)	AIT (°C)	%LFL	%UFL	Vapor Density (Air = 1)	Vapor Pressure[b] (mm Hg)	Class I Zone Group[c]	MIE (mJ)	MIC Ratio	MESG (mm)
Hydrogen	1333-74-0	B[d]	GAS		520	4.0	75.0	0.1		IIC	0.019	0.25	0.28
Hydrogen Cyanide	74-90-8	C[d]	GAS	−18	538	5.6	40.0	0.9		IIB			0.80
Hydrogen Selenide	7783-07-5	C	I						7793				
Hydrogen Sulfide	7783-06-4	C[d]	GAS		260	4.0	44.0	1.2			0.068		0.90
Isoamyl Acetate	123-92-2	D	I	25	360	1.0	7.5	4.5	6.1				
Isoamyl Alcohol	123-51-3	D	II	43	350	1.2	9.0	3.0	3.2				1.02
Isobutane	75-28-5	D[g]	GAS		460	1.8	8.4	2.0					
Isobutyl Acetate	110-19-0	D[d]	I	18	421	2.4	10.5	4.0	17.8				
Isobutyl Acrylate	106-63-8	D	I		427			4.4	7.1				
Isobutyl Alcohol	78-83-1	D[d]	I	−40	416	1.2	10.9	2.5	10.5			0.92	0.98
Isobutyraldehyde	78-84-2	C	GAS	−40	196	1.6	10.6	2.5					
Isodecaldehyde	112-31-2	C	IIIA					5.4	0.09				
Isohexane	107-83-5	D[g]			264				211.7			1.00	
Isopentane	78-78-4	D[g]			420				688.6				
Isooctyl Aldehyde	123-05-7	C	II		197				1.9				
Isophorone	78-59-1	D		84	460	0.8	3.8	4.8	0.4				
Isoprene	78-79-5	D[d]	I	−54	220	1.5	8.9	2.4	550.6				
Isopropyl Acetate	108-21-4	D	I		460	1.8	8.0	3.5	60.4				
Isopropyl Ether	108-20-3	D[d]	I	−28	443	1.4	7.9	3.5	148.7			1.14	0.94
Isopropyl Glycidyl Ether	4016-14-2	C	I										
Isopropylamine	75-31-0	D	GAS	−26	402	2.3	10.4	2.0			2.0		
Kerosene	8008-20-6	D	II	72	210	0.7	5.0			IIA			
Liquefied Petroleum Gas	68476-85-7	D	I		405								
Mesityl Oxide	141-97-9	D[d]	I	31	344	1.4	7.2	3.4	47.6				
Methane	74-82-8	D[d]	GAS	−223	630	5.0	15.0	0.6		IIA	0.28	1.00	1.12
Methanol	67-56-1	D[d]	I	12	385	6.0	36.0	1.1	126.3	IIA	0.14	0.82	0.92
Methyl Acetate	79-20-9	D	GAS	−10	454	3.1	16.0	2.6		IIB		1.08	0.99
Methyl Acrylate	96-33-3	D	GAS	−3	468	2.8	25.0	3.0				0.98	0.85
Methyl Alcohol	67-56-1	D[d]	I		385	6.0	36.0	1.1	126.3				0.91
Methyl Amyl Alcohol	108-11-2	D	II	41		1.0	5.5	3.5	5.3				1.01
Methyl Chloride	74-87-3	D	GAS	−46	632	8.1	17.4	1.7					1.00
Methyl Ether	115-10-6	C[d]	GAS	−41	350	3.4	27.0	1.6				0.85	0.84
Methyl Ethyl Ketone	78-93-3	D[d]	I	−6	404	1.4	11.4	2.5	92.4		0.53	0.92	0.84
Methyl Formal	534-15-6	C[d]	I	1	238			3.1					
Methyl Formate	107-31-3	D	GAS	−19	449	4.5	23.0	2.1					0.94
2-Methylhexane	31394-54-4	D[g]	I		280								
Methyl Isobutyl Ketone	141-79-7	D[d]	I	31	440	1.2	8.0	3.5	11				
Methyl Isocyanate	624-83-9	D	GAS	−15	534	5.3	26.0	2.0					
Methyl Mercaptan	74-93-1	C	GAS	−18		3.9	21.8	1.7					
Methyl Methacrylate	80-62-6	D	I	10	422	1.7	8.2	3.6	37.2	IIA			0.95
Methyl N-Amyl Ketone	110-43-0	D	II	49	393	1.1	7.9	3.9	3.8				
Methyl Tertiary Butyl Ether	1634-04-4	D	I	−80	435	1.6	8.4	0.2	250.1				
2-Methyloctane	3221-61-2				220				6.3				
2-Methylpropane	75-28-5	D[g]	I		460				2639				
Methyl-1-Propanol	78-83-1	D[d]	I	−40	416	1.2	10.9	2.5	10.1				0.98
Methyl-2-Propanol	75-65-0	D[d]	I	10	360	2.4	8.0	2.6	42.2				
2-Methyl-5-Ethyl Pyridine	104-90-5	D		74		1.1	6.6	4.2					
Methylacetylene	74-99-7	C[d]	I			1.7		1.4	4306		0.11		
Methylacetylene-Propadiene	27846-30-6	C	I										0.74
Methylal	109-87-5	C	I	−18	237	1.6	17.6	2.6	398				
Methylamine	74-89-5	D	GAS		430	4.9	20.7	1.0		IIA			1.10
2-Methylbutane	78-78-4	D[g]		−56	420	1.4	8.3	2.6	688.6				
Methylcyclohexane	208-87-2	D	I	−4	250	1.2	6.7	3.4				0.27	

Table A-1. Selected Chemicals [Reproduction of Table 4.4.2 from NFPA 497; reprinted with permission of NFPA]

Chemical	CAS No.	Class I Division Group	Type[a]	Flash Point (°C)	AIT (°C)	%LFL	%UFL	Vapor Density (Air = 1)	Vapor Pressure[b] (mm Hg)	Class I Zone Group[c]	MIE (mJ)	MIC Ratio	MESG (mm)
Methylcyclohexanol	25630-42-3	D		68	296			3.9					
2-Methycyclohexanone	583-60-8	D	II					3.9					
2-Methylheptane		D[g]			420								
3-Methylhexane	589-34-4	D[g]			280				61.5				
3-Methylpentane	94-14-0	D[g]			278								
2-Methylpropane	75-28-5	D[g]	I		460				2639				
2-Methyl-1-Propanol	78-83-1	D[d]	I	−40	223	1.2	10.9	2.5	10.5				
2-Methyl-2-Propanol	75-65-0	D[d]	I		478	2.4	8.0	2.6	42.2				
2-Methyloctane	2216-32-2	D[g]			220								
3-Methyloctane	2216-33-3	D[g]			220				6.3				
4-Methyloctane	2216-34-4	D[g]			225				6.8				
Monoethanolamine	141-43-5	D		85	410			2.1	0.4	IIA			
Monoisopropanolamine	78-96-6	D		77	374			2.6	1.1				
Monomethyl Aniline	100-61-8	C			482				0.5				
Monomethyl Hydrazine	60-34-4	C	I	23	194	2.5	92.0	1.6					
Morpholine	110-91-8	C[d]	II	35	310	1.4	11.2	3.0	10.1				0.95
Naphtha (Coal Tar)	8030-30-6	D	II	42	277					IIA			
Naphtha (Petroleum)	8030-30-6	D[d,i]	I	42	288	1.1	5.9	2.5		IIA			
Neopentane	463-82-1	D[g]		−65	450	1.4	8.3	2.6	1286				
Nitrobenzene	98-95-3	D		88	482	1.8		4.3	0.3				0.94
Nitroethane	79-24-3	C	I	28	414	3.4		2.6	20.7	IIA			0.87
Nitromethane	75-52-5	C	I	35	418	7.3		2.1	36.1	IIA		0.92	1.17
1-Nitropropane	108-03-2	C	I	34	421	2.2		3.1	10.1				0.84
2-Nitropropane	79-46-9	C[d]	I	28	428	2.6	11.0	3.1	17.1				
n-Nonane	111-84-2	D[g]	I	31	205	0.8	2.9	4.4	4.4	IIA			
Nonene	27214-95-8	D	I			0.8		4.4					
Nonyl Alcohol	143-08-8	D				0.8	6.1	5.0	0.02	IIA			
n-Octane	111-65-9	D[d,g]	I	13	206	1.0	6.5	3.9	14.0	IIA			0.94
Octene	25377-83-7	D	I	8	230	0.9		3.9					
n-Octyl Alcohol	111-87-5	D						4.5	0.08	IIA			1.05
n-Pentane	109-66-0	D[d,g]	I	−40	243	1.5	7.8	2.5	513		0.28	0.97	0.93
1-Pentanol	71-41-0	D[d]	I	33	300	1.2	10.0	3.0	2.5	IIA			
2-Pentanone	107-87-9	D	I	7	452	1.5	8.2	3.0	35.6				0.99
1-Pentene	109-67-1	D	I	−18	275	1.5	8.7	2.4	639.7				
2-Pentene	109-68-2	D	I	−18				2.4					
2-Pentyl Acetate	626-38-0	D	I	23		1.1	7.5	4.5					
Phenylhydrazine	100-63-0	D		89				3.7	0.03				
Process Gas > 30% H₂	1333-74-0	B[j]	GAS		520	4.0	75.0	0.1			0.019	0.45	
Propane	74-98-6	D[d]	GAS	−104	450	2.1	9.5	1.6		IIA	0.25	0.82	0.97
1-Propanol	71-23-8	D[d]	I	15	413	2.2	13.7	2.1	20.7	IIA			0.89
2-Propanol	67-63-0	D[d]	I	12	399	2.0	12.7	2.1	45.4		0.65		1.00
Propiolactone	57-57-8	D				2.9		2.5	2.2				
Propionaldehyde	123-38-6	C	I	−9	207	2.6	17.0	2.0	318.5				
Propionic Acid	79-09-4	D	II	54	466	2.9	12.1	2.5	3.7				
Propionic Anhydride	123-62-6	D		74	285	1.3	9.5	4.5	1.4				
n-Propyl Acetate	109-60-4	D	I	14	450	1.7	8.0	3.5	33.4				1.05
n-Propyl Ether	111-43-3	C[d]	I	21	215	1.3	7.0	3.5	62.3				
Propyl Nitrate	627-13-4	B[d]	I	20	175	2.0	100.0						
Propylene	115-07-1	D[d]	GAS	−108	455	2.0	11.1	1.5			0.28		0.91
Propylene Dichloride	78-87-5	D	I	16	557	3.4	14.5	3.9	51.7				1.32
Propylene Oxide	75-56-9	B(C)[d,e]	I	−37	449	2.3	36.0	2.0	534.4		0.13		0.70
Pyridine	110-86-1	D[d]	I	20	482	1.8	12.4	2.7	20.8	IIA			
Styrene	100-42-5	D[d]	I	31	490	0.9	6.8	3.6	6.1	IIA		1.21	
Tetrahydrofuran	109-99-9	C[d]	I	−14	321	2.0	11.8	2.5	161.6	IIB	0.54		0.87
Tetrahydronaphthalene	119-64-2	D	IIIA		385	0.8	5.0	4.6	0.4				
Tetramethyl Lead	75-74-1	C	II	38				9.2					
Toluene	108-88-3	D[d]	I	4	480	1.1	7.1	3.1	28.53	IIA	0.24		

Table A-1. Selected Chemicals [Reproduction of Table 4.4.2 from NFPA 497; reprinted with permission of NFPA]

Selected Chemicals

Chemical	CAS No.	Class I Division Group	Type[a]	Flash Point (°C)	AIT (°C)	%LFL	%UFL	Vapor Density (Air = 1)	Vapor Pressure[b] (mm Hg)	Class I Zone Group[c]	MIE (mJ)	MIC Ratio	MESG (mm)
n-Tridecene	2437-56-1	D	IIIA			0.6		6.4	593.4				
Triethylamine	121-44-8	C[d]	I	−9	249	1.2	8.0	3.5	68.5	IIA	0.75		
Triethylbenzene	25340-18-5	D		83			56.0	5.6					
2,2,3-Trimethylbutane		D[g]			442								
2,2,4-Trimethylbutane		D[g]			407								
2,2,3-Trimethylpentane		D[g]			396								
2,2,4-Trimethylpentane		D[g]			415								
2,3,3-Trimethylpentane		D[g]			425								
Tripropylamine	102-69-2	D	II	41				4.9	1.5				1.13
Turpentine	8006-64-2	D	I	35	253	0.8			4.8				
n-Undecene	28761-27-5	D	IIIA			0.7		5.5					
Unsymmetrical Dimethyl Hydrazine	57-14-7	C[d]	I	−15	249	2.0	95.0	1.9					0.85
Valeraldehyde	110-62-3	C	I	280	222			3.0	34.3				
Vinyl Acetate	108-05-4	D[d]	I	−6	402	2.6	13.4	3.0	113.4	IIA	0.70		0.94
Vinyl Chloride	75-01-4	D[d]	GAS	−78	472	3.6	33.0	2.2					0.96
Vinyl Toluene	25013-15-4	D		52	494	0.8	11.0	4.1					
Vinylidene Chloride	75-35-4	D	I		570	6.5	15.5	3.4	599.4				3.91
Xylene	1330-20-7	D[d]	I	25	464	0.9	7.0	3.7		IIA	0.2		
Xylidine	121-69-7	C	IIIA	63	371	1.0		4.2	0.7				

Notes:

[a]Type is used to designate if the material is a gas, flammable liquid, or combustible liquid. *(See 4.2.6 and 4.2.7.)*

[b]Vapor pressure reflected in units of mm Hg at 25°C (77°F) unless stated otherwise.

[c]Class I, Zone Groups are based on 1996 IEC TR3 60079-20, *Electrical apparatus for explosive gas atmospheres — Part 20: Data for flammable gases and vapors, relating to the use of electrical apparatus*, which contains additional data on MESG and group classifications.

[d]Material has been classified by test.

[e]Where all conduit runs into explosionproof equipment are provided with explosionproof seals installed within 450 mm (18 in.) of the enclosure, equipment for the group classification shown in parentheses is permitted.

[f]For classification of areas involving ammonia, see ASHRAE 15, *Safety Code for Mechanical Refrigeration*, and ANSI/CGA G2.1, *Safety Requirements for the Storage and Handling of Anhydrous Ammonia*.

[g]Commercial grades of aliphatic hydrocarbon solvents are mixtures of several isomers of the same chemical formula (or molecular weight). The autoignition temperatures of the individual isomers are significantly different. The electrical equipment should be suitable for the AIT of the solvent mixture. *(See A.4.4.2.)*

[h]Certain chemicals have characteristics that require safeguards beyond those required for any of the above groups. Carbon disulfide is one of these chemicals because of its low autoignition temperature and the small joint clearance necessary to arrest its flame propagation.

[i]Petroleum naphtha is a saturated hydrocarbon mixture whose boiling range is 20°C to 135°C (68°F to 275°F). It is also known as benzine, ligroin, petroleum ether, and naphtha.

[j]Fuel and process gas mixtures found by test not to present hazards similar to those of hydrogen may be grouped based on the test results.

Table A-1. Selected Chemicals [Reproduction of Table 4.4.2 from NFPA 497; reprinted with permission of NFPA]

Chemical Name	CAS No.	*NEC* Group	Code	Layer or Cloud Ignition Temp. (°C)
Acetal, Linear		G	NL	440
Acetoacet-p-phenetidide	122-82-7	G	NL	560
Acetoacetanilide	102-01-2	G	M	440
Acetylamino-t-nitrothiazole		G		450
Acrylamide Polymer		G		240
Acrylonitrile Polymer		G		460
Acrylonitrile-Vinyl Chloride-Vinylidenechloride copolymer (70-20-10)		G		210
Acrylonitrile-Vinyl Pyridine Copolymer		G		240
Adipic Acid	124-04-9	G	M	550
Alfalfa Meal		G		200
Alkyl Ketone Dimer Sizing Compound		G		160
Allyl Alcohol Derivative (CR-39)		G	NL	500
Almond Shell		G		200
Aluminum, A422 Flake	7429-90-5	E		320
Aluminum, Atomized Collector Fines		E	CL	550
Aluminum—cobalt alloy (60-40)		E		570
Aluminum—copper alloy (50-50)		E		830
Aluminum—lithium alloy (15% Li)		E		400
Aluminum—magnesium alloy (Dowmetal)		E	CL	430
Aluminum—nickel alloy (58-42)		E		540
Aluminum—silicon alloy (12% Si)		E	NL	670
Amino-5-nitrothiazole	121-66-4	G		460
Anthranilic Acid	118-92-3	G	M	580
Apricot Pit		G		230
Aryl-nitrosomethylamide		G	NL	490
Asphalt	8052-42-4	F		510
Aspirin [acetol (2)]	50-78-2	G	M	660
Azelaic Acid	109-31-9	G	M	610
Azo-bis-butyronitrile	78-67-1	G		350
Benzethonium Chloride		G	CL	380
Benzoic Acid	65-85-0	G	M	440
Benzotriazole	95-14-7	G	M	440
Beta-naphthalene-axo-dimethylaniline		G		175
Bis(2-hydroxy-5-chlorophenyl) Methane	97-23-4	G	NL	570
Bisphenol-A	80-05-7	G	M	570
Boron, Commercial Amorphous (85% B)	7440-42-8	E		400
Calcium Silicide		E		540
Carbon Black (More Than 8% Total Entrapped Volatiles)		F		
Carboxymethyl Cellulose	9000-11-7	G		290
Carboxypolymethylene		G	NL	520
Cashew Oil, Phenolic, Hard		G		180
Cellulose		G		260
Cellulose Acetate		G		340
Cellulose Acetate Butyrate		G	NL	370
Cellulose Triacetate		G	NL	430
Charcoal (Activated)	64365-11-3	F		180
Charcoal (More Than 8% Total Entrapped Volatiles)		F		
Cherry Pit		G		220
Chlorinated Phenol		G	NL	570
Chlorinated Polyether Alcohol		G		460
Chloroacetoacetanilide	101-92-8	G	M	640
Chromium (97%) Electrolytic, Milled	7440-47-3	E		400
Cinnamon		G		230
Citrus Peel		G		270
Coal, Kentucky Bituminous		F		180
Coal, Pittsburgh Experimental		F		170
Coal, Wyoming		F		
Cocoa Bean Shell		G		370
Cocoa, Natural, 19% Fat		G		240

Table A-2. Selected Combustible Materials [Reproduction of Table 4.5.2 from NFPA 499; reprinted with permission of NFPA]

Chemical Name	CAS No.	*NEC* Group	Code	Layer or Cloud Ignition Temp. (°C)
Coconut Shell		G		220
Coke (More Than 8% Total Entrapped Volatiles)		F		
Cork		G		210
Corn		G		250
Corn Dextrine		G		370
Corncob Grit		G		240
Cornstarch, Commercial		G		330
Cornstarch, Modified		G		200
Cottonseed Meal		G		200
Coumarone-Indene, Hard		G	NL	520
Crag No. 974	533-74-4	G	CL	310
Cube Root, South America	83-79-4	G		230
Di-alphacumyl Peroxide, 40-60 on CA	80-43-3	G		180
Diallyl Phthalate	131-17-9	G	M	480
Dicyclopentadiene Dioxide		G	NL	420
Dieldrin (20%)	60-57-1	G	NL	550
Dihydroacetic Acid		G	NL	430
Dimethyl Isophthalate	1459-93-4	G	M	580
Dimethyl Terephthalate	120-61-6	G	M	570
Dinitro-o-toluamide	148-01-6	G	NL	500
Dinitrobenzoic Acid		G	NL	460
Diphenyl	92-52-4	G	M	630
Ditertiary-butyl-paracresol	128-37-0	G	NL	420
Dithane m-45	8018-01-7	G		180
Epoxy		G	NL	540
Epoxy-bisphenol A		G	NL	510
Ethyl Cellulose		G	CL	320
Ethyl Hydroxyethyl Cellulose		G	NL	390
Ethylene Oxide Polymer		G	NL	350
Ethylene-maleic Anhydride Copolymer		G	NL	540
Ferbam™	14484-64-1	G		150
Ferromanganese, Medium Carbon	12604-53-4	E		290
Ferrosilicon (88% Si, 9% Fe)	8049-17-0	E		800
Ferrotitanium (19% Ti, 74.1% Fe, 0.06% C)		E	CL	380
Flax Shive		G		230
Fumaric Acid	110-17-8	G	M	520
Garlic, Dehydrated		G	NL	360
Gilsonite	12002-43-6	F		500
Green Base Harmon Dye		G		175
Guar Seed		G	NL	500
Gulasonic Acid, Diacetone		G	NL	420
Gum, Arabic		G		260
Gum, Karaya		G		240
Gum, Manila		G	CL	360
Gum, Tragacanth	9000-65-1	G		260
Hemp Hurd		G		220
Hexamethylene Tetramine	100-97-0	G	S	410
Hydroxyethyl Cellulose		G	NL	410
Iron, 98% H_2 Reduced		E		290
Iron, 99% Carbonyl	13463-40-6	E		310
Isotoic Anhydride		G	NL	700
L-sorbose		G	M	370
Lignin, Hydrolized, Wood-type, Fine		G	NL	450
Lignite, California		F		180
Lycopodium		G		190
Malt Barley		G		250
Manganese	7439-96-5	E		240
Magnesium, Grade B, Milled		E		430
Manganese Vancide		G		120
Mannitol	69-65-8	G	M	460

Table A-2. Selected Combustible Materials [Reproduction of Table 4.5.2 from NFPA 499; reprinted with permission of NFPA]

Chemical Name	CAS No.	*NEC* Group	Code	Layer or Cloud Ignition Temp. (°C)
Methacrylic Acid Polymer		G		290
Methionine (l-methionine)	63-68-3	G		360
Methyl Cellulose		G		340
Methyl Methacrylate Polymer	9011-14-7	G	NL	440
Methyl Methacrylate-ethyl Acrylate		G	NL	440
Methyl Methacrylate-styrene-butadiene		G	NL	480
Milk, Skimmed		G		200
N,N-Dimethylthio-formamide		G		230
Nitropyridone	100703-82-0	G	M	430
Nitrosamine		G	NL	270
Nylon Polymer	63428-84-2	G		430
Para-oxy-benzaldehyde	123-08-0	G	CL	380
Paraphenylene Diamine	106-50-3	G	M	620
Paratertiary Butyl Benzoic Acid	98-73-7	G	M	560
Pea Flour		G		260
Peach Pit Shell		G		210
Peanut Hull		G		210
Peat, Sphagnum	94114-14-4	G		240
Pecan Nut Shell	8002-03-7	G		210
Pectin	5328-37-0	G		200
Pentaerythritol	115-77-5	G	M	400
Petrin Acrylate Monomer	7659-34-9	G	NL	220
Petroleum Coke (More Than 8% Total Entrapped Volatiles)		F		
Petroleum Resin	64742-16-1	G		500
Phenol Formaldehyde	9003-35-4	G	NL	580
Phenol Formaldehyde, Polyalkylene-p	9003-35-4	G		290
Phenol Furfural	26338-61-4	G		310
Phenylbetanaphthylamine	135-88-6	G	NL	680
Phthalic Anydride	85-44-9	G	M	650
Phthalimide	85-41-6	G	M	630
Pitch, Coal Tar	65996-93-2	F	NL	710
Pitch, Petroleum	68187-58-6	F	NL	630
Polycarbonate		G	NL	710
Polyethylene, High Pressure Process	9002-88-4	G		380
Polyethylene, Low Pressure Process	9002-88-4	G	NL	420
Polyethylene Terephthalate	25038-59-9	G	NL	500
Polyethylene Wax	68441-04-8	G	NL	400
Polypropylene (no antioxidant)	9003-07-0	G	NL	420
Polystyrene Latex	9003-53-6	G		500
Polystyrene Molding Compound	9003-53-6	G	NL	560
Polyurethane Foam, Fire Retardant	9009-54-5	G		390
Polyurethane Foam, No Fire Retardant	9009-54-5	G		440
Polyvinyl Acetate	9003-20-7	G	NL	550
Polyvinyl Acetate/Alcohol	9002-89-5	G		440
Polyvinyl Butyral	63148-65-2	G		390
Polyvinyl Chloride-dioctyl Phthalate		G	NL	320
Potato Starch, Dextrinated	9005-25-8	G	NL	440
Pyrethrum	8003-34-7	G		210
Rayon (Viscose) Flock	61788-77-0	G		250
Red Dye Intermediate		G		175
Rice		G		220
Rice Bran		G	NL	490
Rice Hull		G		220
Rosin, DK	8050-09-7	G	NL	390
Rubber, Crude, Hard	9006-04-6	G	NL	350
Rubber, Synthetic, Hard (33% S)	64706-29-2	G	NL	320
Safflower Meal		G		210
Salicylanilide	87-17-2	G	M	610
Sevin	63-25-2	G		140

Table A-2. Selected Combustible Materials [Reproduction of Table 4.5.2 from NFPA 499; reprinted with permission of NFPA]

Chemical Name	CAS No.	*NEC* Group	Code	Layer or Cloud Ignition Temp. (°C)
Shale, Oil	68308-34-9	F		
Shellac	9000-59-3	G	NL	400
Sodium Resinate	61790-51-0	G		220
Sorbic Acid (Copper Sorbate or Potash)	110-44-1	G		460
Soy Flour	68513-95-1	G		190
Soy Protein	9010-10-0	G		260
Stearic Acid, Aluminum Salt	637-12-7	G		300
Stearic Acid, Zinc Salt	557-05-1	G	M	510
Styrene Modified Polyester-Glass Fiber	100-42-5	G		360
Styrene-acrylonitrile (70-30)	9003-54-7	G	NL	500
Styrene-butadiene Latex (>75% styrene)	903-55-8	G	NL	440
Styrene-maleic Anhydride Copolymer	9011-13-6	G	CL	470
Sucrose	57-50-1	G	CL	350
Sugar, Powdered	57-50-1	G	CL	370
Sulfur	7704-34-9	G		220
Tantalum	7440-25-7	E		300
Terephthalic Acid	100-21-0	G	NL	680
Thorium, 1.2% O_2	7440-29-1	E	CL	280
Tin, 96%, Atomized (2% Pb)	7440-31-5	E		430
Titanium, 99% Ti	7440-32-6	E	CL	330
Titanium Hydride (95% Ti, 3.8% H_2)	7704-98-5	E	CL	480
Trithiobisdimethylthio-formamide		G		230
Tung, Kernels, Oil-free	8001-20-5	G		240
Urea Formaldehyde Molding Compound	9011-05-6	G	NL	460
Urea Formaldehyde-phenol Formaldehyde	25104-55-6	G		240
Vanadium, 86.4%	7440-62-2	E		490
Vinyl Chloride-acrylonitrile Copolymer	9003-00-3	G		470
Vinyl Toluene-acrylonitrile Butadiene	76404-69-8	G	NL	530
Violet 200 Dye		G		175
Vitamin B1, Mononitrate	59-43-8	G	NL	360
Vitamin C	50-81-7	G		280
Walnut Shell, Black		G		220
Wheat		G		220
Wheat Flour	130498-22-5	G		360
Wheat Gluten, Gum	100684-25-1	G	NL	520
Wheat Starch		G	NL	380
Wheat Straw		G		220
Wood Flour		G		260
Woodbark, Ground		G		250
Yeast, Torula	68602-94-8	G		260
Zirconium Hydride	7704-99-6	E		270
Zirconium		E	CL	330

Notes:

1. Normally, the minimum ignition temperature of a layer of a specific dust is lower than the minimum ignition temperature of a cloud of that dust. Since this is not universally true, the lower of the two minimum ignition temperatures is listed. If no symbol appears between the two temperature columns, then the layer ignition temperature is shown. "CL" means the cloud ignition temperature is shown. "NL" means that no layer ignition temperature is available, and the cloud ignition temperature is shown. "M" signifies that the dust layer melts before it ignites; the cloud ignition temperature is shown. "S" signifies that the dust layer sublimes before it ignites; the cloud ignition temperature is shown.

2. Certain metal dusts may have characteristics that require safeguards beyond those required for atmospheres containing the dusts of aluminum, magnesium, and their commercial alloys. For example, zirconium, thorium, and uranium dusts have extremely low ignition temperatures [as low as 20°C (68°F)] and minimum ignition energies lower than any material classified in any of the Class I or Class II groups.

Table A-2. Selected Combustible Materials [Reproduction of Table 4.5.2 from NFPA 499; reprinted with permission of NFPA]

PURGED AND PRESSURIZED TYPE "p" PROTECTION

This is a type of protection which prevents the entry of the surrounding atmosphere into the enclosure of the electrical apparatus by maintaining a positive pressure within the enclosure of a protective gas (air, inert, or other suitable gas) at a higher pressure than the surrounding atmosphere.

Purging is the process of supplying an enclosure with a protective gas at a sufficient flow and positive pressure to reduce the concentration of any flammable gas or vapor initially present to an acceptable level. This technique can be used to change a Class I or Class II, Division 1 location into a nonhazardous location or into a Division 2 location, or to change a Class I or II, Division 2 location into a nonhazardous location. It requires a noncombustible enclosure (which may be a control room or a machine room) that is first purged of any combustibles or flammables that may be present, and is then maintained at a positive pressure sufficient to assure that combustibles or flammables cannot enter the enclosure and be ignited by electrical equipment within the enclosure. The purging may be a continuous purge or a single purge with a positive pressure maintained to make up for leaks. The pressurizing medium may be either air, commonly used in a control room where people will be working, or a nonflammable gas. In tanker ships at sea, flue gas is a common purging and pressurizing medium. In instrument enclosures in locations with corrosive atmospheres, specially processed and dried air or gas is used to protect the enclosed equipment against corrosion as well as to provide protection against ignition of exterior flammable gases and vapors, or combustible dusts.

TYPE	EXPLANATION
X	Changes the area within the unit from Division 1 to nonhazardous
Y	Changes the area within the unit from Division 1 to Division 2
Z	Changes the area within the unit from Division 2 to nonhazardous

POWDER FILLING TYPE "q" PROTECTION

This protection system is permitted in Zone 1 and 2 locations. There is no equivalent system recognized in the US NEC 500 electrical code. In this type of protection system the enclosure or the electrical apparatus is filled with a material in a finely divided granulated state so that, in the intended conditions of service, the arc occurring within the enclosure of an electrical apparatus will not ignite the surrounding atmosphere. Further, no ignition can be caused either by flame or excessive temperature of the surfaces of the enclosure. This protection system is used for protection of the components in junction boxes. It is sometimes called "sand filling".

SPECIAL PROTECTION

Some countries permit special protection systems consisting of combinations of other systems or other special systems. UL listed flashlights and lanterns for use in hazardous locations would be an example of such a special protection system.

ENVIRONMENTAL PROTECTION NEMA ENCLOSURE TYPES AND CSA TYPES

DEFINITIONS PERTAINING TO NONHAZARDOUS LOCATIONS

The term NEMA enclosure is common in the US, although products are normally tested to a UL standard. The following are environmental protection designations, which are specified in addition to electrical or hazardous location requirements.

Type 1 Enclosures
Type 1 Enclosures are intended for indoor use primarily to provide a degree of protection against limited amounts of falling dirt. This type is not specifically identified in the CSA Standard.

Type 2 Enclosures
Type 2 Enclosures are intended for indoor use primarily to provide a degree of protection against limited amounts of falling water and dirt.

Type 3 Enclosures
Type 3 Enclosures are intended for outdoor use primarily to provide a degree of protection against rain, sleet, windblown dust; and damage from external ice formation.

Type 3R Enclosures
Type 3R Enclosures are intended for outdoor use primarily to provide a degree of protection against rain, sleet; and damage from external ice formation.

Type 3S Enclosures
Type 3S Enclosures are intended for outdoor use primarily to provide a degree of protection against rain, sleet, windblown dust; and to provide for operation of external mechanisms when ice laden.

Type 4 Enclosures
Type 4 Enclosures are intended for indoor or outdoor use primarily to provide a degree of protection against windblown dust and rain, splashing water, hose directed water; and damage from external ice formation.

Table A-3. Hazardous Locations Data   Courtesy of Hubbell/Killark

Type 4X Enclosures

Type 4X Enclosures are intended for indoor or outdoor use primarily to provide a degree of protection against corrosion, windblown dust and rain, splashing water, hose directed water; and damage from external ice formation.

Type 5 Enclosures

Type 5 Enclosures are intended for indoor use primary to provide a degree of protection against settling airborne dust, falling dirt, and dripping noncorrosive liquids.

Type 6 Enclosures

Type 6 Enclosures are intended for indoor or outdoor use primarily to provide a degree of protection against hose directed water, the entry of water during occasional temporary submersion at a limited depth; and damage from external ice formation.

Type 6P Enclosures

Type 6P Enclosures are intended for indoor or outdoor use primarily to provide a degree of protection against hose-directed water, the entry of water during prolonged submersion at a limited depth; and damage from external ice formation.

Type 12 Enclosures

Type 12 Enclosures are intended for indoor use primarily to provide a degree of protection against circulating dust, falling dirt, and dripping noncorrosive liquids.

Type 12K Enclosures

Type 12K Enclosures with knockouts are intended for indoor use primarily to provide a degree of protection against circulating dust, falling dirt, and dripping noncorrosive liquids.

Type 13 Enclosures

Type 13 Enclosures are intended for indoor use primarily to provide a degree of protection against dust, spraying of water, oil, and noncorrosive coolant.

DEFINITIONS PERTAINING TO HAZARDOUS (CLASSIFIED) LOCATIONS

The following NEMA type enclosures occasionally appear on specifications and product literature however, they are not used by CSA. These NEMA types are specific to the US only.

Type 7 Enclosures

Type 7 Enclosures are intended for indoor use in locations classified as Class I, Groups A, B, C, or D, as defined in the NEC®.

Type 8 Enclosures

Type 8 Enclosures are for indoor or outdoor use in locations classified as Class I, Groups A, B, C, or D, as defined in the NEC®

Type 9 Enclosures

Type 9 Enclosures are intended for indoor use in locations classified as Class II, Groups E, F, and G, as defined in the NEC®

Type 10 Enclosures

Type 10 Enclosures are constructed to meet the applicable requirements of the Mine Safety and Health Administration (MSHA).

- *Refer to NEMA Standards Publication No. 250 Enclosures for Electrical Equipment (1000 Volts Maximum) or other third party certification standards for specific requirements for product construction, testing and performance such as Underwriters Laboratories Inc.®, Standard UL 50 "Standard for Enclosures for Electrical Equipment", and UL 886 "Outlet Boxes and Fittings for use in Hazardous (Classified) Locations".*

Table A-3. Hazardous Locations Data Courtesy of Hubbell/Killark

COMPARISON OF SPECIFIC APPLICATIONS OF ENCLOSURES FOR INDOOR NONHAZARDOUS LOCATIONS

PROVIDES A DEGREE OF PROTECTION AGAINST THE FOLLOWING ENVIRONMENTAL CONDITIONS	TYPE OF ENCLOSURE									
	1*	2*	4	4X	5	6	6P	12	12K	13
Incidental contact with the enclosed equipment	X	X	X	X	X	X	X	X	X	X
Falling dirt	X	X	X	X	X	X	X	X	X	X
Falling liquids and light splashing	—	X	X	X	X	X	X	X	X	X
Circulating dust, lint, fibers, and flyings**	—	—	X	X	—	X	X	X	X	X
Settling airborne dust, lint, fibers, and flyings**	—	—	X	X	X	X	X	X	X	X
Hosedown and splashing water	—	—	X	X	—	X	X	—	—	—
Oil and coolant seepage	—	—	—	—	—	—	—	X	X	X
Oil and coolant spraying and splashing	—	—	—	—	—	—	—	—	—	X
Corrosive agents	—	—	—	X	—	—	—	—	—	—
Occasional temporary submersion	—	—	—	—	—	X	X	—	—	—
Occasional prolonged submersion	—	—	—	—	—	—	—	—	—	—

* These enclosures may be ventilated. However, Type 1 may not provide protection against small particles of falling dirt when ventilation is provided in the enclosure top.

** These fibers and flyings are nonhazardous materials and are not considered as Class III type ignitable fibers or combustible flyings. For Class III type ignitable fibers or combustible flyings see the National Electrical Code®, Article 500.

COMPARISON OF SPECIFIC APPLICATIONS OF ENCLOSURES FOR OUTDOOR NONHAZARDOUS LOCATIONS

PROVIDES A DEGREE OF PROTECTION AGAINST THE FOLLOWING ENVIRONMENTAL CONDITIONS	TYPE OF ENCLOSURE						
	3	3R***	3S	4	4X	6	6P
Incidental contact with the enclosed equipment	X	X	X	X	X	X	X
Rain, snow, sleet*	X	X	X	X	X	X	X
Sleet**	—	—	X	—	—	—	—
Windblown dust	X	—	X	X	X	X	X
Hosedown	—	—	—	X	X	X	X
Corrosive agents	—	—	—	—	X	—	X
Occasional temporary submersion	—	—	—	—	—	X	X
Occasional prolonged submersion	—	—	—	—	—	—	X

* External operating mechanisms are not required to operate when the enclosure is ice covered.

** External operating mechanisms are operable when the enclosure is ice covered.

*** These enclosures may be ventilated.

COMPARISON OF SPECIFIC APPLICATIONS OF ENCLOSURES FOR INDOOR HAZARDOUS (CLASSIFIED) LOCATIONS

PROVIDES A DEGREE OF PROTECTION AGAINST ATMOSPHERES TYPICALLY CONTAINING HAZARDOUS GASES, VAPORS, AND DUSTS***	TYPE OF ENCLOSURE NEMA 7 & 8, CLASS I GROUPS**					TYPE OF ENCLOSURE NEMA 9 & 10, CLASS II GROUPS**			
	Class	A	B	C	D	E	F	G	10
Acetylene	I	X	—	—	—	—	—	—	—
Hydrogen, manufactured gases	I	—	X	—	—	—	—	—	—
Diethyl ether, ethylene, cyclopropane	I	—	—	X	—	—	—	—	—
Gasoline, hexane, butane, naptha, propane, acetone									
Toluene, isoprene	I	—	—	—	X	—	—	—	—
Metal dusts	II	—	—	—	—	X	—	—	—
Carbon black, coal dust, coke dust	II	—	—	—	—	—	X	—	—
Flour, starch, grain dust	II	—	—	—	—	—	—	X	—
Fibers, flyings *	III	—	—	—	—	—	—	X	—
Methane with or without coal dust	MSHA	—	—	—	—	—	—	—	X

* Due to the characteristics of the gas, vapor, or dust, a product suitable for one Class or Group may not be suitable for another Class or Group unless so marked on the product.

** For Class III type ignitable fibers or combustible flyings refer to the National Electrical Code® Article 500.

*** For a complete listing of flammable liquids, gases, or vapors refer to NFPA 497 - 1997 (Recommended Practice for the Classification of Flammable Liquids, Gases, or Vapors and of Hazardous (Classified) Locations for Electrical Installations in Chemical Process Areas and NFPA 325 - 1994 (Fire Hazard Properties of Flammable Liquids, Gases, and Volatile Solids). Reference also NFPA 499 – 1997 Classifications of Combustible Dusts and of Hazardous (Classified) Locations for Electrical Installations in Chemical Process Areas.

Table A-3. Hazardous Locations Data   Courtesy of Hubbell/Killark

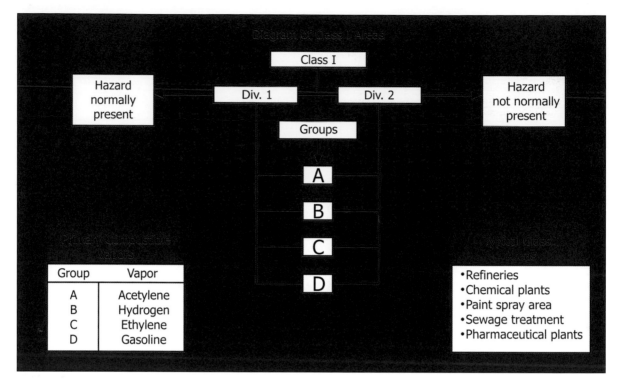

Figure A-01. Diagram of Class I Areas (Concept courtesy of Appleton EGS Electrical Group)

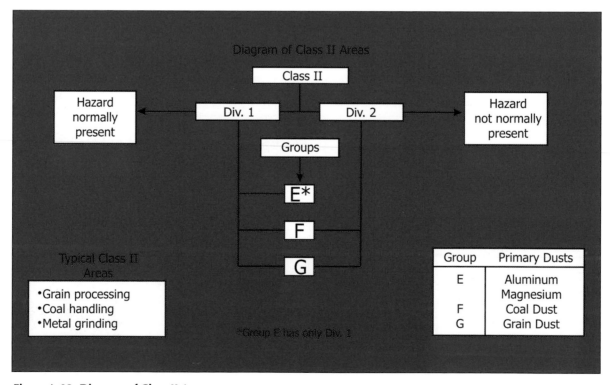

Figure A-02. Diagram of Class II Areas (Concept courtesy of Appleton EGS Electrical Group)

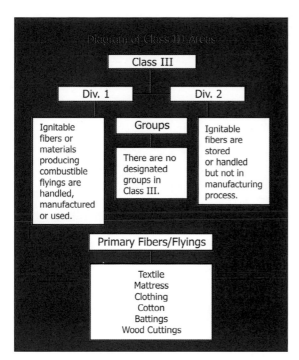

Figure A-03. Diagram of Class III Areas (Concept courtesy of Appleton EGS Electrical Group)

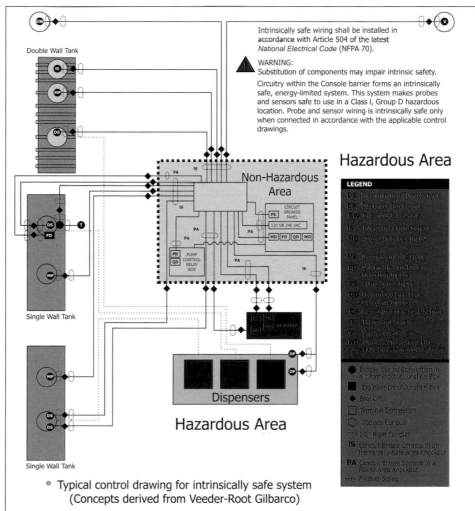

Intrinsically safe wiring shall be installed in accordance with Article 504 of the latest *National Electrical Code* (NFPA 70).

WARNING:
Substitution of components may impair intrinsic safety.
Circuitry within the Console barrier forms an intrinsically safe, energy-limited system. This system makes probes and sensors safe to use in a Class I, Group D hazardous location. Probe and sensor wiring is intrinsically safe only when connected in accordance with the applicable control drawings.

Figures A-04 through A-08 are conceptual drawings only and should not be used for actual field installations. Consult manufacturer's actual control drawings with the equipment used in the field.

Figure A-04. Typical control drawing for intrinsically safe system

*For example use only.

* Typical control drawing for intrinsically safe system
(Concepts derived from Veeder-Root Gilbarco)

Figure A-05. Typical control drawing for intrinsically safe system

*For example use only.

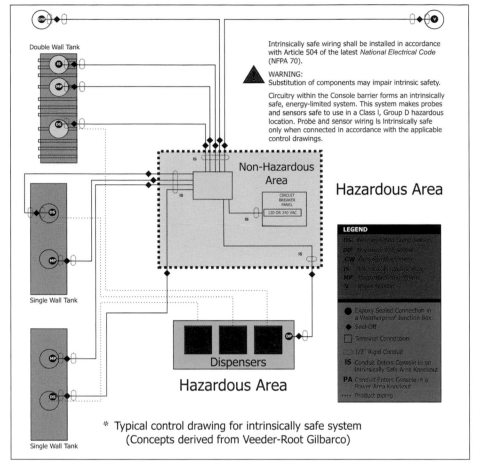

Intrinsically safe wiring shall be installed in accordance with Article 504 of the latest *National Electrical Code* (NFPA 70).

⚠ WARNING:
Substitution of components may impair intrinsic safety.

Circuitry within the Console barrier forms an intrinsically safe, energy-limited system. This system makes probes and sensors safe to use in a Class I, Group D hazardous location. Probe and sensor wiring is Intrinsically safe only when connected in accordance with the applicable control drawings.

Non-Hazardous Area

CIRCUIT BREAKER PANEL

120 OR 240 VAC

Hazardous Area

Double Wall Tank

Single Wall Tank

Single Wall Tank

Dispensers

Hazardous Area

LEGEND

● Epoxy Sealed Connection in a Weatherproof Junction Box
◆ Seal-Off
☐ Terminal Connection
1/2" Rigid Conduit
IS Conduit Enters Console in an Intrinsically Safe Area Knockout
PA Conduit Enters Console in a Power Area Knockout
···· Product piping

* Typical control drawing for intrinsically safe system
(Concepts derived from Veeder-Root Gilbarco)

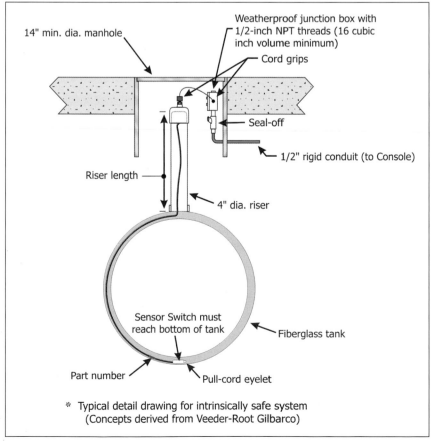

14" min. dia. manhole

Weatherproof junction box with 1/2-inch NPT threads (16 cubic inch volume minimum)

Cord grips

Seal-off

1/2" rigid conduit (to Console)

Riser length

4" dia. riser

Sensor Switch must reach bottom of tank

Fiberglass tank

Part number

Pull-cord eyelet

* Typical detail drawing for intrinsically safe system
(Concepts derived from Veeder-Root Gilbarco)

*For example use only.

Figure A-06. Double wall tank detail

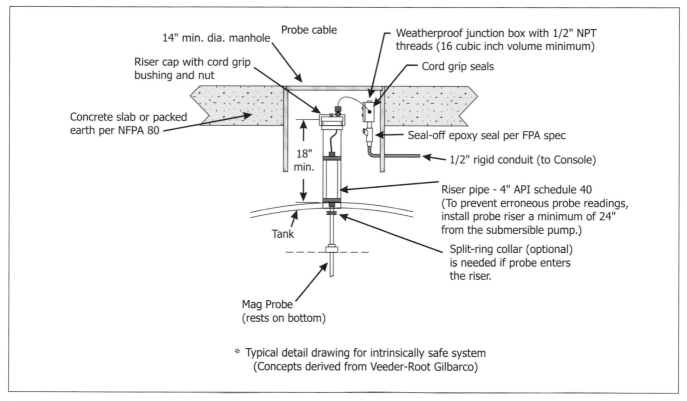

14" min. dia. manhole

Probe cable

Weatherproof junction box with 1/2" NPT threads (16 cubic inch volume minimum)

Riser cap with cord grip bushing and nut

Cord grip seals

Concrete slab or packed earth per NFPA 80

Seal-off epoxy seal per FPA spec

18" min.

1/2" rigid conduit (to Console)

Riser pipe - 4" API schedule 40 (To prevent erroneous probe readings, install probe riser a minimum of 24" from the submersible pump.)

Tank

Split-ring collar (optional) is needed if probe enters the riser.

Mag Probe (rests on bottom)

* Typical detail drawing for intrinsically safe system (Concepts derived from Veeder-Root Gilbarco)

Figure A-07. Underground tank detail *For example use only.*

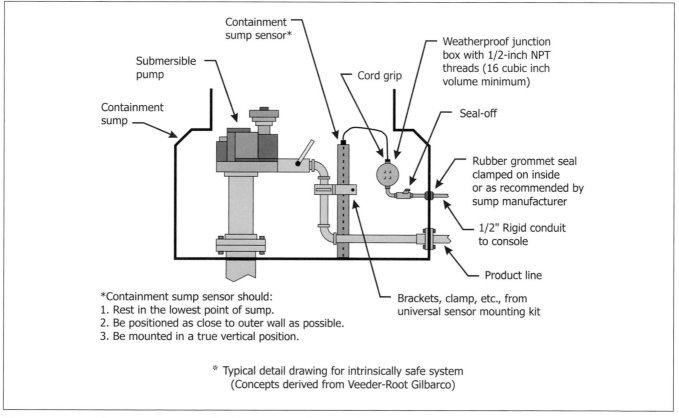

Containment sump sensor*

Submersible pump

Cord grip

Weatherproof junction box with 1/2-inch NPT threads (16 cubic inch volume minimum)

Containment sump

Seal-off

Rubber grommet seal clamped on inside or as recommended by sump manufacturer

1/2" Rigid conduit to console

Product line

*Containment sump sensor should:
1. Rest in the lowest point of sump.
2. Be positioned as close to outer wall as possible.
3. Be mounted in a true vertical position.

Brackets, clamp, etc., from universal sensor mounting kit

* Typical detail drawing for intrinsically safe system (Concepts derived from Veeder-Root Gilbarco)

Figure A-08. Containment sump sensor detail *For example use only.*

Hazardous Locations

INDEX

INDEX

Chapter 1

1. c. In textbook
2. c. In textbook
3. a. In textbook
4. c. In textbook
5. d. In textbook
6. b. In textbook, *NEC*, 500.5(B)(2)
7. a. In textbook, *NEC*, 505.5(B)(2), 505.6(A)
8. a. In textbook, *NEC*, 500.6(A)(4)
9. d. In textbook
10. b. In textbook
11. a. In textbook
12. d. In textbook
13. b. In textbook
14. c. In textbook
15. d. In textbook
16. c. In textbook, *NEC*, Article 502
17. a. In textbook, *NEC*, Section 506.1
18. d. In textbook, *NEC*, 500.2 Definition of "Unclassified"
19. b. In textbook, *NEC*, Article 505
20. b. In textbook, *NEC*, Article 506

Chapter 2

1. b. In textbook
2. b. In textbook
3. a. In textbook
4. d. In textbook
5. a. In textbook
6. d. In textbook
7. a. In textbook
8. a. In textbook
9. b. In textbook
10. d. In textbook
11. b. In textbook
12. a. In textbook, NFPA 77 and NFPA 780
13. a. In textbook
14. c. In textbook
15. d. In textbook

Chapter 3

1. d. In textbook
2. b. In textbook
3. c. In textbook, *NEC*, 500.2 Definition of purged and pressurized
4. a. In textbook, *NEC*, 500.7
5. c. In textbook, *NEC*, 500.7(A)
6. c. In textbook, *NEC*, 500.7(G), 500.6(B)(1)
7. a. In textbook, *NEC*, 500.8(A)(1)
8. d. In textbook
9. a. In textbook
10. b. In textbook
11. b. In textbook
12. a. In textbook
13. b. In textbook
14. b. In textbook
15. a. In textbook

Chapter 4

1. c. In textbook, *NEC*, 504.10(B), 501.105
2. b. In textbook, *NEC*, 505.20 Exception No. 4
3. a. In textbook
4. b. In textbook, *NEC*, 502.115(A)(1)
5. d. In textbook, *NEC*, 502.130(A)(3)
6. a. In textbook, *NEC*, 502.100(A)(3)
7. b. In textbook, *NEC*, 502.115(B)
8. d. In textbook, *NEC*, 503.5
9. b. In textbook, *NEC*, Article 501, Part III
10. a. In textbook
11. b. In textbook
12. b. In textbook, *NEC*, 500.8(B), Table 500.8(B)
13. b. In textbook, *NEC*, 504.30(B)(3)
14. b. In textbook, *NEC*, 505.8(A)
15. a. In textbook, *NEC*, 501.145

Chapter 5

1. d. In textbook, *NEC*, 501.10(A)(1)(c)
2. d. In textbook, *NEC*, 501.10(B)

3. a. In textbook, *NEC,* 501.10(B)(2)
4. b. In textbook, *NEC,* 502.15
5. d. In textbook, *NEC,* 503.30(A)
6. b. In textbook, *NEC,* 503.10(A)
7. a. In textbook, *NEC,* 502.10(A)
8. a. In textbook, *NEC,* 502.40
9. c. In textbook, *NEC,* 501.10(B)(1)
10. a. In textbook, *NEC,* 501.20
11. a. In textbook, *NEC,* 501.15(F)(3)
12. b. In textbook, *NEC,* 501.15(B)(2)
13. a. In textbook, *NEC,* 501.15(E)(4)
14. c. In textbook, *NEC,* 501.15(C)(6)
15. a. In textbook, *NEC,* 502.15

Chapter 6

1. b. In textbook, *NEC,* 511.1
2. c. In textbook, *NEC,* 511.3(A)(7)
3. b. In textbook, *NEC,* 511.12
4. b. In textbook, *NEC,* 513.4 and 514.7
5. d. In textbook, *NEC,* 513.12
6. a. In textbook, *NEC,* 513.8(A)
7. b. In textbook, *NEC,* 513.3, 514.4(A) and (B)
8. a. In textbook, *NEC,* 514.3, Tables 514.3(B)(1) and 514.3(B)(2)
9. b. In textbook, *NEC,* 514.11(A)
10. d. In textbook, *NEC,* 514.13
11. a. In textbook
12. a. In textbook, *NEC,* 514.3(A)
13. b. In textbook, *NEC,* 515.8
14. a. In textbook, *NEC,* 516.3(A), (B), or (C)
15. a. In textbook, *NEC,* 516.1 also NFPA 33
16. a. In textbook, *NEC* 514.11(B)
17. c. In textbook, 514.11(C)
18. d. In textbook, 514.3(B)(1) and Table 514.3(B)(1)
19. c. In textbook, 514.3(B)(2) and Table 514.3(B)(2)
20. B. 514.3(B)(1) and Table 514.3(B)(1)

Hazardous Locations

Contributors: Michael J. Johnston
                Paul A. Dobrowsky
                Donald R. Cook

Technical Edit and Review:
    Michael J. Johnston
    Paul A. Dobrowsky
    Donald R. Cook
    Edward M. Briesch, P. E.
    James W. Carpenter

Technical Drawings: Michael J. Johnston
                      Brady M. Davis

Graphic Production: John Watson
                      Laura Hildreth

Cover design: John Watson

Production Manager: Laura Hildreth

Project Manager: Michael J. Johnston

Associate Editor: Laura Hildreth

Technical Editor: Michael J. Johnston

Art Director: John Watson

Managing Editor: Kathryn Ingley

Editor in Chief: James W. Carpenter

Photos / Illustration Reprints:
    Appleton EGS Electrical Group
    Alagasco (Alabama Gas Corporation)
    Chevron (FW Cottrell)
    Cooper Crouse-Hinds
    Emerson Process Management, Rosemount
    Gilbarco/Veeder-Root
    Hubbell/Killark
    IAEI Archives
    Michael J. Johnston
    National Fire Protection Association
    OZ Gedney
    Southwire Company
    Schneider Electric/Square D
    Thomas & Betts
    Tyco Thermal Controls
    Underwriters Laboratories

Composed at: International Association of Electrical Inspectors in Kepler Std, Optima Lt Std, and Arial
Printed: Mosaic Print, Cheverly, Maryland, on Luna Matte text and bound in C1S White Tango cover